Second Edition

Coaching the Offensive Line: By the Experts

Edited by
Earl Browning

COACHES CHOICE™

ISBN: 1-58518-930-8
Library of Congress Control Number: 2005922510
Cover design: Jeanne Hamilton
Book layout: Jeanne Hamilton
Front cover photo: Jeff Gross/Getty Images

Coaches Choice
P.O. Box 1828
Monterey, CA 93942
www.coacheschoice.com

Contents

Offensive Line Techniques and Drills

George Belu
Ohio State University
2001

It is good to be here. I appreciate high school football coaches. I coached at LSU for five years. When someone uses the term coach, regardless of where you are, it means something special. Wherever you are and you have that coach tag, you are something special to those young kids. I have been able to see this all through the years.

I am going to talk about offensive line play and how I teach the offensive linemen. I think the progression in which you teach is very important. This is true if you are a line coach or a linebacker coach. It is important to believe what you teach. These kids can spot a phony a mile away. If you are not sold on what you are teaching, the players will know it. They will have a little doubt in their mind.

Another important point in coaching offensive linemen is that you talk the same language. When you talk to the players and they answer you, it has to be in the same language. I started coaching at Marshall University in 1965, and I have been at several schools since that time. In all of those years, I have never let the kids say, "Probably," or, "I think." When you ask them a question, they need to give you the answer in terms that both of you understand. The worst thing for an offensive lineman is to come to the line of scrimmage and have doubt in his mind about what he is to do. We want them to be able to go to the line of scrimmage and carry out their assignment without having to think what they are doing. It has to be like they are walking and chewing bubble gum. They do not have to think about what they are doing; they just do it out of habit. If you have the players prepared to carry out their assignment, they develop the attitude they can't wait to get after the defensive man.

The thing I like about offensive linemen is toughness. The first day of practice at Ohio State, we talk about toughness. You have to explain to the offensive line what toughness is. Some players think toughness is pushing around a pile, or that toughness is a cheap shot. Some players think toughness is running off at the jaws. To me, toughness is sticking your nose in the block. It is getting a clean block and getting after the defender. Even when things are not going well, you must stay after the defender. By the time the fourth quarter comes around, you will own the defender. You have to tell the kids what toughness is.

I want to talk about some requirements for a good blocker. The first point we talk about is strength. In the running game, the lineman must be strong enough to move a defender of equal size by brute force. In the passing game, the lineman must be strong enough to stop the defender's charge at the line of scrimmage and maintain that position.

The second point is mobility. I am talking about initial quickness, feet, agility, coordination, body balance, and control. In the running game, the lineman must be quick enough to meet defenders on his side of the line of scrimmage and mobile enough to stay on the block when the defender is trying to escape. In the passing game, they must have enough mobility to slide, mirror, and maintain the inside position on a pass rusher—giving ground grudgingly until the ball is thrown.

The blocker has four advantages. I want to list these advantages. Four advantages a blocker has:
- Knowing the snap count.
- Direction of the ball.
- Proper use of leverage.
- Proper alignment.

I want to touch on the proper use of leverage. Leverage is when the blocker strikes his initial blow at a point. The blocker must be low enough to create a lifting force on the defender. He must be close enough to neutralize his charge. The force must be continued to get the defender on his heels, so he is unable to make a counter move.

We want to teach the blocker to hit up and through the defender. Line of force is that 45-degree angle up and through the defender in which we channel all our force.

Diagram 1

Let me get to the teaching progression for the base block. We believe the base block is the most important block of an offensive lineman. This block is used when blocking at the point of attack. The objective is to get movement, option blocking the defender the way he wishes to go. You must maintain contact.

Following is the sequence of how we teach this drive block. First we teach stance and start, and then sequences are taught in reverse order to ensure the athlete experiences the perfect block.

First Phase—Stance/Starts

We start off with a good base. We want a base at least armpit width but never wider than your shoulders. We want a staggered stance with the toes in and the heels out. We want the feet lined up in a toe-to-instep or toe-to-heel relationship. If you are a right-handed player, we like to put the right foot back. The right toe will be on the instep of the left foot, or possibly to the heel. That is the way we want them to line up. Some of the kids you get may be a little different. Some kids may be 6'6", and some kids will be 5'10". You may have to be lenient with those types of players. You want them to feel comfortable. The players are the ones that have to play, so they need to be comfortable. The players are the ones that have to feel comfortable. If they have to get into a different stance in order to feel comfortable, that is fine.

We have had a lot of fun with this over the years. We tell the players that all of us are either from the country or the city. I ask them how many of them are from the country. They raise their hands. I ask those country players if they ever took a crap in the woods. "Yes, I did coach." They look pretty good from that point. Then, we get the city players up front. I ask them to squat down like they are going to take a dump in the woods. I tell them to look at their heels. "You are going to get 'do-do' on your heels." Tell them to get down and get the butt out of the way.

The thing about offensive linemen is the fact they play from an uncomfortable position. In the off-season, we start them off by having them squat down just like they are going to take a crap in the woods. Have them squat for 30 seconds and then have them stand up. We keep doing that, but we add a few seconds each time, until they can stay in the squat position for one minute. Then, we have them do a quarter-eagle squat. We put a line on a wall, where they can put their hands on the wall in that squat position. Then, we have them walk down the line in that squat position with their hands flat on the line as they move down the line. They have to be low. It is an unnatural position for the linemen. They have to learn to play that way.

Their weight is on the inside balls of the feet. Their knees are in and over their ankles. We want a "Z" in their knees. The power-producing angles are created by the bend in the ankles and knee joints.

We have them put their down hand slightly inside their rear foot. Their weight is extended comfortably from their shoulder. We want them to reach out far enough to create a balanced stance with 60 percent of their weight forward and 40 percent of their weight back. We still like to use the tripod with the fingers of the down hand on the ground.

We want the head cocked back slightly. We tell them to get into a bull neck position. We want them to have some peripheral vision, so they can see the feet of the defender. We like to use the phrase look through the eyebrows.

The next point is the off hand. We take the off hand and put the wrist on the left knee. When they take that first step, we want the off hand and everything else to be going in the same direction.

It is important in teaching stance to have a system and to be consistent with the way you teach it. The way we like to teach this is by having all of the offensive linemen together. We give them commands—"feet shoulder-width apart, stagger the stance, squat down, right hand down, left hand on the knee." Then, we get them up and start again. When I clap my hands, I want them to clap their hands and then take two steps and get down in their stance. "Ready, break." We call, "Set"—and they get down in their stance. We keep them down in that stance. They have to be comfortable. We walk around as they sit in their stance. Make them sit in that stance until they are comfortable.

Our initial movement must be forward—not upward. It is like a sprinter going out of the starting blocks. If the defender is over the offensive lineman, we want the blocker to drive off the up foot and step with the rear foot. If the defender is to either side, the blocker must step with the foot nearest him.

Here are the coaching points for the rear foot lead. Mentally shift the weight to the push foot and step with the near foot. I will show you a tape of the drill we use to teach this. It is our one step drill.

One-Step Drill

- The first step should be a three-inch step out and slightly up, attacking the line of scrimmage.
- The knee of the up foot should point toward the ground (it should roll over the toe of the up foot).
- Arm action should be like a sprinter coming out of the starting blocks.
- The back should be flat, and the chest should be on the thigh.
- The blocker should bull the neck and sight the target.
- The blocker should follow up quickly with his third step.
- The blocker should stay down low and maintain his lift leverage.

Next, we work on the up foot lead. We want to mentally shift the weight to the push foot and step with the up foot. Then, we do the one-step drill. The first step should be a three-inch step out and slightly up, attacking the line of scrimmage.

Second Phase—Fit Position

The purpose of this phase is to show the blocker ideal blocking position, utilizing power-producing angles. We must put the defender in a challenge position and have the offensive blocker fit into him.

- The offensive blocker is in a good position.
- Feet parallel—toes in—heels out.
- Good bend in the knees—create power-producing angles.
- Knees in over the ankles.
- Butt down.
- Back arched.
- Good bull neck.
- Eyes in the solar plexus of the defender.
- Arms are in a blocking position; fists of the hands at the bottom of the defender's breast plate, forming a triangle with the hairline and both fists.
- The defender is in a challenge position.
- The defender's feet are slightly staggered—up foot at the edge of the board.
- The defender holds the blocker under his arm.
- The defender gives resistance.

Third Phase—Follow Through

The purpose of this phase is to have the player experience an ideal block (i.e., to teach the proper use of leverage, the hip roll, the acceleration of the feet and the maintenance of a block).

The offensive blocker will align in a fit position, his toes at the end of the board. The defender will be in a challenge position, holding the blocker in place.

Walking down the board, the blocker will walk the defender down the board with a bulled neck, power-producing angles, and, feeling pressure at the small of his back, he should never raise up. The defender must give steady resistance.

Hip Roll

- The blocker will roll his hips and accelerate his feet. When executing a block, he will make contact and have a stalemate.
- In order to get movement, the blocker must roll his hips and accelerate to dominate a defender.
- The hip roll is the underneath action—the snapping of his knees straight out and the shooting of his hips through.
- His feet should be underneath his shoulder pads to guard against overextension.

Hold

- Half way down the board on the command, "Hold," the blockers will stop.
- The position of the blocker should be checked.

Finish

- On command, the blocker stays locked on and sustains.

Fourth Phase—Contact

The purpose of this phase is to teach the contact phase of the drive-block technique. We want to emphasize the use of his arms and the timing of the pop.

The offensive blocker in a down position situates himself one step from the defender. The defensive man will assume a challenge position. The defender should be in a good two-point stance, bending his knees as much as possible with his chest out and his head tucked. He will catch the blocker rather than deliver a lick.

The offensive blocker takes only one step—jolting the defender backwards. He should concentrate on ripping his arms and taking a short, powerful step.

Fifth Phase—Hit and Drive

The purpose of this phase is to put all aspects of the drive block together. The offensive blocker is aligned in a three-point stance, a foot away from the defender, his toes at the end of the board. To start, the defender will be in a two-point stance. As the drill progresses, he will move to a three-point stance without boards.

The offensive blocker will explode out of his stance and drive the defender down the board. Employing a good base and acceleration of the feet are emphasized. The defender will make a good collision and then allow the blocker to drive him down the board while giving ground slowly. As the drill progresses, the distance is varied between the blocker and the defender to aid in the development of a rhythm of blocking a defender at varied distances away.

The two whistle drill can be used in this phase. The first whistle is to check body position; the second whistle is to release the athletes from the drill.

Sixth Phase—Second Effort

The purpose of this phase is to teach the blocker to maintain contact when the defender is spinning out or disengaging the blocker.

The coach will give the defender a direction spin. When the defender reaches the end of the board, he will spin out of the block in the direction indicated by the coach. The blocker must step with his near foot in the direction of the spin, aggressively attacking the defender. The blocker should never cross his feet or kick his heels together. He should maintain a good base.

Seventh Phase—versus Shade Alignments

The purpose of this phase is to teach the drive on opponents who are aligned in shaded or off-set alignments. This phase is the same as the hit and drive phase, except that the blocker and the defender start from a position with their inside foot on the outside of the board. The blocker's first step must be perfect in order to get to the solar plexus of the defender. His second step must be upfield, while maintaining his base. Practice inside to outside shades of the offensive blocker.

The second block we teach is the lead block. This is an aggressive block that is used to prevent a defender from pursuing the ball. Our teaching sequence for this block is as follows.

First Phase—Stance and Start

The stance is exactly the same as for the drive block. In the start, the first step will depend on the defender's alignment (45 percent head up, 30 percent shade, etc.). During the first step, the blocker's shoulders will turn and the chest will be kept on the thigh.

Second Phase—Point of Aim

All linemen and tight ends should use the armpit for their point of aim versus a down lineman. They should drive to the playside, their hand to the defender's outside hip.

Third Phase—Three-Step Drill

The coach should use a slow count (i.e., one – two – three) to exaggerate each step of lead block. The blocker's first step must be at an appropriate angle, his chest on his thigh while turning his shoulders.

His second step is a power step, driving it down the crotch of the defender. He rips his backside arm as he steps. He should not let his step hang; he must get it down quickly.

His third step is upfield, trying to square his shoulders. He should get to the point of his aim. A sled can be used to work various aiming points of aim of the lead block.

After each pass is thrown, all offensive linemen must run quickly to their assigned coverage area and locate the ball. If the pass is completed, they must sprint downfield and block for the receiver. If the pass is intercepted, they must sprint to the ball and surround the interceptor.

Sets—Pass

Pass Protection Techniques

Stance: proper stance for offensive linemen was discussed previously, but it must be emphasized that a blocker must always use the same stance. Any adjustment in stance that gives away our intention to pass gives the advantage to the defense. However, the blocker should mentally shift his weight to his push foot, so he is prepared to make his initial step when getting set.

Getting set: a pass blocker's success depends upon his ability to move from his stance to his set position. He should move into position as quickly as possible. The concept of sets is designed to tell the blocker the initial movement he should take on the snap to put himself in the best position to block his man. His set position prior to contact must be in direct line between the defender and the quarterback.

Footwork: the blocker's footwork (set) is based on a rusher's alignment.

Versus head-up alignment: the blocker should drop step four inches with his outside foot. He should keep square with the defender. His inside foot always remains in front of his outside foot. He should pull back his hips, with his butt still slightly up, and squat, thrusting his head and shoulders back.

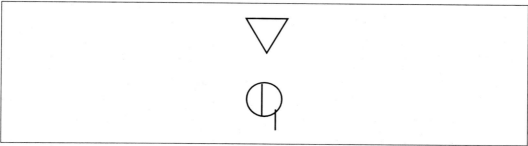

Diagram 2

Versus outside alignment: the blocker should kick step with his outside foot (30 degrees) to where his foot now is aligned with the in-step of the defender's outside foot. He should keep his shoulders square and move his inside foot to keep his balance, always keeping the inside foot up.

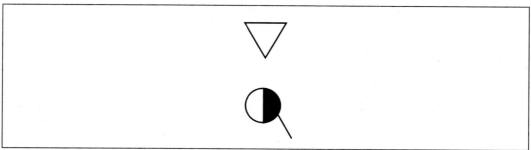

Diagram 3

Versus inside alignment: The blocker should slide his inside foot to gain a head-up position. His outside foot is again on the in-step of the defender's outside foot. He should keep his inside foot up.

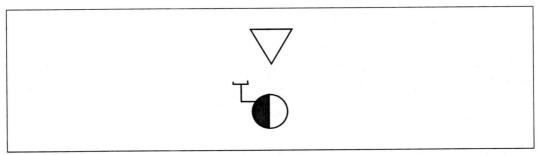

Diagram 4

Body position:

- Head—thrown back with the chin up and the eyes focused on the bottom of the numbers of the defender.
- Back—straight or flat, but never rounder.
- Feet—shoulder-width apart.
- Knees—bent in power-producing angles, but never straightened.
- Butt—down and tucked, to keep his center of gravity low.
- Hands and elbows—the hands are at eye level, armpit-width apart; the thumbs are up; the elbows are near the body.
- Shoulders—always square to the line of scrimmage.

Teaching Sequence—Pass

General information:

- Two men work together.
- We teach the four phases in reverse order.
- We show each player the ideal position (set and fit) for pass protection.

Fit position (first phase): we put the defender in a pass-rush position and have the offensive blocker fit into him.

Offensive blocker fit:

- Head is back with shoulders square.
- Butt is tucked with knees bent.
- Back is straight; lower back is arched.
- Feet are shoulders-width apart with toes pointing straight ahead. Inside foot is always up.
- Open hands are placed in armpit area.
- Arms are extended but slightly bent.
- Eyes are focused on base of defender's numbers.

Pressure (second phase):
- From fit position, the defender moves in either direction laterally.
- The blocker will slide and apply pressure by locking arms and pushing to the direction the defender is moving. The blocker should not allow his opposite arm to become lazy and lose contact with the defender.
- Always maintain a shoulder-width base. Keep your head and shoulders back and stride with the knees bent. Do not get overextended.
- Four-way pressure can be practiced by allowing the defender to pull rush or pull the blockers, as well as move laterally.

Pop (third phase):
- The blocker is in a ready position.
- As the defender approaches, the blocker will thrust or pop his arms forward and, at the same time, replace a foot. This foot replacement ensures a strong, solid base.
- Contact is made with the heel of his palms to control and stop the charge of the defender. The defender's shoulders should snap backwards.
- The timing of the pop should be emphasized (i.e., arms thrusting forward and replacing a foot). The timing of the pop on the defender should be practiced by approaching from different angles and utilizing the pop in shuffle drill.

Full go (fourth phase):
- The offensive blocker is now in a three-point stance.
- The defender will rush from a three-point stance.
- We now combine all teaching phases of pass protection.

You have to work every single day to drive block and angle linemen. This comes in the individual period. You have to constantly work on the first step and where the defender is angling. The blocker's second step has to go in the direction the defender is going. You have to work on this everyday. I also think you have to work on the combination blocks every single day. If you do a lot of gap blocking or step blocking, I think you have to work on those blocks everyday. If you do not work on them everyday, it will get sloppy.

If I could say something on the gap block, it may help. I will explain what we do on the gap block. We can look at the center blocking back on the 2 technique man. The center does not know if the 2 technique man is going to plow into him or go upfield and read the block. This could be a tackle blocking down on a 3 technique, a guard blocking down on a 1 technique, or the center blocking on the backside. The key to the block is the first step. The step must be really flat. It is a short, flat, quick step. It is really quick. The second step is the adjustment step. If the man plays into the blocker, the second step is into the defender and the contact point is the near armpit and the near number. The next step is to get the near foot in the center of the defender and get the head into the man and knock him out of the hole.

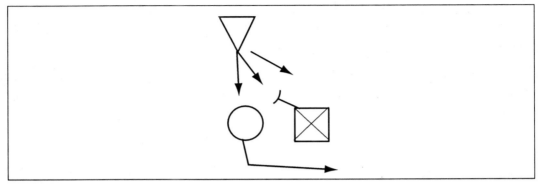

Diagram 5

The next block is the combination block. It does not matter which two linemen we are talking about. It could be a center and a guard, a guard and a tackle, or a tackle and the tight end. We are working on a combo block on the linebacker.

In the diagram here, we have a defender in the shade technique on the offensive player on the left. We use the terms thick and thin. It means who is going to hit thick and who is going to hit thin. The inside man is going to hit the down man thick with his near foot. The step is almost straight upfield. He is going to the near number of the down defender.

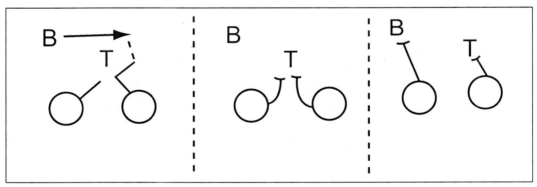

Diagram 6

The step of the outside blocker is upfield, where he will slide inside slightly. He is the outside man, and he steps with his inside foot. His second step is very important. That step must be parallel to his first step to keep his shoulders squared. You have to rep, rep, rep this in practice. The outside blocker is going to combo block on the linebacker inside. He makes contact with the down lineman on his near number. The footwork becomes a little different. His shoulders must be square to the line of scrimmage. If the linebacker comes over the top, we tell the outside man not to come off the block on the down man until the linebacker comes to his near ear hole. At that point, the outside blocker starts working off his man. He keeps his inside shoulder low and runs through the defender to the linebacker. The big mistake the outside blocker often makes is to get too loose with his hips, thereby opening a gap between him and the inside man. That allows the down defender to come upfield where the inside blocker cannot control him.

If the second step of that outside man is not parallel with his first step, his shoulders get turned and the linebacker comes over the top. The outside blocker then has a hard time getting squared up to make that block on the linebacker.

This block is used on cutback plays. You want to get the linebackers moving on those plays. This is how we want to come off the block and square up on the linebacker.

If the linebacker hangs in the same position, we stay in our double-team block. We want good movement on the play. If the linebacker runs a blitz, the inside man can make contact on the line of scrimmage.

I wanted to get into the three-step pass protection out of the one-back set and a five-step pass protection out of the two-back set. The rules for the offensive linemen are almost the same for all three positions. I do not have time to get into that now.

I really enjoy talking about the offensive line. When you break it down and show the kids what you want them to do, you have the opportunity to work with them even though they may not have as much athletic ability as some of the other players on the field. They are fun kids to work with and fun kids to coach. Hopefully, you have gotten something out of this that you can take back and use in your program. Thank you very much.

2

Line Blocking Schemes

Mike Cummings
Central Michigan University
1995

I will show you three main blocking schemes that we use to move the ball on the ground. We refer to them as base, lead, and gap schemes. We try to keep our blocking scheme as simple as possible.

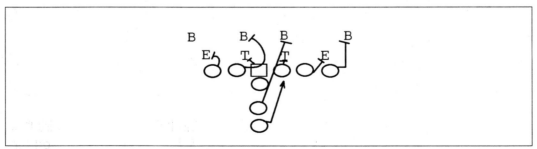

Diagram 1. Base block

The second scheme we use is our lead blocking scheme for inside running plays. In this scheme, our offensive linemen will zone block. They will all step toward the point of attack and block the man in that zone. The adjacent linemen all work toward the playside and are responsible to block the defender in their frontside gap or the adjacent lineman's backside gap.

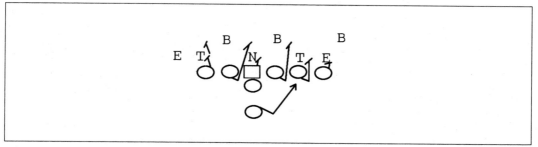

Diagram 2. Lead block inside

We also use a lead blocking scheme for an outside play. The offensive linemen use zone blocking principles in this scheme as well. However, the zone they will work through is designated differently to account for the outside course of the ballcarrier. The linemen still step toward the playside and block the zone and man in that zone and still have the adjacent backside lineman covering their backside gap.

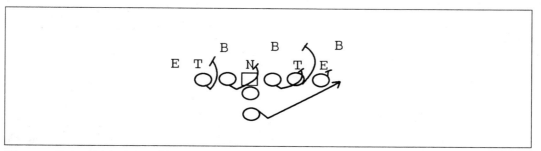

Diagram 3. Lead block outside

The third blocking scheme we use to run the football is our gap blocking scheme. This is also a zone blocking scheme, but, in this scheme, our linemen will step away from the point of attack and work toward the backside of the play. We will leave a defender to be trapped/logged on the frontside. We can trap with our fullback, guard, center, or tackle.

What is most relevant and important to all these schemes is not how each play is blocked precisely against each front. It is the techniques involved in each scheme that make it so successful. It is our ability to practice them, drill them, correct them the greatest number of times, while still becoming more and more aggressive. The greatest concern is how to practice and drill these techniques that make the scheme work so well.

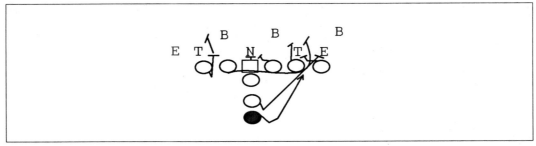

Diagram 4. Gap block

I will give you the techniques that we use at the point of attack in each of our three main schemes (base, lead, gap), and I will show you what we use as our base drills to develop these schemes while we develop our linemen. I will give particular attention to the combination blocks and the points we emphasize on each of these.

There are some concerns with using three different blocking schemes. The biggest concern, besides simply to teach them, is the raising of the pad level on the lead schemes. Leverage is not only a commodity at your place, but at ours as well. We are concerned with our players playing higher on lead schemes than they do on base and gap Schemes.

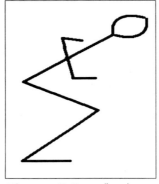

Diagram 5. Zone/lead

Diagram 6. Balanced

Diagram 7. Option/veer

We understand that the lead schemes cause offensive linemen to play with their pads somewhat higher than in gap or base schemes, but we don't want them *much* higher. We especially don't want our linemen to *think* that they should be playing higher. We develop our linemen to knock people off the ball *first*, then we get into other stuff. We *will not* bump and shove. We use boards and chutes; every day, we work on leverage. We teach, we indoctrinate, we demand leverage first; if your linemen learn to play low and play hard first, you can teach them zone blocking. But, if you teach zone blocking first, you're going to have a problem getting them into a good mind-set on short yardage and goal line to knock someone off the ball.

If we only used lead schemes (zone run), we would have a different philosophy on our teaching of run blocking and leverage. Our offensive philosophy dictates that we do this (run everything), so we feel we must work on the toughest aspect of blocking first, which is leverage. Then, we work on lead schemes and gap schemes and employ the principles of leverage to these schemes.

Let me talk about blocking in general. We talk about going back to the basics when talking about blocking. Blocking can be improved to a greater degree than any other phase of the game. Let me list these basics concerning blocking.

- Stance—Fit what you do offensively: power=narrow, balance=wide. We must be able to do it all from the stance.
- Feet/footwork—Emphasize frequency, not length (don't pick them up too high, losing frequency). Kill the cat? Pound the feet on the ground. Teach where the first, second, and third steps should go. *Why?* The offensive lineman can't take a wrong step. Give them landmarks and aiming points. Make contact on the second step (never on the first step). The first step is timing and weight transfer; the second step is power, and then punch.
- Surface—Identify the surface to be used: helmet, hands, shoulder/forearm. Aim point with surface. Give the offensive lineman part of the defender's body to aim at for the best chance (shoulder, hip, sternum—be specific). Our general rule is this: hands at the point of attack, control. Shoulder forearm—BS=power.
- Fit position—It is a constant struggle to keep the knees bent and the butt up. Gather ability; adjust ability. It is important to keep the back flat on contact. The hips will roll naturally. We teach the stalemate: rolling the hips *isn't* the key.
- Repetition—We do the same drills every day. We make the drills fit our scheme and technique. Conditioning is achieved by going full speed. We want more reps than any other player. The tough part is practice; the game is easy. Again, consistency is our goal.
- Motivation—Individual and team goals are used. We want measurable goals. Our goal is to be the best line in the Mid-American Conference. When we grade our film, we give extra credit on blocking. We can give it, and we can take it away. A pancake or knockdown block gets extra credit.
- Enthusiasm—The coach has to build enthusiasm. We can grind them, run them, and then we must love them. We want to know them as individuals, because they will play harder if they feel close to the group. The more we know about them, the more we can help them. If we know them as individuals, we can tell if they are having a good day or not. We must make the right things important. If everything is important, then nothing is important. There are certain things to pick out that are important.
- Patience—We feel this is very important. How would you want your child to be treated? Every once in a while kids need a kick in the rear. We run a tight ship. We set the rules early and stay with them.

- Blocking triangle—This is our philosophy on blocking. We want them to know *who* to block. We want to make it simple for them. We stress these three points: *who—how—aggressive!*
- Keep it simple—We have a 20-hour rule in college, and we cannot spend a lot of time doing nothing. The 20 hours include the games and everything else we do. We want to knock people off the ball. It is easier said than done. We want to run north and south to win. If things are not working, we subtract a play instead of adding more plays. Also, we do less talking and spend more time on the practice field.

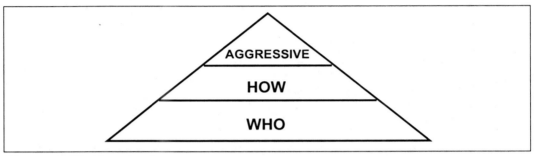

Diagram 8. Blocking triangle

I will show you how we teach each point of attack technique and how we drill it. Our base block is a man block and is used primarily at the point of attack. We tell our linemen, who have the assignment of base blocking, that the ballcarrier is directly behind him and will make his cut depending on which way he takes the defender. In our base block, we allow our offensive lineman to take the defender any way he wants to go. That is the block used on our basic Isolation play.

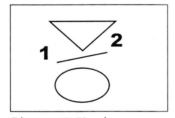

Diagram 9. Head up

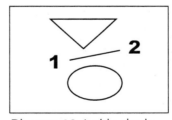

Diagram 10. Inside shade

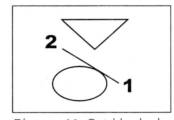

Diagram 11. Outside shade

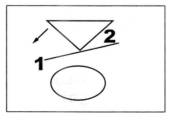

Diagram 12. Angle inside (head-up)

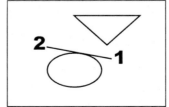

Diagram 13. Angle inside (outside shade)

The first step is with the inside foot, or near foot. The inside foot is used, if the defender is head-up or inside. We will step with the near foot, if the defender is outside. The first step should get the offensive lineman square to the defender and not to the line of scrimmage. The first step should be halfway to the defender, and make contact on the second step.

The second step is upfield at the defender. We make contact on the second step. We are already square to the defender, so we want to get into the defender. Our first step will take care of any slant or angle. We punch on our second step at the defender.

The aiming point for our headgear is the sternum of the defender. We will focus into the sternum to see any movement. It is the middle of the defender, and we can continue contact regardless of movement of the defender.

The surface we aim for is the helmet and hands. We want to punch and shock the defender and get control. We want to maintain a flat back, tail slightly higher than our shoulders. We get on the insteps with high frequency. Drive the defender by driving the knees inside. Our hips will roll with movement of the defender. We base block primarily on isolation plays.

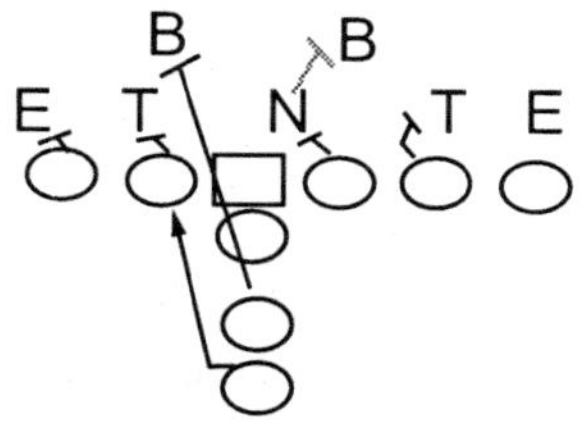

Diagram 14. Isolation play

Next is our lead blocking or zone blocking. We use a pick blocking scheme when our ballcarrier is using an inside course; and the cut may go inside or outside the combination block on the frontside. Let me go over the lead blocker. His first step is in the bucket; then he turns his shoulders far enough so that the second step comes down on the ground at the crotch of the defender. The second step is on the ground at the crotch of the defender; the punch comes through on the second step. The second step designates the zone. We refer to this as the track. We want to stay on track.

We use the hands and helmet, if the defender slants to the lead blocker. We use the shoulder and forearm, if the defender angles away. We want to finish the block. We stay on course unless we are using a scoop block by the trail blocker. The ballcarrier makes his cut off of the combination block. If the scoop is used, we stay on course to the linebacker. Once he is on the linebacker, he has him man-to-man.

Let me go over the trail blocker. His first step is in the bucket. He turns his shoulders enough so that on the second step he can contact the ground while being pointed at the crotch of the defender. We want to establish tandem relationship or get the trail blocker behind the lead blocker. The second step in underneath his own hip. It will be pointed at the defender's crotch, with the playside hand extended.

Next, we look at what happens when the *reads* take place. First, *scoop*—if defender is coming inside, shove the lead blocker off and helmet adjust to defender's playside number and take the defender over. Second, *base*—if the defender is going outside, continue on zone (tracks), established by the second step on the way to the linebacker. On the slant course by the tailback, we use the shoulder and forearm. On the cutback by the tailback, we use the helmet and hands. Third, *shove*/double—if the defender is hanging inside but has not declared inside or outside, shove with the hand over to the lead blocker. Double-team while staying on course to the linebacker.

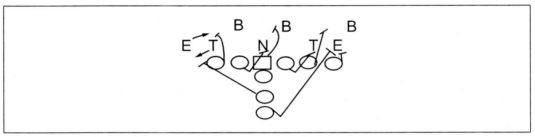

Diagram 15. Pick inside play

Next are our lead schemes. We use the scoop block on outside running plays. The ballcarrier is going outside the combination block. We have two blockers: lead and trail. On the first step, the lead blocker drop-steps and turns his shoulders enough to get the second step on the ground just inside the playside foot to the defender. We may lose more ground if the defender is farther outside. We lose ground to gain ground.

On the second step, we contact the ground at a point just inside the playside foot of the defender. Contact is made on the second step, and we want to establish a zone, or tracks. We want to knock the defender off the ball.

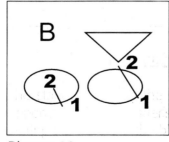

Diagram 16

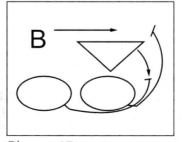

Diagram 17

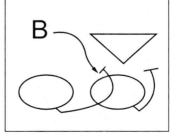

Diagram 18

We use our hands to the helmet to the playside number of the defenders on defensive linemen or the linebacker. We use a shoulder forearm against fast-flowing linebackers. To finish the block, we bring the playside arm into the outside of the defender's playside number and maintain a lateral position. When scooped off, we maintain lateral position on the linebacker with the strong playside arm.

Our trail blocker's first step is a drop step. He turns his shoulder enough so that on the second step he contacts the ground underneath his own hip with his foot pointed at the inside of the defender's playside foot. The second step is underneath his hip point at the inside of the defender's playside foot, with the playside hand extended. On the second step, the trail blocker will read the man on the lead blocker. He feels the linebacker.

To finish, he brings his hand into the ribs and shoves the adjacent offensive lineman off to go to the frontside linebacker. He adjusts his helmet to the defender's playside number and takes over the defensive lineman with the strong playside hand and helmet adjusts.

Our third blocking scheme is our gap scheme. We double-team at the point of attack.

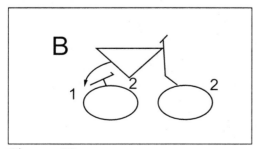

Diagram 19

We trap with the fullback or guard (center). We use a *swipe* combination/double-team on our gap scheme when we have a trap by a fullback or guard and an off-tackle aiming point by our ballcarrier. We use a zone scheme away from the point of attack.

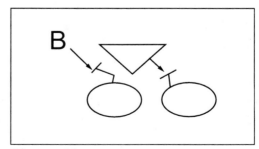

Diagram 20   Diagram 21

We use two blockers: the lead or chipper and the trail or swiper. The lead blocker is referred to as the chipper. On his first step, he slides and steps inside. The slide should be far enough to get the second step down on the ground in the crotch of the defensive lineman. If the defender is aligned such that the second step would go in the crotch now, he will use a settle or weight transfer step and gain no ground inside. On the second step, we contact the ground at the defender's crotch. As contact is made on the second step, we establish the zone on the second step and work straight upfield.

We want the shoulder and forearm on the surface of the defender. We want the head out of the block, with the eyes on the backside linebacker.

On the finish, we want to take a waddle step and knock the defensive lineman straight back off the ball. We want to stay into the defensive linemen, until we are on the linebacker level. We keep the surface on the defensive lineman as long as possible.

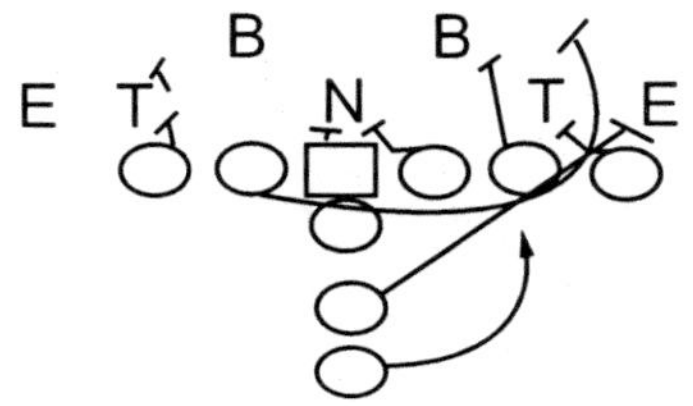

Diagram 22

The trail blocker is the swiper. His first step is a lateral and upfield/lead step at the inside of the defensive lineman's playside foot. We gain ground to get to the defender. The lead blocker is ahead of him. He must keep his shoulders square to the linebacker. His second step is upfield. He should bring his feet to a parallel position (toe to toe). The second step cannot be past the parallel position or it will cause a down block on the defensive lineman and squeeze the chipper off his block.

On the blocking surface, we want the helmet on the playside number, with the hands inside on the man's shoulder pads with the stronger playside arm. To finish the block, we want to knock the defensive lineman off the ball, straight back. We tell him to block the defensive lineman as if he had no help. If the defensive lineman angles inside, he must stay on course and work upfield to the linebacker.

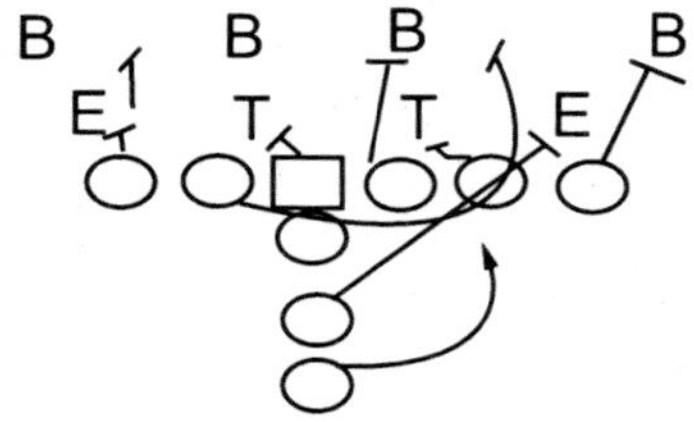

Diagram 23

3

Offensive Line Play

Dan Haley
Bowling Green (Ky.) High School
1996

My topic is offensive line play. I will start out by providing a context from which our ideas have evolved. First, I want to tell you this is not a scheme talk. If you want to get out of here, you can. This is not a scheme lecture. It is not a philosophy talk about all of the things we believe in. Best of all, this is not a talk where a coach comes up and puts on a ton of overlays with a list of 10 things we are going to do. This is going to be a technique talk. I will cover in detail the feet, eyes, and head, and how-to-deliver-a-blow talk. I am not trying to tell you this is the best way to teach or coach offensive linemen or how to teach the drive block. I am saying what I think is the best way to teach the drive block.

We have been a triple-option football team for more than 20 years now. We went through the split-back veer era and the wishbone era. As the defenses adjusted and caught up, we tried to evolve the offense rather than ditch the concept altogether. The main reason we have embraced the offense and stayed with it over the years is the blocking scheme. It allows us to block with five people on four people. It allows us to come off the football at full throttle. What I am saying is that the way we teach blocking is a function of the offense that we run. With a different scheme, we might believe different things, but, for our scheme, we believe in the following six points:

- We use a three-point stance with our weight equally distributed.
- At the line of scrimmage, our down hand is grounded three inches from the neutral zone, not back like most teams. We are up on the line, crowding the line of scrimmage.
- We use the snap count to get a jump on the defense.
- We want to explode in the face of the defense. We want to explode a vertical release through the aiming point, somewhere on someone's body. We want to make a vertical release to an aiming point, to what we call a level five. That is just five yards downfield. Level one, two, three, four, and five are the number of yards downfield we strive for.
- We make a commitment with our players that we are going to come off the football better than anyone else in football. We are going to measure this commitment. We look at the films and show them coming off the line of scrimmage. The way we measure this is by checking the feet on the snap of the football. We want 11 feet moving on the snap of the football. We want to see 11 sets of feet moving on the ground before you can see any evidence of the defense reacting. That is what we mean by coming off the football.
- We believe we have to knock a hole in the defense. From that hole, we are going to attack horizontally and vertically. Those are the principles we operate on.

We teach several types of blocks and several blocking combinations, but everything we do in the running game is based upon the drive block. I want to take you through the coaching points and some drills that we use in teaching the drive block. Then, I want to take those principles and use them to develop the zone blocking combination as we teach it.

In the drive block, we start with stance and start. We simply believe that a three-point stance allows us to be more explosive than a four-point stance. We think a four-point stance rounds the shoulders more, and rounded shoulders tend to round the back, and a rounded back diminishes explosiveness.

We believe in the three-point stance. We teach it with the toes at 12 inches and the heels at 13 inches, which makes us slightly pigeon-toed. We have a slight foot stagger. Why do we want to be narrow in our stance? We want to be narrow in our stance because it facilitates a better takeoff, and being slightly pigeon-toed allows for better push-off, especially when taking a slight angle. We want to move forward. If you watch most sprinters in track, you can see how they get down. They have a narrow base, because they want to go forward. We want the ankles close and the Z's in the knees. We want the hips cocked into what we call a power position, slightly higher than the shoulders, and hand placement such that the natural line of sight for the eyes is a point on the ground 1.5 yards in front of that hand. We call that point on the ground the basic spot for the eyes.

We do go at angles. We have to take that fact into account. The reason we are slightly pigeon-toed is so when we are not going forward we can make that step at an angle. If we are going to the right, we want to step with the near foot, just as most of you do. We want to attack with the near foot. If we are going to the left, we want to lead with the left foot first.

When you strike a blow, regardless if you are a tackler or blocker, there are two components. There is the power that goes into it and the explosion that comes on top of it. I use Hank Aaron as an example to our players. He weighed 165 pounds, but, when he swung the baseball bat, he was generating power. When he got the wrist turned, he got the explosion into the swing. That was how he was able to hit more than 700 home runs. So, when we are blocking, we want power and explosion. I want them coordinated. We tell our kids the power comes from the waist down. The power comes from the butt and the legs. The explosion comes from the upper body.

The question is this: if all of the power comes from the lower body, how do you get the power into the explosion? The answer is this: it has to be transferred, just like electricity, right through the body. The power of the lower body, if it is going to get into the blow, must come through the trunk of the body. If the trunk of the body is rounded, it will not go through. It is just like lifting weights. On the dead lift, we can get 500 pounds on the Olympic bar. They can't just reach over and pick up the 500 pounds. You have 500 pounds in the lower body, and it has to come through the trunk. If you get the back in a power position and get your hips under the bar, you can come straight up and get those 500 pounds.

It is fundamental in the winter program. Make sure they learn how to get down in position. We do not want the banana back. That position is a non-aggressive position. He can't hit from that position. We want the head to be an extension of the body. We want the eyes to be focused on what we call the basic spot. The basic spot for the eyes is 1.5 yards in front of the hand. We tell them to look through their eyebrows to the basic spot. We keep our free arm on the knee. We do not carry it sidesaddle. We feel it makes us more explosive; it may not be, but that is our thinking.

We tell our players to store the snap count in their memory and then concentrate on the ultimate objective of their assignment. We want them to concentrate on their assignment. We want them to concentrate on their objective and allow the snap count to trigger them. The definition of concentration is *oneness*—one thought. We do not want them to concentrate on the snap count. We want them to concentrate on the objective they have on the play. We want them to concentrate on what they are asked to do on the play.

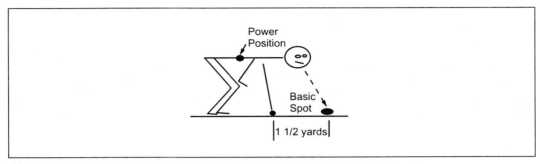

Diagram 1

We try to get on the defense before they can move. Everyone has a prescribed first step, and we take pride in getting it on the ground before there is any noticeable defensive reaction. We want to come off the ball better than anyone in football and attack aiming points.

Let's talk about the drive block. I will break the block down into three components: the approach, contact, and follow-through.

First is the approach. We come out of the stance with a four-inch step. We come off hard, but we don't want to overstride. I have talked about the concentration that gets you out of your stance. When we come out of our basic stance, our eyes go from the basic spot to the landmark. The landmark is the aiming point of the defender we are attacking. That will be the breastbone or the playside number, depending on the play called. When we drive block, we will not aim at the armpit or the knee; we are aiming at the breastbone or the playside number. We want their eyes to go from the basic spot to the landmark in zero seconds. It is, "Hike"—*bam*! There is no in between. I will stress one additional point. Coach Blanton Collier always said, "The most important thing in blocking is the eyes." He was a brilliant coach and a great technician. When I started coaching, I used this point. "The most important thing in blocking is the eyes." I was not sure about this when I first started coaching. Over the years, I have become a firm believer in this point.

We come out of our stance with a four-inch step. We come off hard, but we don't want to overstride. If we overstride on the first step, it is difficult for us to adjust to an aiming point that moves laterally. With a four-inch first step, we can adjust to lateral defensive movement and still strike the target vertically. The short first step makes it physically possible to block movement, but the key to doing it lies with the eyes. The most important thing in blocking is the *eyes*. Eyes tell your feet what to do, and eyes time the delivery of the block. We want the eyes to go from the basic spot to the aiming point in the instant of the first movement. The *eyes* are the blocker's guidance system.

The first step gets us in the frame of the defender, and the second step establishes the base spot. Film studies clearly show that offensive linemen who don't establish base with the second step lose balance on the third step. Some players have more trouble than others, but I believe a significant part of coaching the drive block is the coaching of the second step. In addition to blocking on the boards every day, we have a little block movement drill that we do at thud speed that helps us train the feet, so they respond to what their eyes tell them.

A blocker may step-hit, step-step-hit, or step-step-step-hit, but, regardless of the distance he must travel, he is in the delivery area when he is within three steps of the defender. In the hit area, he must eye the target, be on track, in frame, beneath the target plane, hips lower than the head, and in a power position, and all levers cocked. We say he comes into a hitting position. His head should be an extension of his body.

We call the area we are aiming for the target plane. We want the blocker to approach the target in the delivery area, where he can block the defender. He must be lower than the target plane. He must keep his eyes on the target.

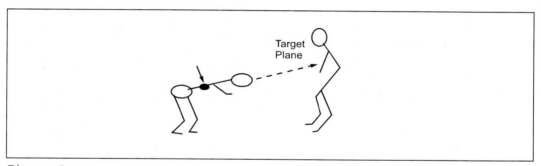

Diagram 2

When he comes out of his stance and attacks the defender, he must be beneath the man, his eyes must be on the target, and his hips must be lower than his head. His feet must be on track. His body must be on his frame, and he must be in a power position in his hips.

Next is contact. As the eyes tell the feet what to do, they also tell the body when to deliver the blow. As the blocker enters the delivery area, the eyes say when the hips should roll under, steps shorten, body extend, and power transfer to the hitting surface. Then, the eyes say when the upper body should explode into the target. If the blocker eyes the target and if all the levers are in the right place, then the blocker generates tremendous power and explodes it up through the aiming point with perfect timing.

The aiming point for a drive block should be either the breastbone or the playside number. The blocker should deliver an ascending blow, up through it, and movement will occur. The blow is delivered with the pads and hands.

If the blocker delivers the blow properly, the defender will be moved backward. Now comes the follow-through. To finish the block and drive him vertically backward, the blocker must sustain the pressure of the initial blow with strong leg drive. We coach him to hit through and sustain, working upward as he goes.

It takes more power to cause movement than to sustain it, so the blocker must trade some power for balance, as he drives the defender backward. He should widen his base slightly and work up as he drives. He cannot give his man the opportunity to recover or disengage. We like to finish the block with our man in the reach position. Being physically superior is a tremendous advantage, but hard work on quality repetitions will develop mechanics that, coupled with toughness and effort, can make an average player into an excellent blocker.

Let's look at blocking combinations that we get into. I will go over the veer against the 4-3 defense. The rule for our offensive linemen on the backside of the veer play is zone playside gap or Z.P.G. That means that each player is responsible for blocking the defender who is responsible for the playside gap. Usually, there is a lineman and a linebacker in the area, aligned so that they could switch their gap control from one play to the next. We want to zone them or come off the ball and pick them up regardless of how they react.

On the frontside, we have two basic rules. First, we want to collapse the 3 technique area. Second, we do not want any leakage on the frontside when we run the veer. On the backside, everyone is zone blocking to the onside gap. Those are the two basic blockers I want to cover.

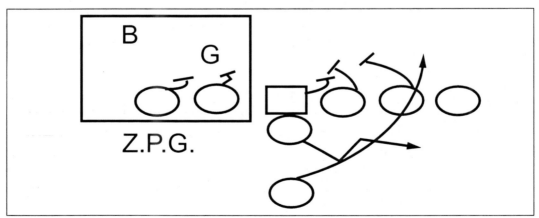

Diagram 3

Let's take a 4-3 defense for example, and let's Z.P.G with our left guard and left tackle, as we would do if the play went to the right. We would operate on the assumption that the 2 technique and the Will linebacker would become backside A and B for defenders on the flow away. If Will scraped to the backside A gap, then the 2 technique would defend the backside B gap for the cutback. We want our backside guard to block the A gap defender and our backside tackle to block the B gap defender.

The guard attacks the playside armpit of the 2 technique, using drive blocking principles. The tackle attacks the breastbone of the 2, also with a drive block principle. With the eyes leading the way, the guard picks up the A gap defender in the "V" of his left shoulder. They drive to level five without permitting the defenders to cross their blocks.

If you are primarily a running football team, I do not think you can run the veer from a split-back alignment. With the defenses today, you will have a hard time outnumbering the alignments on the corner. We have embraced the three-back triple-option concept. We do not want to line up in the three-back set because it places restrictions on the passing game. We line up in the broken bone alignment, a lot. Our two basic schemes against a 50 defense, as far as blocking is concerned, are these. If the tackle is in a 5 Technique on the callside and we make a 5 call, we are going to drive block on the linebacker and nose. It is a 3-on-2 situation. We explode the fullback off the hip of the guard and read the tackle first and the end second.

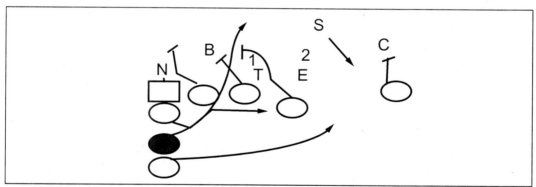

Diagram 4

If the defense has two men outside in the secondary, we have a problem. If we bring the ball outside, we have only one blocker blocking on two defenders. One of the defenders will come up, and one will be deep. The wideout must block the defender who comes up. You have to live with the other man, if you are going to run the play into that defense.

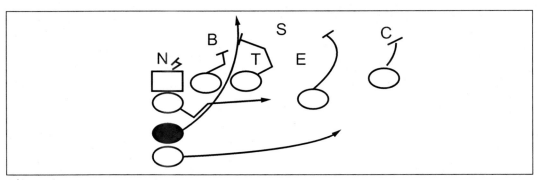

Diagram 5

If the defensive tackle is in a 4 technique and we make a 4 call, the tackle will step around the 4 technique and the slot will arc outside on the deep man inside. We are in a better situation now because we can block 2-on-2 on the outside. We still Z.P.G. on the backside. Those are the two basic schemes we use against the 50 defense. You know there is a lot more to the offense than this. You must have an adjustment for each situation. The basic block is the drive block, and the zone block fits in with the scheme. This is where it all starts from. We want to knock a hole in the defense, collapse the 3 technique, and prevent leakage.

4

Line Blocking Techniques

Jerry Hanlon
University of Michigan
1991

How many times have you heard the comment that, "Defense wins games"? If that statement was true, then Bo Schembechler would have been coaching on that side of the football. He coached offense. *Offensive football is what wins games*. I want my offensive linemen to know that. If anyone wants to meet a real football player, then 90 percent of the time it is an offensive lineman. Think about this. The defensive coaches will grab a player and tell him to go in the game and stuff the offense for three plays, and then he can come back over on the bench and sit down. Those kids don't get to play any football. I tell my players to stay out there for eight or 10 plays. I tell them to stay out there eight to 10 minutes if they want to play. I do not care how long they are on the field. I tell them just be sure to put some points on the board while they are out there. The only people who will know the offensive linemen are out on the field will be the moms, dads, uncles, and other relatives. It will not be their girlfriends, because they are too ugly to have a girlfriend. That is the attitude the offensive line has to have. What are these guys looking for? They are looking for respect from their teammates. That is what we strive for and what we are looking for.

If you can teach blocking and teach technique, you can move the football. What I want to move on to is how we teach some of the blocking techniques at Michigan. The first block is the base block. This is a 1-on-1 block. You have to start to teach technique of any block with the stance. I have changed my viewpoint on the stance somewhat. I used to say I wanted my feet as far apart as the width of my armpits. Now, I want the feet as wide as the shoulders. I have widened the stance somewhat. We did that because we pass the ball more. It is easier to get into the pass block fundamental position from a wider stance. To the side, they put their hand down. I let them stagger their feet somewhat, not an awful lot, but I let them drop one foot back. I want about a heel-to-toe relationship.

Getting the offensive linemen into the proper position is extremely important. Everything starts with a good stance. I do not want them too comfortable in the stance, because I want them to get the hell out of it when the ball is snapped. I do not want comfort. I want effectiveness.

The next thing we teach is the buddy system. We have two players working together. The blocker has to know what it feels like to be in the perfect drive block position before he can make a perfect drive block. The partners work together to get into a form blocking position, which teaches all the fundamentals of contact, leverage, and technique. When the blocker makes contact with his partner, he whips his fist up inside the shoulders of the defender. He leads with his forearms but brings his fist up inside. We have to center the head on the defender. We don't teach the butt block. We don't teach the shoulder block. If the defense would stand still, we should teach a shoulder block. But, they don't. Lead with the forearms, rip the fist up inside, and center the helmet on the chest. The last thing is the follow-through. That comes when the defender tries to get off the block. The offense and defense may get into a stalemate. That is fine, because the defense must try to tackle the ballcarrier. He is going to have to get rid of the blocker to make the tackle. When he attempts to do that, the follow-through takes place. The time to really get after the defense is when he tries to disengage with the blocker. That is when the blocker finishes his block.

The next block we teach is the read technique. We use that technique when the defensive man is trying to seal him inside. I start from the basic stance. I am going to fire in such a way as to put my helmet right through the defender's outside hip. If the defender plays straight, we have him in a shoulder block. If the defender plays the head of the offensive blocker, we are back in the base block. If the defender goes inside, we listen to the ancient Chinese philosopher, Confucius. Confucius says, "When one goes in, one goes out." The offensive blocker lets him go in, and he goes out. He looks for the man outside. That is the linebacker scraping. That is the lead technique when the lineman is covered.

If the lineman is not covered and he is looking at the linebacker, he runs a different aiming point. His aiming point becomes the inside hip of the down lineman outside him. If the down lineman plays straight or goes outside, the offensive blocker is in perfect position to seal the linebacker. If the down lineman comes inside, the offensive lineman locks on him and drives him inside on a drive block.

We use a little different type of block when teaching the gap blocking. To block a gap, the first thing the blocker has to do is control his inside area. If I am gap blocking, I am blocking the first defender to my inside between me and the ball. The first thing I have to do is prevent penetration through the gap. The fastest way the blocker can cover the inside is to step down immediately. We don't aim at the hips. We take a lateral move. As I am taking a lateral move to the inside, I read the defender's charge. The first thing I want to do is to read the stance of the defender. If his head is down and his butt up, he probably is coming hard into the gap. If he is back in his stance, he is probably reading. As I lateral step to the inside and as the defender comes into my gap, I want to get the biggest piece of him as I can. If I get my head inside on him, that is great. If I don't, I take the biggest piece of him I can get. If he is reading, my next step is upfield. I try to get my hands inside and drive him down inside. If the defender loops into the face of the blocker, it is back to the base block.

The next type of block is the hesitation block. This is a technique used by the offensive guard to keep from getting picked off by a slanting defensive tackle when he is trying to block a linebacker. The offensive tackle blocks his man anywhere he wants to go. The guard steps to the defensive tackle and reads his movement. If the tackle is playing straight or going outside, the guard comes up and attacks the linebacker. If the tackle slants to the outside, the guard comes and attacks the linebacker. If the tackle slants to the inside, the guard reaches with his outside hand, puts it on the butt of the offensive tackle, pulls himself around, and attacks the linebacker on his side of the line of scrimmage. If the linebacker is at his normal depth, we use this technique. If he is on the line of scrimmage, we go get him right now.

The last technique I want to show you is when two offensive linemen can block one gap control defender and linebacker, when he shows. It is two linemen controlling the line of scrimmage and then blocking the linebacker later. The two linemen take a move so that they can control the gap area. We have an inside and outside control area. We can control the inside with the inside man coming off for the linebacker. Or, we can control the line with the outside man coming off for the linebacker.

The next thing I am going to talk about is pass protection. We could spend all day here talking about 101 ways to pass block. You know what I want to do with the ball? I want to run that ball. I do not want to take away from my running game by spending a lot of time learning how to protect the passer. I had to find something that fits into my scheme that would allow me to become a great pass protector, without taking away from my running game. We wanted our linemen to fire out but still stay under control. We wanted the linebackers and defensive backs to see run from our offensive line, even when we pass.

The first thing we teach our linemen in pass protection is how to read a rush from a defender. If he has his head down, his rush will be hard and physical. If he raises up in the air with the body, his rush will be some kind of finesse move.

As soon as the lineman straightens his legs in pass protection, he is dead. We eye the defender in the numbers. We want to know where the quarterback is going to set up. We want to know where the point of no return is. And, we want to stay between the defender and the passer. We must be patient, have good feet, and good initial movement.

Let me talk about four different sets we teach in our pass protection. This allows me to coach my players by the numbers so they know what I am talking about.

- The 1 set is the inside blocking technique. The key to this set is to keep the weight off the inside foot. I also want to maintain a power move position. That is a slight stagger in my feet with a good base. That allows me to shuffle down inside. The initial move is down inside, maintaining good weight distribution and a power position.
- The 2 set is for a head-up technique by the defender. It is like the 1 set in that my first responsibility is inside, but I don't step to the inside. I simply move my feet up, and I am already in the proper position.
- In the 3 set, the responsibility is for the outside move. That is the reverse of the 1 set. My weight distribution is on the inside and outside foot light.
- The 4 set is for a wide charge from the defender. I want to take him on as close to the line of scrimmage as possible. We want to stay parallel with the line of scrimmage and take him on as quickly as we can. The weight has to be on the inside foot. We want to shuffle and take this move deep and out of the passing lane. If the defender comes inside, the blocker has his power move with the weight on the inside.

I don't like to lock up with a rusher. When we do that, we tend to forget about our feet. When the rusher moves, we tend to fall and try to drag him down. I want to lock out, recoil, and take him on again. That keeps my feet moving. You don't block a man with your hands and arms. You block him with your feet. You want to move your feet and legs and maintain your position.

When we set up, we want the elbows in. We don't want the defender to touch our shoulders. We want our hands active enough to keep the defender's hands off our shoulders.

Now, what do you do with all of this material I have just covered? What I want you to do is go home and teach the techniques that fit into your system of offense. When you coach offense, you must know *why* something doesn't work. You can't grab bag and try to find something that works. When the play breaks down, you have to know why, so the next play can take advantage of what happened.

5

Offensive Line Techniques and Drills

Danny Hope
Purdue University
1998

I am going to talk a little about techniques and drills and how to transfer techniques onto the playing field. I would like to talk a little about philosophy. You must know where you are coming from to get where you want to go. You must have something to hang your hat on. With coach Joe Tiller, our number one team goal was to have fun. It may sound elementary, but it works for us at Purdue. We don't fear failure. Coach Tiller told me, for most of his career, he did not focus on having fun, but, for the latter part of his career, he wants to have fun first. It carries over into the attitude of the players, as enthusiasm is contagious. Having fun is the philosophy our head coach hangs his hat on.

As an offensive line coach with coach Howard Schnellenberger, I spent a lot of time teaching assignments on the football field. Coach Schnellenberger pulled me aside and told me that in order to be a good offensive line coach, I shouldn't hang my hat on being an assignment football coach. If I only teach assignments, there are a few things happening. One, I have too many plays and I need to condense my schemes, or my players are stupid and I cannot teach. You don't want to focus only on assignments, because the things that make a difference in offensive line play are technique and tempo. In practice if you are spending a lot of time on who a player is going to block, you are not watching what they are doing technique-wise and you are not pushing them to get away from the defense.

The philosophy I adopted in the last several years is to keep it simple, reduce the number of schemes, improve as a technique coach, and try to make a difference in the tempo. After every practice, I ask myself this question, "Did I make a difference in the technique or tempo of the practice?" Some days when I walk off the field, I am a little disappointed in myself. Asking this question encourages me to assert myself from the start to the end of practice. To win on the offensive line, you need to practice technique and tempo.

When I coached the line at Louisville, Wyoming, Oklahoma, and Purdue this year, there were three elements I wanted the offensive linemen to hang their hats on. The number one fact with offensive linemen is want to. Want to is the overriding factor in how good a player is. Guys who are average athletes can be the best players, as they have the most heart. I have had great athletes who were average players because they have less heart. We try to emphasize want to in our group and make it a part of us. You have to critique it and point it out on the field. When you are running sprints, you have to challenge the guys to be first and show the players how important want to really is.

The second element that is important is tempo. Being politically correct, we use the word vaginal as an adjective. If you have a vaginal offensive line, then there is a good chance you may be a vaginal offensive line coach. Think about it. Now, the players they gave to you are not natural-born butt kickers. You have to take your guys and insist that they play aggressive. You must teach them how to be aggressive. We want that to be our trademark. The best compliment for an offensive line coach is to have another coach tell you this: "Your guys play hard, and your guys play really tough."

The tempo is very, very important to me. There are some things you can do in practice to make the linemen tough and more aggressive. In individual periods, we spend a lot of that time working on individual drills. We try to go on a high tempo and try to get it on during that period. For example, every day, we work on cut blocking. I like to start every day with that drill for a couple of reasons. I want to get the players running full speed, lunging forward, being reckless, and getting on the ground. A lot of times, linemen are afraid to get on the ground. Every day for about 10 minutes, we work on running down the field,sawing the defensive players down. It is a high-tempo-type drill.

Another thing we do every single day is boards and bags. This is where the players are working on their footwork on the inside zone. They have to be very physical because we do not stop. We will go over that drill later, but it has to be a physical drill. A lot of people run the drill, but they do not make the drill aggressive. We use boards and bags as an aggressive drill.

During the spring, we do a lot of shoot drills. For fear of injury, I don't do them during the season much. There seems to be a problem with offensive linemen, now, in that they do not want to put their face on anyone. In the pass protection, they put their hands in front of themselves. In the springtime, we want the guys to accelerate through the shoots against air. Then, we put the offensive linemen against the linemen in the shoot. We do it in the spring, so in the season when we come off the ball and run the inside zone, our linemen are hitting as hard as they can. We do a lot of shoot work in the spring, because we think it makes them aggressive and encourages them to go in and hit people with their faces.

We do a drill we call the fill block, where a player works on stepping forward like a center, if he as going to go back on somebody, or the tackle gapping down. We do a fill drill, where we are firing off the ball with a point of aim where we are making contact with each other.

The tempo makes the difference in the offensive line. This year, we had a player named Mark Fisher. He is an offensive line coach's dream. He was as tough as they come. He was such an aggressive player that he gave the other players someone to emulate.

The last element is the us aspect. It is the us or togetherness as a group. This year, I had a very efficient offensive line. Individually, they were not outstanding players but worked well as a group. In order to have a cohesive offensive line, I think you have to give them something a little special. We will ask the line to do something extra as a team, whether it is sit-ups or pass sets. I am always trying to give them something extra to do together. Anytime you give them something extra to do, that will bond them closer and the more they will feel special.

I think you are kidding yourself if you think you are just going to show up and coach. I think that is a crime in our profession today. For some coaches, the only time they are around the players is when it is time to coach them on the field. Coaching requires more personal interaction with the players, especially when you have a large support staff, so when you have to get salty with them, they know you love them and they can trust you. We hang our hat on the want to, the tempo, and the us thing. If you do not do all three things, you will not overachieve on the offensive line. You will not play well enough to win all of your games. The players you get on the offensive line are not good enough to play to their ability. They have to play above their ability. They need these three elements.

Let me cover the stances. We do not spend a lot of time on stances. We vary our stances based on down and distance, whether or not the play is going to be a five-step drop or a third-and-long situation.

If you are going to put them in an up stance, they are going to be in an up stance. If it is third-and-one and you are going to run the ball and they have their butt up in the air, that is fine. It is when you don't want them to know if you are running or passing is when you have a problem with the stance. If you run the ball all of the time, no one would have any problem with the stance, because everyone would have their butts up in the air. The same is true if you throw the ball all of the time and you have your butt down all of the time.

We do a drill that we call run or pass—check-with-me. We run this drill during the off-season. The linemen get in their stance and wait for a run or pass call and then shift their weight forward. If it is a pass, they shift the weight back. We work on shifting their weight without adjusting their hands. We do not worry on how high or low their hips are. We tell them we are going to run right or pass right. We get them down in their stance and tell them, "Set." I will call out, "Pass right," and on, "Hut," they have to get their hands up, and, boom, they have to get over here and set up for a pass. If I call, "Run right," they have to do run steps when I call, "Set." We work on an up stance, and we do not give a darn if they know we are going to throw the ball. Then, we will get in a three-point stance, and we do not care if they know we are going to run the ball. The rest of the time, we are in a balanced stance. We try to shift our weight around a little without changing our hand placement on the ground.

I think you have to work on stance and starts a lot during the off-season. During the season, you want to work on football. You can't spend half of your time working on stance during the season. The linemen must be disciplined enough to get together and go outside and work on their stance on their own. On Thursdays and Fridays during the season when we do not practice as much, I try to take the first five minutes of individual work to get them back into a regular stance. Typically, as the season progresses, their stances get sloppier. I see them in the film, and I can't believe some of the players in their stances. We want to prevent bad habits.

I want to talk about fill blocking. Some of you may call it gap down blocking. If you want to make an offensive line coach nervous, just ask him how to gap block down. He is nervous because he can never be right. The best way to block a gap block, where you can cut off protection and also the back door, is to take the inside foot and step at the defender's far foot. That is your point of aim. You have to gain ground, or the defender will get penetration. So, if I am going to gap block down on my inside, I put the weight on my outside foot and I push with my outside foot and step toward his far foot and try to put my face in the "V" of the defender's neck. I try to drive his butt out of there.

When we teach the basic gap block, we will come out with two lines of defensive players. We have one line of offensive players. We have the defensive line get down first. Then,, we have the offensive blocker line up. We can gap block left or right. You can stand behind the blocker to see that he is right with his technique. You have to watch his feet. We always have the defensive players line up first in order to give you a true look. We work either gap blocking to the left or right. We make the guy standing behind the blocker watch to make sure he sees what is going on and that he is right with the technique. If you don't do a lot of filling or gap blocking, it is still a good drill to teach you to push off as you step. I have a tape here that will shows our center's gap blocking.

Gap block drill and technique. Step at the defender's far foot with your inside foot. Put your face in the "V" of defender's neck. The offensive man can gap block in either direction. Both defenders penetrate with movement by the offensive lineman.

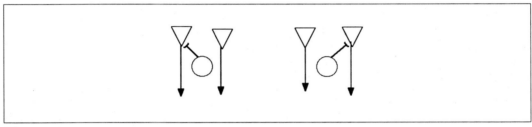

Diagram 1

The center must be aggressive and obtain his block in the trap block in gap blocking. When we go out in the pre-game warm-up before a game, there are several different drills we do. One of them is gap block.

Another drill we use is pass protection on a sled. I believe there are two reasons why you get beat on pass protection. Take missed assignments and players not getting off on the snap, and this is what we find: first, you get outside your center of gravity, and, two, you set up in the wrong place.

All the drills we use in season and out of season as far as pass protection goes are things that are going to help you get out of your stance and maintain your center of gravity. We choreograph the sets based on the steps of the quarterback's drop and the alignment of the defender.

I want to get into the drills that help us keep our center of gravity. In order to keep their center of gravity, we tell our linemen this: we want them to imagine they have a seven-foot steel rod stuck in the top of their head. Then, we run the rod down the player's body. He has two feet of the rod sticking from his head. If we would stand behind the player, we would see his center of gravity can be maintained by keeping the bar vertical. It should be straight up and down.

Another drill we have is a sled drill, where we ask them to change direction and do some things on the sled. We think this drill helps them with their pass protection techniques and it also helps to keep their center of gravity on blocks. We do this drill every day.

We have them bend the knees and keep their heels on the ground, as well as their butt to the grass. You have to keep the heels flat on the ground. Then, we work on sitting down in the sweet spot in a position where we feel comfortable to take on the defender. We work on stabbing the bag, straight line shots, from our breast to their breast. We emphasize taking the triceps and squeezing the front of your rib cage, so the elbows are not dropping before you stab. This means our hands get on the defender faster. We ask them to lock the bag out, to sit down and separate, and to squeeze the edge of the bag.

We run the inside zone play. It is our 34 and 35 sprint. We use the board and bag drills to help with these plays. I really want you to see this drill first. When we line up on the line of scrimmage, we want our helmet on the bottom of the center's numbers. That is how deep we have our offensive linemen off the ball. The rule is that they have to break the center's hip. If you line up at the center's numbers, you are about as close as you can be. We want them back off the ball, so they can get over in front of the defender before he knocks the crap out of them. They have to get over on the defender at their point of aim. If you crowd the ball, contact is made before the blocker can get over on the defender. When we are working on our drive block, which we used on our inside zone play, we give the linemen a point of aim. We tell them to take their nose and split the defender's sternum at the outside numbers. We want his inside foot slightly inside the defender's inside foot. That is the fit that we want. We feel if we can get back off the ball we can get over in position to get our face on the defender. We feel the contact will happen on the second step. So, when we do boards and bags, we back them off just enough to make the drill effective. We tell the bag holder to move forward. That is what the defense does. We do not want the bag holder to stand back and let the blocker drive him 15 yards off the ball. We want the blocker to go over and then up. The defender with the bag steps forward and jams the bag into the blocker as hard as he can. The last time we played, the defense was coming across the line as hard as they could. So, we want the man with the bag doing the same thing. If the man holding the bag does not make it an aggressive drill, we will take the bag away from him and make it live for him. The guy holding the bag is the key to the drill. The blocker does not get anything out of the drill if the defender does not do the drill right. This is a good assessment of what we are going to get.

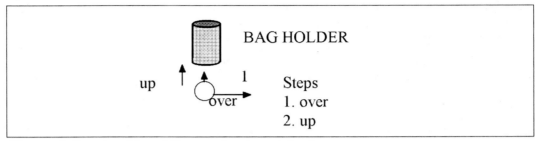

Diagram 2. Board and bag drill versus head-up defender

We have established the fact that contact will take place on the second step. We have backed the offensive man off the ball. We want them to dip the shoulders as they take that first step to get their pads low. We emphasize this a lot, but you do not see them dropping down very much, but we do not see them raising up a lot. The first step, which we call the set step, is the one that gets them over. We want them to lower their pads. If they can lower the pads one inch instead of raising them by three inches, that is four inches of leverage. That is a lot of leverage.

Next, we offset the board and block at an angle. This would be a right guard on a 3 technique defender, or it could be a tackle on a 5 technique, or an end on a 9 technique. Now, for the blocker to get his face outside and up into the defender's numbers, he has to move over and back a little. We take a bucket or drop step. We bucket step, gaining width and depth. Then, we step up. We offset the board in order to emulate the defender lining up off the outside shoulder of the lineman. We do a lot of work with boards and bags. We work on the bags both right and left.

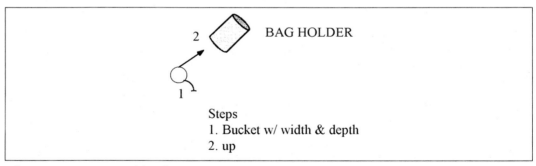

Diagram 3. Versus outside alignment

The next drills are the cut drills. I know you cannot cut in high school. However, there is some carryover in this drill. We are cutting the linebacker in this drill. We offset him so it is more like a game situation.

We tell the blocker to get on top of the defender. We want to take the arm and rip it through the crotch of the linebacker. We want the shoulder pads coming up. We want

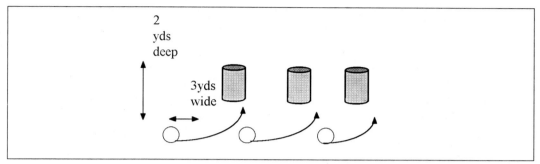

Diagram 4. Linebacker cut or climb drill

to get as close to the defender as possible. We throw off the outside foot. We want to get on top of the man before we throw. We tell them to run to their legs and get on top of them before we throw. A coaching point is this: when we land on the ground, we get up running. We do not lay on the ground. We do this for two reasons. One, we can continue to tie the man up. Second, we can get downfield and get another man.

We use our reach block on our outside zone plays, which are our 38 and 39 sprint. We also use the block on the toss play. The thing on the reach block is what you teach as the point of aim and what you are making contact with. We want to take our backside pad and get it on the defender's outside pad. A lot of people teach the block by telling the blocker to take his face and get it on the outside of the numbers. By teaching the block by getting the backside pad on his outside pad, I think two things happen for you:

- If I am trying to reach a real wide man and I am trying to get my backside pad on his outside pad, it will usually take care of where my feet should go in order for me to get the angle on the defender. You do not have to teach a lot of lead step footwork, if you are teaching backside pad on outside pad. They will step wide if they do this.
- If I get my backside pad on the defender's outside pad, the defender has to fight through my neck and head in order to get to the ballcarrier. If we just put our nose on him, he can slip off and get to the play. When we teach the reach block, we want that backside pad on the outside pad. We try not to cross over for our second step. We do not teach it, but it happens at times. We teach them on the reach block to never step past their midline. We want them to get their foot down and never step over the midline. We teach them to take a big drop step, a bucket step, and I want to make sure we are getting depth and width. We want the back pad on the outside pad. Once I get that leverage, it is critical that I get heavy with my outside arm and then fight to get north and south.

Another drill I picked up from a former Illinois coach is very helpful in teaching this block. We take two offensive linemen and line them head-up on each other. We have

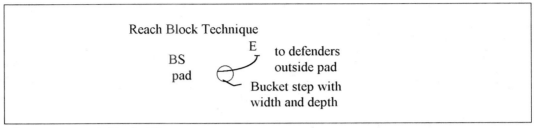

Diagram 5. Reach block drill

both offensive linemen try to reach each other at the same time. They try to get their backside pad on the outside pad of the other man. This is a great drill. The man that gets off the ball first has the advantage. They are both doing the same drill, and they are using the same technique. They really work on getting off on the snap count. It teaches the blockers to fight to get to the outside on the reach block. They have to get their feet moving, and they have to stay up on the man. This has been a good drill for us, especially for our centers, who have to do a lot of reach blocking. Also, it has helped our tight ends and our tackles on the openside. When you are talking about reach blocking, the vertical alignment is critical. We review this all of the time. We want the helmet on the center's bottom part of his numbers. By halftime, the officials should come over on the sideline and tell us that we have to move our linemen up on the line more.

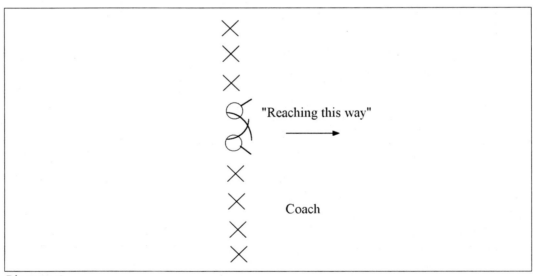

Diagram 6

When we run our outside zone plays, 38 and 39 sprint, we break into two parts. We have two linemen on offense. We have an offensive tackle that is covered and a guard that is uncovered.

When we teach the outside zone, we teach it as covered or uncovered techniques. If I am the guard and we are running the outside zone play and the tackle is covered, then the guard is the uncovered man. The guard will take the defender if he goes inside. We tell the covered man this. If the man is heads up, we want the tackle to overreach and rip pad under pad and try to slow the man down a little for the backside guard. The closer the linebacker gets to the play, the wider you must lead. If a man is head-up or on the inside eye, we expect that blocker to be the one who comes off on the linebacker.

When you are the uncovered man, some people call them the trail man, but we call them the short puller. The reason for this is because the technique we are using is a short pull technique. There are three steps he must use on this technique. The first thing he must do is to open his hips up and point his nose toward the boundary. He must open up all the way. They must be able to go off the tail of the cover man. If they do not open up enough, it is hard to get the head across the bow if the defender pinches.

The second step is to go for the outside number of the defender. He has to be looking for that aiming point.

The third step is an action. If I see his outside number, one of two things happens. Either he takes him over and keeps his head across the bow, or he turns it up at the linebacker.

6

Offensive Line Blocking Techniques and Drills

Bill Legg
Purdue University
2004

I have taken all these ideas from guys I thought were good football coaches. I tried to piece their ideas together into something that fit what I believe. I can take these ideas to the players and teach them with full conviction. I firmly believe it is not what I know that is important. It is what my players can learn, understand, and execute that matters.

You have to teach your players in a manner they can learn, understand, and execute. The game of football comes down to the players on the field, not the coaches in the press box. I believe strongly that fundamentals win football games. We can talk about great schemes, but the guys that block and tackle best usually win the game.

The system in football allows your team to be successful, but it is the players within the system that win games. For the players to win games, they have to be allowed to play. Do not turn your players into robots by overcoaching them. The major concern of the coach should be that the player is getting the job done within the framework of the system.

My topic today is run blocking techniques. At Purdue, the first objective in running the football is for our offensive linemen to cover up the defenders. That means leaving no one unblocked on the defensive line. The second objective in the offensive line is to create movement.

Movement in our philosophy could be laterally down the line of scrimmage instead of off the line. It does not have to be vertical movement for the linemen to be successful.

To accomplish these objectives and goals, we start with the offensive linemen's stance. At Purdue, we are going to run and throw the ball an equal amount of the time. I want our linemen in a stance that does not indicate what they are going to do prior to the snap of the ball.

For us to have a balanced stance, the first thing we have to teach is the base. We have some tall offensive linemen whose stances have to be modified. However, for the average player, his feet are going to be shoulder-width apart. I have two players that are 6 foot −7, and they have to take a wider stance to get their hips down.

The toes in the stance are pointed straight ahead. By pointing the toes straight ahead, it gets the rest of the body pointed in the same direction. Our right side players get into a right-handed stance, and the left side players get into a left-handed stance. We get in those stances to accommodate the passing game rather than the running game.

We stagger our feet in our stance. The guards align in a toe-to-instep stagger. The tackles are in a toe-to-heel type of stagger. That allows the tackle to kick out of his stance quicker in pass protection against the wide outside rusher. That allows him to get his feet in position prior to having to move.

For us to have a balanced stance, the weight must be on the linemen's feet. We use the expression full-footed to teach our weight distribution. The full-footed philosophy of the stance is going to depend on the flexibility in the players' ankles. The guard can get his inside foot flat on the ground because his stance is a toes-to-instep stagger. The outside foot of the offensive lineman has the weight on the ball of the foot. I want as little air as possible under the outside heel of the guard. With the tackles, I am more forgiving with the air under his heel because his stagger and the width of his stance are wider and longer.

After we get both feet as flat on the ground as we can, we talk about loading the spring. I talk to my players about being coiled up like a spring. From that position, they can explode. The linemen set their feet and squat to get down in their stance. We want to create good power angles in their ankles, knees, and hips.

You have to work the two-steps routine into your practices daily. I use T-boards to teach the two-step technique (Diagram 1). You can set the T-board at different angles so the linemen can set their first step at different angles. The objective behind the T-board is to get the first step pointing in the same direction as the T and to get the second step down before the feet cross the T. We get power and explosion, and the base is still underneath the lineman as he moves out into his block. We use the T-boards in conjunction with the chutes as our first drill period of the day.

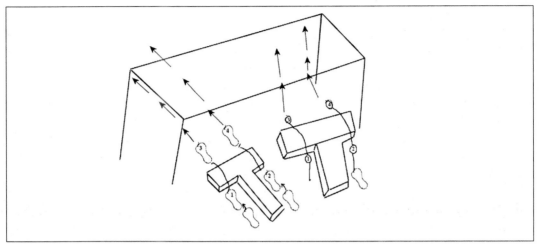

Diagram 1. Chute and T-board drill

My chute does not have any divider under it. It is 25 feet long and 48 inches high, and allows me to create any angles that I want to use. You can also pull and trap in the chute. I set the T-boards in the chute and go through a variety of angles very rapidly. For an offensive lineman to hit the target consistently, he has to understand the take-off. The take-off has to be ingrained.

The next thing in the blocking progression is target practice (Diagram 2). When we take target practice, we use what we call a two-step punch mentality. The type of running play will determine what the target is going to be. If the play is an inside run, the target is the outside number of the defender tight to the sternum. On an outside run, the target is the armpit or the outside shoulder of the defender. On a gap blocking scheme, the target is the near hip of an inside defender.

I always start with the target in close proximity to the blocker. Those techniques put the target at arm's length from the blocker. The blocker takes two quick steps. His nose and eyes should be on the aiming point of the defender.

In offensive blocking, I believe the blocker has to lead with his face. I do not think you should teach hitting with the head, but wherever the head goes, the body will

The body posture in the lineman's stance creates a squatter's arch in his lower back. The forearms are relaxed and resting on the thighs. The lineman's chest is up in his stance. The description of a squatter's arch refers to a weightlifting technique that is done in a leg squat exercise.

If we are going to use a two-point stance, we stop in that position and get ready to play football. This is basically our two-point stance we use in our passing scheme. We can run the ball out of the two-point stance because this is a sound stance with all the fundamentals of a three-point stance.

To go to the three-point stance, we let the appropriate hand drop down and hang in front of the lineman. I tell the lineman to take six, which means to take six inches in front of the dangling hand and put the hand down. The rule is that the lineman is not allowed to use his thumb when he puts his hand down on the ground. If he does not use the thumb in the stance, the offensive lineman cannot put enough weight on his hand to get out of balance. The weight is centered over their hips, legs, knees, and feet.

When the hand is dropped to the ground, the weight will shift slightly forward. However, the hand can be pulled off the ground without the lineman falling forward on his nose. The only time the thumb is allowed to go to the ground is in a short yardage or goal line situations. In those situations, the offensive line will be crowding the ball.

The first thing I teach when we go to run blocking is footwork. The reason I work on the offensive lineman's footwork is to increase the odds of him making a successful block. The first movement in the lineman's footwork is called the set step. The purpose of the set step is to set the angle of the body at the target.

The length of the step depends on the position of the blocking target. If the defender is in front of the offensive lineman, the set step is picked up and put down in almost the same position. If the defender has to be reached, the first step is longer. The first step is not moving the lineman forward; it is putting his body into position to attack the target.

After the set step, the next step is an attack step. If the blocker is going to the right, he pushes off his inside foot and points his toe at the target to set the angle. The next step is an attack step. The offensive linemen attack the target with the second step. If the blocker attacks on the first step, he is going to have problems because of the slanting and twisting defenses. Offensive line schemes are more zone-blocking schemes than man-blocking schemes. If the linemen get too much weight forward, they cannot adjust on the second step to hit the target. The second step is a six-inch power step that regenerates the weight going forward to the aiming point.

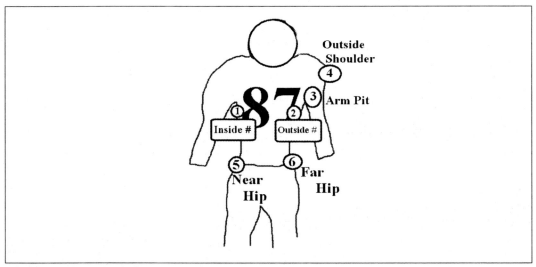

Diagram 2. Target practice

follow. You cannot expect the offensive linemen to put his head on the outside numbers of the defender if he does not lead with his face.

The reason we do so much work in the chute is to stay low. We do not want our body angles to change drastically. We want the butt and head to stay down as we come off the ball. The blocker wants to surround the target with his hands, provided the target is big enough. We are leading with the face, but we want the hands to get to the target before the face.

The blocker, as he takes the set step, pulls his hands off the ground. On the second step, he shoots his hands to the target. We call that pull and shoot. We teach shooting the hands on the second step to get inside the defender's hands. The blocker rips the wrist, drives the elbow, and locks out on the defender. The punch, which comes from shooting the hands, has nothing to do with strength. The punch to lock out is nothing but speed and timing. You can drill the punch in the winter, spring, and fall programs to perfect the lockout.

Sometimes the target is too small to hit with the hands. When a lineman has to gap block on a defender, it is difficult to shoot the hands because the target is too small. To solve that problem we train two points of contact. On the big targets, we teach "hat and hands to the target." On the small targets, we teach that the shoulder and forearm are the points of contact. As the blocker comes down on the hip of the defender, he puts the ear hole of his helmet on the aiming point and brings up the forearm. The blocker is using the front part of the shoulder pad and his chest muscle to get into the defender.

After we work the offensive linemen with the defender in close proximity, we vary the distance. When we start to vary the distance, the target is removed from the area around the lineman. His block could be on a linebacker, a trap, or a log type.

We use what we call an arm's length rule. The rule states no matter how far the blocker has to run, when he gets within an arm's length of the target, he goes back to his two-step scheme. The blocker repeats the same skill as he did when the target was close to him.

After we teach the skill, we time it with target practice. We have the blocker fire up on a linebacker at linebacker's depth and watch his technique. We practice the technique of pulling and logging on a defensive end to perfect the angles of the offensive blocker. We pull a guard on a power play and let him turn up on the linebacker. We give him all the situations he has to handle in his blocking scheme. We rep it and practice it until the blocker has confidence.

In practice, the footwork drills are the first period after stretching. They are part of my warm-up drill every day. On Sunday afternoon, once we get our footwork drills and warm-up completed, we go to target practice drills. We start them on reach blocks and go to linebacker blocks. After that, we cover all the situation blocks that may occur in our scheme.

In the target practice drill we are checking their hats, eyes, hands, and shoulders. We want to make sure they are where they belong. We move the defenders around so the linemen have to work covered principles and uncovered principles in the drill. We call the play and work the two-step movement. We continue on with the drill, working aiming points for covered and uncovered defenders. From there, we work the angles and fits of the hands on the defenders. The key to finding success in these skills is repetition.

After we work on our footwork and fits into the block, we work on uncoiling and exploding on contact. The reason we do this drill is to maximize the leverage of the blocker. Defensive coaches are telling their defensive linemen the same thing I am telling my offensive linemen.

At some point in blocking low, you reach a point of no return. That means if the blockers get too low, all they do is hit the defender and fall on the ground. Most contact between the blocker and defender is going to be like two rams butting each other in the head. When this takes place, the hand placement, forearm extension, and explosion are important to maximize leverage. We have to literally think we are running through the defender. When we do this drill, the contact has to happen fast.

We want to think in terms of diving off a diving board into a swimming pool. The offensive blocker wants to dive through and snap the wrist in the explosion of the block into the defender.

To run through a defender, the blocker has to keep his feet moving during contact. The reason blockers lose their feet at contact is because they try to jump off both feet. To finish the block, the lineman has to explode and take the next step. The step before the lineman hits the defender is important because that is the plant step for the explosion. When that foot hits the ground, the blocker drives his knee up to take the next step and explodes from the toes up through his body. The hips have to unlock because that is where the power is coming from in the block.

We do not teach our players to roll their hips. We do squats, cleans, dead lifts, and vertical jumps, and none of those exercises are hip roll exercises. Those exercises snap the hips and explode out, but they do not invert the hips. We want to use the same kind of movement that is required to perform a standing vertical jump. We want the hips to go through the shoulders.

When you do that type of exercise you maximize the power, and you maintain power angles. We want our butt behind the contact at all times. We want the butt to go through the shoulders.

The blocker wants to feel his arms lock out on the defender. If you were doing this blocking technique on air, it would look like the lineman is diving into a swimming pool and doing a belly flop.

The first thing I am going to do with the linemen to teach this technique is to get them in a six-point stance (Diagram 3). They are going to get down on their hands and knees and rock back on their haunches. If we are not wearing pads, we may want to put a hand shield in front of them to break their falls. On the command, they explode from that position, with their knees going through their hip area, the hips going through the shoulder area, and the hands coming up in the punch. The movement is one motion, and they dive out and catch themselves on their chest.

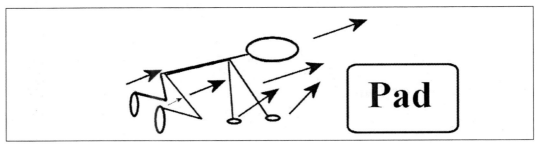

Diagram 3. Six-point explosion

The next part of the drill is to put a player in front of them with a hand dummy about arm's length from the blocker. The linemen do the same thing from the six-point stance, and the blocker can feel it as he explodes through the dummy.

We go to a fit up drill where the block and defender are placed into a fit position just before contact is made (Diagram 4). This is the position a blocker would be in after the two-step punch. His nose is on the target, with his hands surrounding the target. He takes the next step, which is to explode the hips as fast as he can through the defender. The emphasis is on taking the next step so he can finish the block and locking out with his hands.

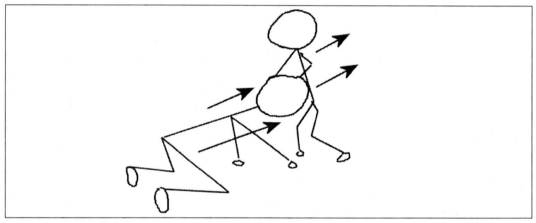

Diagram 4. Fit drill

In that whole process, the blocker is creating explosion, quickness, snap, and lock out. The third phase of the drill is to back them up and take them through the technique of the covered lineman. That allows the linemen to go from the stance through the block.

The defender is going to move at the offensive blocker. Even though we are exploding out and punching our hands, we are not going to get to the perfect lockout position. The blocker will never get completely uncoiled unless the defender is terrible. However, if the blocker can explode violently enough to get to the lockout position, he is in control.

On the second day of practice, we warm up with our footwork drills. We do a few target practice drills, but the primary work is done on explosion drills. The second day of the practice week is a big contact day for the offensive linemen. On Sunday, we did target practice, and on Tuesday, we are going to do the same drills, except we are doing the next step, which is explosion. If you do not do these drills full speed and live, the players will never improve their technique.

The finish to the block is the next part of the progression. Finishing off a block begins with attitude and effort. We want to use a sprinter mentality on the finish because we want to maximize the pressure on the defender. No matter how good the offensive lineman is, chances are the defender is a better athlete than he is. When they hit each other at the same time, there is not going to be much movement.

The fact that there is no movement is fine with the offensive lineman. We are looking for a stalemate with the defense because eventually the defender has to get off the block. If the defender is going to make the tackle, he has to separate from the offensive blocker. If the offensive lineman wants to stay with the block, he has to maximize the pressure on the defender. The sprinter's mentality starts with the movement of the feet, the lower body, and the legs.

As the blocker starts to run through the defender, his toes will slowly move outside. We want to get as many cleats in the ground as possible. This allows the blocker to push an immovable object with maximum pressure. It allows him to change direction when the defender changes direction. The blocker's arms are going to be somewhere near lock out, and his eyes are totally focused on the target. That lets the blocker feel and see what is happening in front of him.

We do a drill to help the blocker finish the block (Diagram 5). When we start the drill, we begin at the point where the blocker has exploded and nearly locked out the defender. On the whistle, the offensive blocker starts to crank his knees up and let the toes go out to get as many cleats in the ground as possible.

Diagram 5. Finish drill

The defenders start out the drill by not exerting much resistance on the offensive lineman. I will tell the defender to exert half pressure on the blocker. As the drill continues, I tell the defenders to load up and not let the offensive blocker move them.

The defender makes the blocker run as hard and fast as he can in place. The defender has to eventually separate to make the tackle.

When the defender tries to separate, the blocker feels the movement. The blocker moves his feet rapidly and will not lose contact on the block. The defender has started the movement the offensive blocker needs to bury him. As the pressure from the defender lessens, the blocker's steps get larger as he maintains contact with the defender and continues to push.

We use a fit drill to practice the finish of the block. We fit the blocker and defender together with the blocker in his coiled position (Diagram 6). The offensive blocker goes from an explosion to a speed finish. We do not narrow the base of our feet when we get into the sprinter's mentality; we simply increase our foot and knee movement. The key to keeping the wide base is the position of the toes. If the feet are pointed straight ahead, the feet will come together. If the toes go outside, the feet stay wider apart. As we did in the other fit drill, the blocker backs up and executes the entire block from two-step to explode and to finish.

Diagram 6. Fit and finish

On the third day of practice, we are three days from the last game and three days until the next game. This is our second contact day of the week. We warm up with footwork drills and take a few shots of target practice, and a couple shots of explosion drill. For the next fifteen minutes of our practice the offensive line will work on finishing blocks. The pancake block comes from the finish of the block.

When we do separation drills, we work a one-on-one drill (Diagram 7). I stand behind the offensive linemen and tell the defenders which way to try to get off the blocks. The offensive and defensive lineman locks up in a stalemated situation. When I blow the whistle, the defenders separate and the blockers work on their finish.

If a blocker is running as hard and as fast as he can, trying to run through a brick wall, his steps are short. However, if a defender is trying to get off a block, to run to the football, the blocker strides lengthen and automatically adjust.

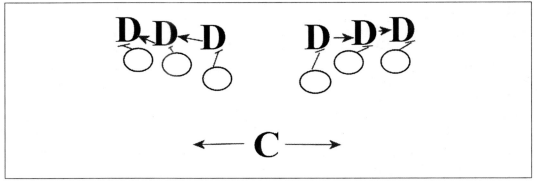

Diagram 7. Separation drill

We are going to do additional drills to improve our technique. We take the target drill and make it a moving target drill (Diagram 8). Defensive linemen are not going to stand in one place and let the offensive linemen come out and hit them. The defenders are going to be moving or stunting to the ball. The key to the moving target is the second step. The first step is our set step. That step gives us direction in our charge. If the defender moves, the second step can adjust to that movement without destroying the base.

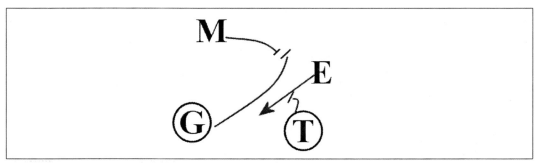

Diagram 8. Moving target drill

The next drill we do is called the replacement drill (Diagram 9). If both players are trying to get their hands inside the other, in reality they end up with one hand inside and one outside. Each player has one hand on the chest and one on the shoulder pad. It is hard to get both hands inside at contact, but if the blocker works hard enough, he can get his second hand inside on the finish of the block. That is what we work on in the replacement drill.

To do the drill, we fit the linemen with one hand on the chest and one hand on the shoulder. I designate one of the players as the blocker and the other the defender. When I blow the whistle, the offensive blocker starts his finish drill and wheels his outside hand up underneath the defender's arm and replaces it inside on his chest. Sometimes the blocker misses with both hands. When the whistle blows, the blocker wheels both hands inside during the finish working one hand inside at a time.

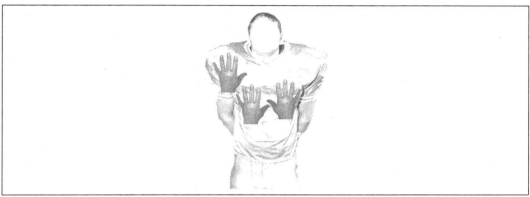

Diagram 9. Replacement drill

Throughout our drill work I am trying to create carryover for our players. If the blocker has a man over him and he is trying to create vertical push, I call that a drive-block. If the blocker is trying to get outside leverage on a defender, that is a reach-block. If a backside tackle has a man over him and he is running away from him, it is a cutoff-block. The drive, reach, and cutoff-blocks are similar blocks in relationship to the aiming point.

When a tackle has to down block on the man inside of him, it is a gap-block. If a tackle has to block out on a defender outside of him, that is a fan-block. The last block is a pulling block where the offensive lineman traps or logs a defender. Those three blocks are similar in the aiming point and punch.

To create carryover with all these blocks, the offensive lineman has to realize that the targets change. The second thing the blocker has to learn is that as the target change, so do the angles. The first step is the set step, and that sets the angle for the blocker. As the target and angle change, the adjustment occurs in the first step only.

The next thing we have to discuss is how that works into our two-man schemes. We have built carry over into every individual block. The individual blocks carry over into the two-man scheme. The offensive linemen have to get used to working with their blocking partner. If we run an inside tight scoop scheme as with the inside zone play, we block that play with a tandem block (Diagram 10). In this scheme there is generally a covered lineman and an uncovered lineman. We have a blocker who base blocks the man aligned on him and a blocker inside of him feeling his way through the playside gap. We tell the covered blocker that the defender covering him is his assignment until he is pushed off by the blocker to his inside. We tell the uncovered blocker to track through the near hip of the down lineman, up to the linebacker, unless the linebacker fires through the gap.

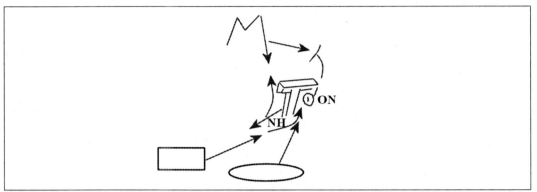

Diagram 10. Tight scoop

If the covered defender slants inside, the blocker adjusts his second step and goes from a two-handed punch to an inside forearm shiver on the slant defender. As the defender slants, he covers the uncovered blocker. Both blockers wedge the slanting defender up to the linebacker. One of the blockers will come off the wedge to block the linebacker. The linebacker will determine which blocker comes off. If the linebacker comes outside, the outside blocker comes off the wedge to block the linebacker. The inside blocker will take over the slanting defender and seal him.

There are several coaching points to this type of block. When the covered defender slants inside, we use the forearm instead of the hands. If the blocker tries to use his outside hand on the defender, his shoulders will turn, and he and the inside blocker will be pushing against one another. If the linebacker comes inside, the inside man comes off on the linebacker, and the outside blocker uses his outside hand to push the defender down the line of scrimmage.

We want to control the line of scrimmage first before we even think about the linebacker. We want to be patient with the tandem block and not be in a hurry to get off for the linebacker. If we are getting good movement on the down lineman, the blockers will not come off their double-team until they get to the same level as the linebacker. If we have a great defensive tackle and we are not getting movement, we stay on the double-team until the linebacker gets all the way up in the hole.

The full scoop goes with our outside zone play or the sweep (Diagram 11). The covered offensive lineman is reach blocking. His aiming point is the outside arm pit of the defender. He is going to open, attack, and track the outside arm pit of the defender.

The uncovered lineman is going to cover up the defensive lineman. His aiming point is the playside number of the defender. He is reading on the run, and has three steps to decide what to do.

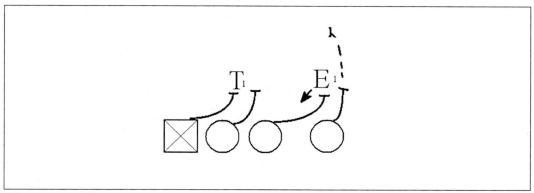

Diagram 11. Full scoop

The covered blocker stays on the defender until he is pushed off by the inside blocker. If the defender slants inside the covered blocker, he stays on top of the block, knowing that the inside blocker is watching the defender and coming to over take him. On the full scoop, we have two reach blocks working together.

When we combo block, we are aiming at the inside half of the defender, with the inside blocker and the outside half of him for the outside blocker. Both blockers are using forearms and not hands to secure the down defender. The inside blocker has his inside hand free and the outside blocker has his outside hand free. When one of them come off for the linebacker both offensive blocker engage the defender with their hands.

I appreciate the opportunity to come to talk to you.

7

Offensive Line Techniques and Drills

Paul Lounsberry
University of South Carolina
2003

I like to talk X's and O's and learn more about that part of the game, but I believe *drill work* is where you improve your team. What I want to do today is talk about our techniques and drill work. I'm going to explain why we do the drills and what we are trying to accomplish from them. The drills have to relate to what you do offensively so they carry over to what you want to accomplish on the field.

I want to start out by talking a little about our *offensive line philosophy*. I was a high school coach and teacher for 12 years. Coaching and teaching are the same things. It doesn't matter if you are coaching on the NFL, college, high school, or junior high levels, coaching is teaching.

Coaching is all about what you are able to convey to your players and what they are able to handle. Coaching is not about telling players how to play; it is teaching them how to play. It is not what you know that counts; it is what they know. You have to get your players to do what you want them to do to improve.

When you have a meeting with your players, make sure you are organized in that meeting. If you are organized in your meetings, it will save lots of misdirection and wasted time. That thought really carries over to the practice field because being organized on the practice field is essential. If you are organized on the practice field you can avoid distractions and get more out of your players. That lets you work on work ethics and tempo on the practice field.

Coaching the small things will lead to player improvements. You have to be big on details. When I teach the first step to a lineman, you don't tell them the step is about six inches. The step is between four and six inches. Be specific on details when you teach a skill or drill. If the eyes are supposed to be focused on the breastplate, make sure that is where the eyes are focused. Let them know that is important. Tell them exactly how much width you want between their hands.

Be demanding when you are coaching your players. Your players will respond to you if you ask them to do something. You don't have to berate them, they will respond to you if you demand that they do things a certain way. If you expect excellence from them, then they will give you excellence. Be demanding of your players on the field and in your meeting room.

We have instilled *accountability* into our players. As an offensive line coach, you have to teach accountability to the offensive linemen. If the ball is intercepted the offensive line should feel it is their fault. The quarterback didn't get to finish his read because of the pressure that was put upon him. He got hit as he was delivering the ball. He threw quickly because he had been knocked down three plays in a row.

The players have to understand their play is an *accumulative* thing. They are part of a unit. How the unit does depends on their individual efforts. They do not succeed as individuals. They succeed when their group does the job. This is a huge thing with the offensive line. They don't get a lot of recognition for the job they do until someone makes a mistake. When you succeed as an offensive line, it gives you and your group a good feeling. But when you fail as an offensive line, you have to be accountable.

The offensive line is the most important group of players on the field. The team wins or loses depending on how the offensive line plays. They are the biggest people on the field. They are the largest segment of players on the field. If you can get your five offensive linemen thinking the same way and winning together, that will spread throughout your entire team. They are the biggest bodies on the team and have the best work ethics. That in itself lends to building leadership within that group and on the team.

Players have to learn to accept *corrective criticism*. But the coach has to understand it is not what he says that is important, it is the way he says it. They have to know the coach cares about them getting better. Coaches need to correct the mistake, not belittle the players in doing it.

We tell our players this all the time: *Players play and the coaches coach*. Since they are the players, they are the ones who have to be coached and you have to coach him. Make sure everyone knows their role. When you are doing your corrective criticism, stay as positive as you can. When an offensive lineman gets beat on a pass-rush block, don't jump down his throat. Tell him, "You did a good job on your pass set and a great job on the first step. However, you need to work on your punch, staying square, and keeping that guy off the quarterback."

Stay positive whenever possible and praise him when he does something well. Outstanding play in the offensive line is all about the coach convincing the players that he cares about the lineman's improvement. Make sure your players understand that and you will have a lot more success teaching them.

When you are coaching your players, you must be honest with them. Don't tell them they are doing a good job when they are not. If they screw up give them something that will help them get better. Sometimes you have to bite your tongue and not say anything when your linemen screw up. He may be the best lineman you have. You just keep your mouth shut and go to the next play.

The offensive line coach has to have a passion for coaching. I really enjoy coming to work every day. I enjoy being in meetings with my players, being with them on the field, and being in the locker room with them. I have a passion for coaching and teaching. That can carry over to your players. If you have a good attitude about coming to work, your players will pick that up.

I'm going to talk about some fundamentals before I get into our drills. The first basic fundamental to an offensive lineman is the stance. We teach a *three-point stance* and a *two-point stance*. The center has to make some adjustments to his stance to perform certain skills. The stance needs to be adjusted to the system being coached.

If your team is a wishbone team, the offensive linemen don't need to be in a two- or three-point stance. They need to be in a four-point stance with a lot of weight forward. All they want to do is come off the ball hard and move straight ahead.

At South Carolina we are a one-back team and we are going to throw the ball about 50 percent of the time. In this system we need to be in a three-point stance as our run stance. In our situation we use the three-point stance for run blocking as well as pass blocking.

In second- and third-down situations where we have long yardage, we are going to screen, draw, and throw the ball down the field. In these situations our linemen may be in a two-point stance.

I know you have heard this before, but it is the truth. Every spring and fall when we start practice, we go back to our stance and make sure we do all the little things right.

We start with a *shoulder-width foot placement*. That seems to be the best position for the body to have balance and be able to move. If a player's girth is bigger, he may have to be slightly wider. We are in a right-handed stance on the right side of the ball and a left-handed stance on the left side of the ball. There are two reasons we do that. We do not flip-flop our line and it is easier to pass block with the outside foot back. The stagger in the stance is slight. I like to have a toe-to-instep relationship with the feet.

When the linemen start to go down in their stance, I tell them to put their forearms on their thighs and bend their knees. When they put their forearms on their thighs, I want their knees over their toes and their toes straight down the field. A lot of people teach the stance with the toes slightly outside. That makes the linemen get into a knock-kneed stance. You can teach it that way if you want because it is sound, however we don't teach it that way at South Carolina.

The thing we are checking as they go down is the *knee-over-the-toes relationship*. We don't want their knees outside or inside their toes. If their knees go outside it is usually because their feet are too close together. If their knees are inside too much, their feet are too far back or too wide. That is what we mean by teaching the details.

If they are in a right-handed stance, we tell them to drop their right hand down to the ground right below their right eye socket. They are in a *fingertip stance*. I never want more than 20 percent of their weight on their hand. If you ask the player to pick up his hand, he should tilt forward slightly but not very fast. The natural thing they want to do is get weight on their hands so they can come off the ball. The off hand in the three-point stance rests against the outside of the left thigh and knee. We don't cross it over our thigh.

The problem with the weight on the hand is coming out of the stance. In the stance I want the lineman to have all the cleats on his up foot in the ground. On the back foot I want all his cleats in the ground with the exception of his heel. If the weight is forward, the first step has to be a big step. In order to take short steps, you can't have too much weight on the hand. Defensive linemen are taught to look for tips from the offensive linemen in their stance. Our defensive linemen call them out when they see a heavy stance or light stance. We work hard on trying to keep 80 percent of our weight on our feet.

You have to work hard on those numbers with some of your lineman. They don't understand what 20 percent of their weight feels like. After we show them film work of themselves, they begin to understand what we are looking for. We have to really give them guidance in those areas.

We want our linemen in their stance to have a *flat back*. We don't want their tails too high or low. The center gets his tail down a little while he is calling our line blocking, but he always comes back to flat before he snaps the ball.

The head in the stance is *up*. We don't want it up so far that there is a bow in the neck. All they need to see is the defensive linemen and the bottom half of the linebackers.

The two-point stance has the same fundamentals as the three-point stance. On the stagger, we allow the tackle to drop his outside foot back a little more in his stagger. We want his back up straight with his chest out. We want his head and shoulders back. I want their hands up in a ready position and actually touching the numbers on their jersey.

The point of concentration in the two-point stance is the *bend in the thigh*. What we like is to have their thighs parallel with the ground. If they don't bend their knees, their stance is too high and their legs are too straight. That good knee bend allows them to come off the ball in a two-point stance and run block.

In the two-point stance, we don't normally put more weight on one foot than the other. We want a *balanced stance*. There are times when we mentally shift the weight on to one foot, but we don't want to tilt and tip the movement.

The guard could be in a three-point stance all the time. The tackle is the one who can take advantage of the two-point stance. He is the one who is being threatened by the rush of a defensive end coming off the edge with speed. He has to kick back quickly and get depth straight back off the line to change the angle of the speed rusher. Obviously if he is already up in his stance, it helps him retreat quicker. The guard does not face that hard speed rusher.

We are a big shotgun team. In his stance, the center will not have any weight on the ball. We do not want him to stagger his feet. We want his hips square so that the shotgun snap comes back straight. We want the tail of the center flat. If he gets his butt up, that causes him to snap the ball high. If his butt is down and flat, the ball will come out low and flat. I want the center to get the ball as far out in front of him as he can. I want him to be able to make a good snap, but I want the defensive front as far away from the offensive line as I can get them.

When the quarterback is under the center and taking a direct snap, it takes thousands of reps to get the snap down. The center, as he snaps the ball, is stepping into his block. The quarterback has to ride the center until he secures the ball. *The center has to put the ball in the same place every time.* He cannot put the ball to the side one time and down the middle the next. The center grips the ball with his thumb on the laces. We don't want the center to think about rotating the ball to give it to the quarterback. We tell him to snap it as fast and hard as he can. The natural rotation of his arm will put the laces of the ball right in the quarterback's hand.

We do the same with the *shotgun snap*. That way the center does not have to readjust the ball regardless of the quarterback being in the shotgun or under the center. The shotgun snap is nothing more than the pendulum swing with the arm without breaking the wrist. This has to be done with thousands of repetitions. An important thing about the shotgun snap is the center and quarterback being aligned properly. The center's stance has to be straight and square and the quarterback has to be directly behind the center.

I try to draw a line from the laces of the ball to the quarterback's belt. We have the center swing the ball down that line and away we go. The ball should come off the center's fingers and spiral just like a pass. He is really throwing a pass, but I don't want the center to think about throwing the ball. I want him to think about swinging the ball down the line. The ball should be in the same place every time. We want pace on the ball. We don't want the ball floating back to the quarterback. It has to come back with some speed to accomplish the purpose of being in the shotgun.

If there is a mistake made in the shotgun snap, I want it low not high. The thing the center has to be careful of is not to raise his hips before he lets the ball go. If he raises his hips and straightens his legs, the ball will go in orbit. If he flips his wrist it will go high. When you practice the snaps make the center step right and left as he is making the snap. Make sure the arm is not going right or left as the centers steps in that direction. That fact that he has to block someone helps keep his hips down. The snap is critical in the passing and running game. If the snap is low or high, it destroys the timing of the run and the pass.

One of the basic fundamentals in offensive line play is *alignment*. To be legally aligned on the line of scrimmage, the offensive guard's helmet must break the belt line of the offensive center. We align with our helmet between the bottom of the center's numbers and his belt line. In the two-point stance, since the lineman is upright, his feet have to be closer to the line of scrimmage. The tackle lines up on the center and not the guard.

We are as far off the football as we can legally get because we run the zone scheme and throw the ball quite a bit. We may cheat back further in some situations, but we never want to get a penalty for not being on the line of scrimmage.

We move up on the ball in certain situations. If we have a certain pass protection we move up on the ball. In some cases we want to cut down on the movement by the defensive line, so we move up on the ball to decrease the distance between the offensive line and the defenders. Getting closer to the ball helps the offensive line in preventing the defense from cross facing on blocks. In a short-yardage or goal line situations, we move up on the ball to cut down on penetration. We adjust the depth of our offensive linemen depending on the situation.

We get off the ball so that we can get our first step on the ground and the second step on the way to the ground before we make contact with the defender. If the defender hits the offensive linemen before he gets his first step in the ground, the offensive lineman loses power.

Our splits between our linemen are two feet. We measure two feet from the outside leg of the guard to the inside leg of the tackle. The split rule comes from trial and error. We found the two-foot split fits what we are doing in our offensive system best.

We adjust our splits slightly if we are in certain situations. If are trying to cut down on penetration, we tighten our splits. If we are going to run outside, we tighten down on the splits. If we are going to run inside, we may widen the split slightly. The split between the tight end and the offensive tackle is two-and-a-half to three feet.

Your splits have to fit your offensive plan. We adjust the splits to the play we are running and to the talent level of our offensive line. There are certain situations that require us to adjust our splits. Make sure you consider all the factors and do what is right for your individual situation.

There some basic fundamentals that must go with *run blocking*. The first thing you have to concentrate on is the first step. The quicker the offensive lineman can get his foot in the ground, the better off he is. We never want to be caught with both feet out of the ground. We never want to hop in anything we do. If the lineman steps underneath himself, he is defeated from the get-go. In the stance, I want all the cleats on the lineman's shoes *in the ground*. Every step the lineman takes he wants to have all his cleats in the ground. We never want to be on our toes. We want the weight on the balls of our feet.

When the lineman gets in a stance, he creates power angles in his ankles, knees, and hips. It is important to release all that power at the proper time. If you release the angles too early, you will be fully extended before the contact is made. We want to *release the power* through the surface of the block, not at the surface of the block. If we get fully extended at the surface of the contact and through the surface, we have maximized the power that has been created in those power angles.

As the lineman comes off the ball using short steps, he wants to keep his feet at shoulder width. If a lineman takes a step underneath his body, his feet are too close together. When that happens he loses his balance and control of the block. We want to *drive with each step* the lineman takes. When the first step is in the ground, the lineman drives out with his second step. When that step is in the ground, he drives out with the next step and continues to repeat the movement. If we can get the defender back on his heels, we have a chance to move him the way we want him to go.

It is important to keep your head up and your tail down. The body will go where the head goes. If the head is down, the body is going to go down. If the head goes down, the tail comes up and the only thing the lineman can do is to fall to the ground.

As the lineman punches out with his hands, he wants to make sure he gets his hands *inside the defender's hands*. The man that gets his hands inside usually wins the battle. If the offensive lineman has his hands inside the defender's, he can lift the defender's shoulder back and up. We want to shoot the hands under and inside the defender's hands with our thumbs up. Every defensive coach is going to coach his players to get their hands inside also. To get their hands inside, the offensive linemen have to work extremely hard at it.

When the powers angles are released, the linemen wants to hit on the rise, lift with his hands, and roll his hips. We don't want his shoulders and chest behind his hips. We want a full extension of the hips when the blow is delivered. Once the offensive linemen get the defender playing back, he wants to climb up the defender and keep him high.

We want to play behind our pads and hit the *proper landmarks* with our face and hands simultaneously. We have four landmarks that we talk about and teach in our technique drills. The first landmark is right *down the middle of the defender*. The hands are shot underneath and up into the sternum. Make sure the linemen strike with the facemask and never with the top of the helmet.

The second landmark is the *breastplate*. The breastplate is located in the pectoral areas. I want to give my players a landmark they can see with their eyes. I want to try to hook the pads and gain control with my hands.

We use the *armpit* as a landmark. The armpit is wider than the breastplate. I want one hand on the sternum and the other on the shoulder. You don't have to coach those positions, because it is a natural movement with the hands.

The last landmark is the *outside shoulder*. That is the landmark we use for a wide-reach block. The linemen have to keep their eyes open and focus on the landmark. When the landmark starts to move, the offensive linemen will move with the landmark if they keep focused on it. It is important to see the landmark the entire way through the block.

To block anyone, the linemen must *maintain* his base and a good football position. At some point during the block, the offensive lineman and defender will reach a stalemate. However, the defender has to get away from the offensive lineman if he is to win the battle. If there is a stalemate, the offense wins. The defender has to disengage to get to the ball. That is what the offensive lineman is waiting for. When the defender tries to get separation, the offensive lineman accelerates his feet and finishes the block.

When the offensive lineman feels the release of pressure from the defender as he attempts to get off the block, he comes alive and drives with his feet as hard as he can to bury the defender. The offensive lineman uses the movement created by the attempt to release from the block to drive and gain ground with the defender. The defender may make the tackle, but it will not be a form tackle. As long as the offensive blocker stays on his landmark, the defender has to deal with the blocker.

When we teach our *pass-blocking techniques*, the first thing we cover is the *set position*. The set position is a football position. We want the hands up and the head and shoulders back. We want the elbows turned in and the thumbs up. We want a good balanced base with the feet staggered with the outside foot back. The guard's stagger is not a big as the tackles. The guard faces a different charge than the tackle and doesn't need as big of stagger. He doesn't have to get wide in his pass protection. The guard and center's job is more of a power step both ways. The tackle has to be able to kick back and stay inside-out on a defender. The most important thing for an offensive lineman to have is flexibility in his knees and ankles. If he has that quality, then he has a chance to be a pretty good athlete.

If the tackle has a man on his outside, he has to force from the inside-out. He has to kick back with his outside foot and slide with his inside foot. He does two *kick-slide movements* and can give a little ground after the kick slides. The weight has to be on his inside foot. He never wants to have his feet very far off the ground. The inside foot is always going to be on the ground.

The kick by the tackle depends on the width and speed of the pass rusher. If the defender is extremely wide or fast, the kick-slide is deeper and faster. Conversely, the tighter the rusher is the less depth the tackle has to get. The rule is the farther away the lineman's pass blocking responsibility, the deeper and faster he sets.

We never want to hop in football. If the defender changes direction, and the offensive lineman has both feet off the ground, he has to come down before he can change direction. If he has his weight on his inside foot and is sliding, he simply steps off on his inside foot and seals the move of the pass rusher.

The other step is the *power step*. That is an inside move by the pass rusher. The power step is a short, quick step inside parallel to the line of scrimmage. After the inside step the lineman is sliding. The center and guards get the power rush inside and outside. They block it with the same technique. If for some reason the center or guard is getting a wide rush, they can use the kick-slide method

In the passing game, the offensive line has to *maintain the pocket integrity*. The tackles are responsibility for the width of the pocket. They have to stop the speed rushers from the outside from collapsing the pocket. The center and guards are responsibility for the depth of the pocket. They have to stop the power rushers from pushing the pocket back into the quarterback's lap. That is their job to maintain a pocket for the quarterback to throw from.

Work your players in the set position. Have them set in that position for 15 seconds. Do it daily and increase the time each day until you have worked your way up to one minute. When you get to a minute, you will have some strong, confident legs in the set position. It is hard to hold that position for any length of time. That is why we have so many false starts unless they are trained to hold in that position for a long time.

The offensive lineman wants to mirror the defender and keep his eyes on the inside breastplate landmark. He needs to keep a knee-to-crotch relationship at all times.

When the offensive lineman is pass blocking, he has to keep his head out of the block and get his hands inside the defender's hands. If the offensive lineman tries to use his head to butt a defender, all he does is destroy his balance. He has to keep his head back to maintain his balance. He punches with his hands and presses the defender away from him. He tries to keep his hands on him if possible.

If you convey this next point to your offensive linemen the way I describe it, they will remember it. Quarterbacks are prima donnas, and like to have their picture in the papers. Linemen are grunts; they never get their picture in the papers. They are the ones taking the pictures. We tell our linemen in pass protection to imagine they have a camera inserted in their anal cavity. It is important they keep their camera pointed at the quarterback so they can take his picture. That is an important point. They have to keep their butts pointed at the quarterback, which means *staying square to the line of scrimmage*.

Drill your players on the defender's *rush moves*. The rips, bull rush, swim, and pull-and-grab are moves you have to work on. You have to teach counter to all those moves. The *punch-and-press* is one move to counter change of direction and spin moves. The punch-and-press technique is alternating hands on the defender. If you have both hands on the defender and he spins, you have nothing to stop him. We punch with one hand and press or ride the defender with the other hand.

There are some *variation blocks* that I want to cover briefly. There are two types of pulls that we use in the run game. The first type of pull is called *kick*. It is a trap-type pull. If the guard is going to trap a gap on the line of scrimmage, he pulls into the line. He rips his elbow and twists his hips and runs on an inside out path to kick out a defensive end or trap a 3 technique. On this pull if the defender runs out of the play, we don't chase him. We turn up in the hole and block the next thing that shows.

The second pull we use is called the *man-eye* pull. That is the type of pull you would use on a toss sweep. With that pull, the lineman takes a deep bucket step to get depth out of the line of scrimmage. The offensive lineman is looking for a linebacker to block. We call it a *man-eye* pull because he has to eyeball the linebacker and mirror his path. The hips are running toward the outside, but the shoulders and head are parallel with the line of scrimmage.

Linebackers are coached to pursue through gaps. The lineman has to watch the linebacker. If he drops his eyes to look for a gap to turn into, he will lose the linebacker. When the linebacker turns into the line of scrimmage, the lineman mirrors that move and goes into the hole to block him. If the guard pulls and the linebacker blitzes the gap on a delayed blitz, he stops his pull comes back to block the linebacker. The depth pull allows him to do that.

On the counter trey, the guard has a trap pull on the defensive end. The pulling tackle has a man-eye pull and is looking for the linebacker as he turns up. Anytime we are pulling to get to the second level, we treat that as a man-eye pull.

We are a *zone team*. On the inside zone, we are using the breastplate as the landmark. We are going to give some ground at the beginning of the play, but we are working to get on our landmark. Once we get to the landmark we are not going to continue east and west. We are going to work north and south and get downfield.

If I have to use a wide-shoulder landmark, I may have to cross over to get to the point. But once I get to the landmark, I am going to work north and south. If the defender keeps going to the outside, I take him where he wants to go.

The *inside zone play* is a slow developing play. If the playside guard blocks the 3 technique to his side, his first step is over and up looking for the outside breastplate. He does not cross over on his second step. He is going for the breasts plate and drive blocks up the field. If the 3 technique widens, the guard stays on him and the ball breaks back inside of him.

On the *outside zone play*, the guard takes a lead step and a crossover step to get on the outside-shoulder landmark. After he gets to his landmark, he drives north and south.

If the guard is uncovered and the center has a shade on him, the guard is taking one step keying the shaded nose. If the nose does not cross the center's face by the time the guard takes his step, the guard is going north and south looking to cut off linebackers.

If we think there is a slant coming from an outside man, the offensive lineman is reading knees. If the knee comes toward the lineman, it is a inside slant. If the knee moves away, the slant is not coming.

In the isolation play, you want to seal the backside and expand the playside. If I am running a weakside isolation play against a reduced 3 technique and a 5 technique, I want to reach both those defenders. I increase my splits and go for the reach block. If the defenders widen, they expand the hole for the linebacker. If they come inside, you bounce the play to the outside.

Those are just some ideas that might help you with a running scheme. I'm running out of time quick, but I want to show you this drill tape.

Let me answer this last question and than we have to go to the film. There are two theories on pass protection and we use both of them. You start with *man-blocking rules* and make *zone adjustments* to them, or start with zone-blocking rules and make man adjustments to them.

Normally we go big-on-big, because we don't want to put the back on a defensive lineman. The depth of the quarterback's drop dictates the type of pass-protection scheme we use. If it is a three-step drop, we may cut at the line of scrimmage.

This first drill you see is called a *slingshot* (Diagram 1). You can do this on a sled and get the same result. This drill is done in a rack with two heavy-duty, elastic tire inner tubes chained at the top of the rack and then stretched and chained to the bottom. The player starts in a six-point stance, which is a kneeling position. We fit him into a perfect blocking position. The player puts his head through the opening of the two tubes. On the snap, the lineman uncoils and extends into the inner tubes catching one tube on each shoulder. He sinks his hips and brings his hands up in the punch. The elastic stretch allows him to experience the feeling of the hip thrust. The apparatus recoils and springs him back to his starting position.

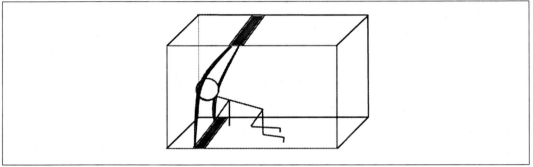

Diagram 1. Slingshot drill

The good thing about this apparatus is if you are not square when you hit the tubes, it will throw you off. It makes you hit it square and hold your balance. The continuation of the drill is to back them out of the fit position and let them hit the straps as if it were a sled. Back them off at a distance of two to three feet and let them attack.

The next drill is a *two-step drill*. The purpose of this drill is work on the short first step. I get the offensive linemen in a stance. I call, "One." I want the linemen to take a short first step, stay low, keep their balance, and freeze. I want them to freeze in their movement so they can see how big a step they took and how high they have gotten. Next I call, "Two." They take the second step and stay low and freeze after that step.

After you do the freeze segment of the drill, you start to increase the interval by going fast in your count. It is a simple drill, but you pointing out the importance of the first and second steps in the blocking sequence is important. After you have gone several times increasing the step movements, let them go on their own without the commands.

The continuation of this drill is to puts dummies into the drill. You are still doing the one/two steps, but on the second step you are punching the dummy. In this drill we start out slow and speed up.

The next drill is called the *hit-position walk*. All we are doing is putting the linemen in a hitting position and making them walk. We want their legs bent and emphasize staying low. The purpose of this drill is to make the lineman keep their feet close to the ground. They are not stomping the ground; they are sliding their feet and keeping good contact with the ground.

The next drill is the same drill, except we add resistance to it. We have them pushing on another lineman to give them resistance. They have to maintain good foot movement, without getting their feet too far off the ground and maintaining a good base. They will find it is hard to keep their feet close to the ground while trying to push against something.

The next things you see are the *chute drills* we do. As you will see in the film, it is almost the two-step drill as far as foot movement goes. We are working on the hit position and taking short steps. We also use the boards in the chutes to keep their feet apart so they can maintain good balance.

We work with air first and then we put defenders in the drill. You can vary the resistance you use. It can go anywhere from passive resistance to live full speed. Those are the two basic tempos we use in this drill.

We do a *z drill* that works on the two basic steps in pass protection (Diagram 2). They start out with a kick step to the left and a power step over to the right and repeat. After they work on the left side, they flip over to the other side and work on their right side.

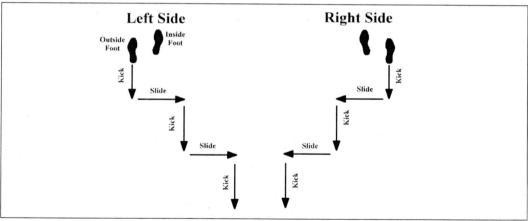

Diagram 2. Z drill

The next drill is the *mirror drill* (Diagram 3). This is a two-man drill. There is one defender and one offensive lineman. The offensive lineman puts his hands behind his back, gets in a good pass-blocking set, and mirrors the defender. This is a non-contact drill. The offensive linemen is staying in front of the defender working on his foot movement, staying low, and keeping balanced.

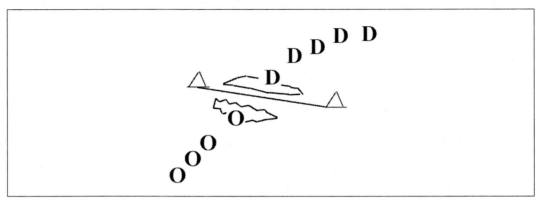

Diagram 3. Mirror drill

The companion drill is called *mirror dodge* (Diagram 4). We line up two cones on a line five- to six-yards apart. The defender is on one side of the line and the offensive blocker is on the other. The defender moves up and down the line trying to fake the blocker and get across the line. The blocker is mirroring the movement of the defender. As the defender tries to cross the line, the offensive blocker uses a punch to prevent him from getting across the line. The blockers are trying to time the punch and keep their hands inside the defender's hands.

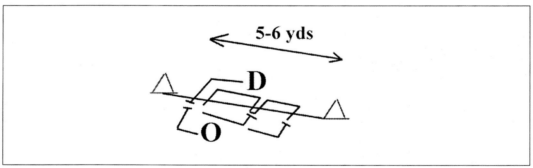

Diagram 4. Mirror-dodge drill

I talked about the *punch-and-press* technique in my lecture (Diagram 5). This is the drill we use to work on those skills. We have a five-yard square box with a defender and blocker at one end of it. The defender can use any part of the square he wants to rush the passer. The blocker has to counter the pass-rush techniques used by the defender. We work on everything from bull rush, swims, rips, and spins. The blocker uses the punch-and-press to keep the defender under control.

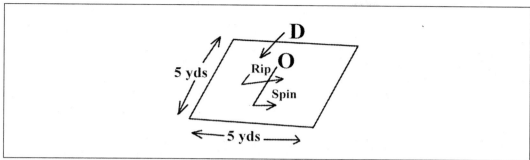

Diagram 5. Punch-and-press drill

The *hit-hit-hit drill* is a bull-in-the-ring type of drill (Diagram 6). The offensive lineman is going to get three punches on targets coming at him from assorted angles. He has to stay alert and deliver a punch on each rusher. The coach stands behind the offensive blocker and points to a designated rusher who charges the offensive blocker. The offensive lineman punches and recoils back into his position waiting for the next rusher.

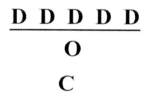

Diagram 6. Hit-hit-hit drill

8

Teaching the Basic Drive Block

Dave Magazu
University of Kentucky
1996

I am going to be talking about offensive line play at the University of Kentucky. First, I will cover the teaching progression of the base block. Next, I will take you through a chute progression. Then, I will talk about a horn block and a gap block. These are basically man blocks that we use in our zone blocking scheme. We call it our inside zone and our outside zone plays, and we incorporated some man schemes depending on the defense.

At the University of Kentucky, we do not have a play in our scheme where we use a base block. However, the base block is the most important block that we teach, and it is the first block that we teach. All of the aspects of the base block are involved in each block that we use. All of the techniques that we use when we teach the base block will carry over into the other blocks, as far as hat placement, hand placement, footwork, and how you get into the block. Every single block needs to have an aiming point, and you need the footwork that allows you to get into your aiming point. Once you get into your aiming point, everything turns into the base block. To say we come out and base block at the point of attack is not true. We just do not do a lot of that.

When we talk about base blocking or any form of blocking, we are talking about option blocking. We really do not try to swing our rear end one way or the other. We try to stay square on most of our blocks. The teaching progression is to teach the base block first and then have that carry over to all of our other blocks. We will teach the base block in the reverse order. The only equipment we use will be chutes. Also, we use a board that is beveled on the side and is 12 feet long.

Blocking Chute—Dimensions

Top—59 X 70
Bottom—54
Front—46
Back—58

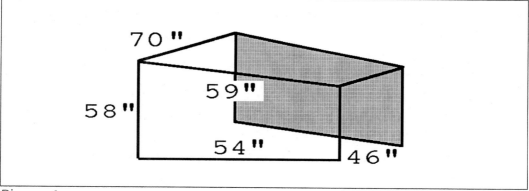

Diagram 1

We have two points that we stress at Kentucky as far as offensive line play. First, we will be the toughest line on the field. Second, we will never quit on a block any time during the game. There are a lot of techniques to be concerned with in coaching offensive linemen.

Teaching Progression—Base Block

We believe that the base block is the most important block of an offensive lineman. This is used when blocking at the point of attack. The objective is to get movement, option blocking the defender the way he wishes to go. You must maintain contact, allowing the runner to option run defenders.

Following is the sequence of how we teach this drive block. First, we teach stance and start, then sequences are taught in the reverse order to ensure the athlete experiences the perfect block.

First Phase

Stance/Start—Lineman Stance

- Feet
    - Good base—at least armpit-width, but never wider than your shoulders
    - Toes in—heels out (depends upon technique being used)
    - Feet—toes to instep or toe-to-heel relationship
- Power-producing angles
    - Weight on the inside balls of the feet
    - Knees in and over the ankles
    - Want Z in the knees
    - The power-producing angles are created by the bend in the ankle and knee joints.
- Down hand
    - Placed slightly inside the rear foot.
    - Extended comfortably from the shoulder.
    - Reach out far enough to create a balanced stance, 60 percent forward, 40 percent back.
    - Five fingertips on ground
- Off hand
    - Wrist to the side of the knee
    - Make a light fist with hand.
- Shoulder—parallel to the line of scrimmage
- Back—parallel to the ground
- Tail—slightly higher than the shoulders
- Head
    - Cocked back slightly.
    - In a bull neck position
    - See feet of defender.

I think stance is important. It does not matter what position you coach in football; a coach has to emphasize stance every day and on every play. It has to happen automatically. We spend a lot of time with this every day. We believe in a stance where you are going to be bunched up. The players will feel a little uncomfortable at first. We do not want them to overextend. I still cannot figure out why the pro players get their legs spread so far apart. We are just the opposite of that type of stance. We start off toe to instep. We never let them get more than toe to heel. The reason we do this is because we are going to be pulling, and we have a horn technique, and we have to set up to pass block. If we have our feet under us, we can go in either direction.

The next phase is the start. Every coach in America yells at his players, "We must stay low. We must come out of our stance low, and we play with leverage." How do you get your players to do this? It is not bending at the waist. It is bending at the knees. Linemen must have the flexibility to bend at the knees. If you come and watch us practice, you will hear me tell our linemen on their first step to pick their foot up and set it back down where they start from. They can't do that. I am trying to get them to pick up that first step and try to put it back where they started. They will only take a three- to six-inch step. If we tell them to take a six-inch step, they step out 12 to 18 inches. We want a short step on the start. We spend a lot of time on this phase.

Lineman Start

- Initial movement must be forward, not up.
- Like a sprinter going out of the blocks, you are trying to create force.
- Step with appropriate foot when firing out to block:
    o Man over—drive off the up foot and step with the rear foot,
    o Man either side—step with the foot nearest him.
- Coaching points—rear foot lead
    o Mentally shift the weight to the push foot and step with your rear foot.
    o One-step drill:
- First step should be three-inch step out and slightly up, attacking the line of scrimmage.
- The knee of the up foot should point toward the ground (it should roll over the toe of the up foot).
- Arm action—like a sprinter coming out.
- Back flat—chest on the thigh
- Bull your neck—sight your target.
    o Follow up quickly with second and third steps.
    o Stay low and maintain lift leverage.
- Coaching points—up foot lead
    o Mentally shift the weight to the push foot and step with the up foot.
    o One-step drill—first step should be three-inch step out and slightly up attacking the line of scrimmage.

Second Phase—Fit Position

The second phase is the *fit position*. We are still talking about the base block. The purpose is to show the blocker the ideal blocking position, utilizing the power-producing angles.

Fit Position

- We must put the defender in a challenging position and have the offensive blocker fit into him.
- Offensive blocker
    - Feet are in a toe-instep relationship (stance).
    - Good bend in knees—create power-producing angles.
    - Knees in over the ankles
    - Butt down
    - Back arched.
    - Good bull neck
    - Eyes in the solar plexus of the defender
    - Arms are in a blocking position, elbow points must break the plane of your hips, heels of the hands at the bottom of the defender's breastplate, forming a triangle with hairline and both fists (thumbs up/fingers through).
- Defender—challenge position
    - Feet slightly staggered—up foot at the edge of the board.
    - Hold blocker under the arm.
    - Give resistance.

Third Phase—Follow-Through

The purpose is to have the player experience an ideal block, to teach the proper use of leverage, the hip roll, the acceleration of the feet, and the maintenance of a block.
- The offensive blocker will align in a fit position, toes at the end of the board.
- The defender will be in a challenging position holding the blocker in place (the defender must give steady resistance).
- Walking down the board
- The blocker will walk the defender down the board with a bulled neck, power-producing angles, and feeling pressure at the small of his back; never raise up.
- Walk the defender off the board, driving knees into the ground. The blocker's weight should be on the instep of each foot (do not be up on your toes).

- Hip roll
  - The blocker will roll his hips and accelerate his feet. When executing a block, he will make contact and have a stalemate—in order to get movement, the blocker must roll his hips and accelerate his feet to dominate a defender.
  - Hip roll is the underneath action—the snapping of your knees straight out and the shooting of your hips through.
  - The feet should be underneath your shoulder pads to guard against overextension.
- Hold
  - Halfway down the board, on the command, "Hold," the blockers will stop.
  - Check the position of the blocker.

Fourth Phase—Contact

Of all of the phases we do, the players struggle on this more than on any of the others. The purpose is to teach the contact phase of the drive block technique. Emphasize arm and timing of the pop.

- The offensive blocker is in a down position and situates himself one step from the defender.
- The defensive man will assume a challenging position.
- The defender should be in a good two-point stance, bending his knees as much as possible with his chest out and head tucked.
- He will catch the blocker rather than deliver a lick.
- The offensive blocker takes only one step, jolting the defender backward.
- Concentrate on ripping the arms and taking short, powerful steps.
- Follow through by driving the defender off the board.

Fifth Phase—Hit and Drive

The purpose of the drill is to put all aspects of the drive block together. We start at the back end of the chute and work under it with the blockers. We do this every Tuesday and Wednesday when we are in pads. You can set the tempo of the drill.

- Align the offensive blocker in a three-point stance, a foot away from the defender, toes at the end of the board.
- To start, the defender will be in a two-point stance; as the drill progresses, he will move to a three-point stance without the boards.
- The offensive blocker will explode out of his stance and drive a defender down the board. Emphasize good base and acceleration of the feet.

- As the drill progresses, vary the distance between the blocker and the defender to aid in the development of a rhythm of blocking a defender at varied distances away.
- Use two-whistle drill—first whistle to check body position; second whistle to release athlete from the drill.

Sixth Phase—Second Effort

The purpose is to teach the blocker to maintain contact when the defender is spinning out or disengaging the blocker.
- The coach will give the defender a direction to spin.
- When the defender reaches the end of the board, he will sprint out of the block in the direction indicated by the coach on the second whistle.
- The blocker must step with the near foot in the direction of the spin, aggressively attacking the defender.
- Never cross your feet or kick your heels together. You must maintain a good base.

Seventh Phase—Versus Shade Alignments

The purpose is to teach the drive block on opponents aligned in shaded or offset alignments.
- Same as hit-and-drive phase, except we start from a position with the inside foot on the outside of the board.
- First step must be perfect to get to solar plexus of defender. Second step must be upfield, maintaining a good base.
- Practice inside-to-outside shades of offensive blocker.

The aiming point on the base block is through the bottom of the numbers. That is where we want to form that triangle I talked about earlier. When you go through blocking drills, you must tell the blocker where his aiming point is. We take the premise of stepping to the alignment and incorporate that into all of our zone blocking.

Next, I want to cover the horn block. Some people call it a fold block. This block is on the frontside of a play, and it can turn into a part of our zone scheme. The purpose of the horn block is to enable an offensive lineman to block linebackers going under or around the blocker to his outside (the technique will vary according to the play).

A man horn block locks up a horn person on the linebacker and another offensive lineman on the defensive down lineman. It enables a lineman to go around or under a block to block a linebacker.

- Bucket step with depth, cross over (or hop) to stay square. Keep your toes pointed upfield.
- Keep shoulders square and read the defensive tackle.
- If the tackle plays straight or outside, take easiest course to the linebacker.
- If the tackle comes inside, release around drive block for the linebacker.
- Sustain contact, smother the linebacker.
- Man horn—the guard on the linebacker all the way, through or around.
- Zone horn—the guard blinks the tackle for slant move. No slant, block the linebacker through or around.

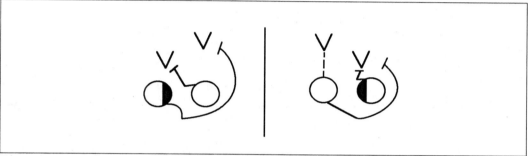

Diagram 2. Man horn

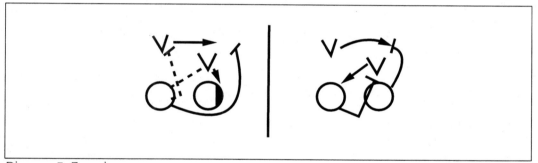

Diagram 3. Zone horn

Now, I want to talk about the gap block. We are going to put this into our zone scheme. We will coordinate the gap block with the man horn block.

Gap Block

The purpose of this block is to be able to block a defender to our inside gap, stopping all penetration at the point of attack (man blocking). Coaching points include the following.

- Take a flat step to the inside. Use the defender's hands as an aiming point (three- to six-inch step).
- Freeze the second step until you read the reaction of the defender.
- If the defender tries to penetrate across the line of scrimmage, pivot and bring your outside foot across and shoulder block the defender's hip. Rip your outside arm and try to punch the defender's hip and work to his armpit.
- If the defender starts to work across your face, step straight upfield on your second step and base block his outside number.
- Stay up on the block—it is not a scramble.

Inside Zone Blocking

Purpose: this is one of our basic blocking schemes. Our approach to zone blocking is to come off on the down defender with two blockers on one defender to get maximum push off the line of scrimmage, providing a pocket for the ballcarrier to run into. We want to knock the first level defenders into the linebackers. At the second level (depth of the linebacker), we either push the first level defender into the linebacker or the blocker to the linebacker side comes off on him. This play attacks the first down defender from the guard to the outside. The back plays a major role in the success of this play. He must run up behind the zone block on the first level defender before making his break to daylight. If he makes his cut too early, the linebacker flows too fast and the come-off blocker can't get him blocked. The key is for the back to run up behind the zone and then explode into a seam with power. Hold the linebackers in there.

Let me go over the coaching points. First is the lead blocker. The lead blocker comes off with power and quickness, aiming to a point that puts his hat on the outside hip of the first level defender. The blocker must stay low with a flat, level back and good base during this come-off. Against a wide-aligned defender, the blocker can use a flat or bucket step, depending on the defender's width. The path established by this come-off is the lead blocker's *track*. He must fight to stay square on the *track* throughout the block.

Unless he has a run through, the trail blocker will be joining the lead blocker at this point, helping him knock the first level defender off the line of scrimmage into the second level. The lead blocker must have his head and eyes up, looking for the linebacker to show up on his side. If he shows up, the lead blocker comes off square on him. Patience is the key to coming off on the linebacker. If the blocker comes off too early, we won't get the necessary push on the first level defender. Let the running back bring the linebacker to you.

If the first level defender slants inside, the lead blocker stays on the *track*, immediately looking for and blocking the linebacker scraping off the slant man's hips. Don't overrun the scraper; be under control—stay square. If he is frozen inside, turn inside and wall him off.

If the down man plays into the path of the lead blocker, the blocker has him by himself. He stays square with the track, working the defender off the line of scrimmage. He can't be flattened; he wants to stay square and *stretch* the defender to the outside. A wide-aligned defender will most likely widen when the blocker bucket steps.

Let me go over the trail blocker. The trail blocker will use a horn technique, taking a bucket step with the foot nearest the lead blocker. He drops this foot back and to the outside, pointing the toe down the *track*. It is important to get the shoulders perpendicular to the *bucket step*—get in position to look down the *track*. Stay low and have good vision; you must read the actions of the defenders while bucket stepping.

The first threat the trail blocker could have is the linebacker run through. A presnap read can help establish the run through possibility. If the linebacker is close and up on his toes leaning toward the line of scrimmage, there is a good chance for the run through. The deeper he aligns, the less chance there is. If the run through develops, drive off the bucket step foot and snap your shoulders off upfield and take on the linebacker square.

The next threat to the trail blocker is for the first level defender to slant toward him. If this occurs, the blocker drives off the bucket step and shoulder spears the slant man with his hat to the playside.

If there is no run through or slant threat, the trail blocker drives off the bucket step foot on a track, which puts his hat on the near hip of the first level defender. If the defender is playing tough into the lead blocker, the trail blocker shoulder spears, arm rolls, lifts, and drives him down the track to the second level. It is important to stay square running along the *track*.

During this maneuver, the blocker's head and eyes must be up so he can keep vision on the linebacker. When reaching the linebacker's depth, with the linebacker still on his side of the block, the trail blocker comes off square into the linebacker. If the linebacker flows behind or across the block on the first level defender, the trail blocker concentrates all his attention and force to driving him down the track.

If the down defender stretches the lead blocker, the trail blocker should stay square on his track to the linebacker. Front up the linebacker, keeping shoulders square.

A wide-aligned first level defender is already stretched, and the trail blocker continues off the bucket step along the track to the linebacker.

When the linebacker aligns in an *up position*, the run through has been committed. The trail blocker has his man and comes directly off the ball on his outside number.

The techniques for the backside of the inside *zone* are basically the same as the frontside. The only technique change is that the *track angle* is sharper. The lead blocker takes off on a track with half of his shoulder pad on the first level defender's playside hip. The trail blocker comes off on a track, which would put him through the middle of the first-level defender's initial alignment.

This technique will vary according to the linebacker's alignment. The lead blocker will use more of a rip technique. The tighter the linebacker is to the play, the thinner the lead blocker is; therefore, the more the aiming point of the trail blocker will change. The trail blocker may go from the defender's middle to far number to armpit.

Let me go over some blocking schemes on the inside zone.

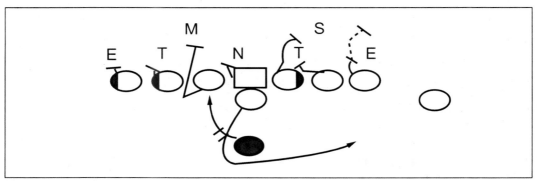

Diagram 4. Inside zone versus 5-2

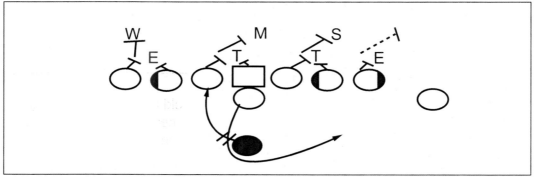

Diagram 5. Inside zone versus 4-3

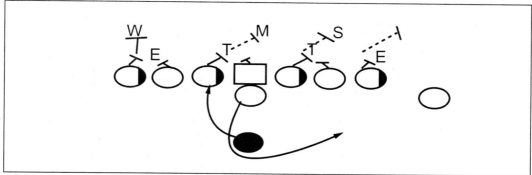

Diagram 6. Inside zone versus 4-3

Very quickly, let me get to the outside zone blocking. Coaching points on the lead block include the following. The lead blocker will use a rip technique or a lead technique (depending on position) on outside *zone*. He is trying to miss the first-level defender by ripping under him to the side of the play; he then works for a wall-off position on the linebacker. He releases on a *track angle* that is outside the first-level defender to the side of the play. If he makes it through, he works upfield and backside to wall the linebacker. He must not overrun the linebacker. He should have his head and eyes up, looking for him immediately as he clears the down defender. He should be especially alert if he feels the first-level man slanting away.

If, as the lead blocker releases, the first-level defender works into him tough, he must work hard to redirect his track upfield. Second effort is important here to keep the defender from playing across the blocker's head. If the blocker will keep driving to get through, he will cut off the first-level defender. If the linebacker is up on the trail blocker or in a tight run through position, the lead blocker takes a cutoff angle on the man.

The trail blocker will use a horn technique by taking a deep bucket step, reading the defenders. If he gets early linebacker run through, he turns up on him and wheels him away from the play.

If the down lineman slants to the trail blocker, he turns upon the slant man and wheels him away from the play. If the slant man is penetrating deep, push him by and release upfield to wall the next defender.

If there is no run through or slant at the trail blocker, he drives off the bucket step foot on a deep pulling path, running a course that would allow him to get his hat on the far knee of the first-level defender. As the lead blocker starts to clear the defender, the trail blocker drives his upfield shoulder, stabbing the playside leg. On contact, he drives up the field hard with second effort, wheeling him inside.

If the lead blocker is stretched, the trail blocker will try to horn around the stretch to the linebacker. As the trail blocker starts his horn, he must get his depth and width. As he attacks the line of scrimmage, it is very important for him to keep his shoulders square and attack the linebacker's outside number. If the down lineman stretches too far, the trail blocker must get inside the stretch and run the linebacker by the play.

On the outside zone plays, don't be afraid to cut the defense. Let me cover some blocking schemes on the outside zone play.

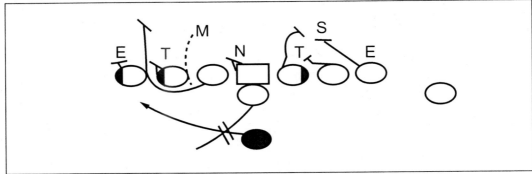

Diagram 7. Outside zone versus 5-2

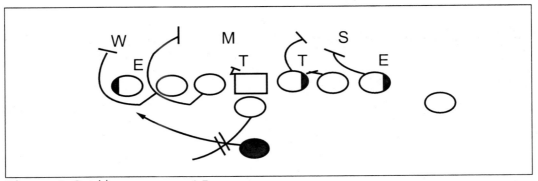

Diagram 8. Outside zone versus 4-3

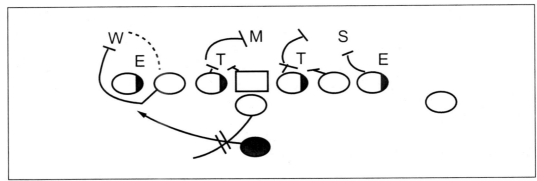

Diagram 9. Outside zone versus 4-3

I will talk about our inside zone play and look at the outside zone play. You will see the play from the wide angle first, and then you will see the tight copy.

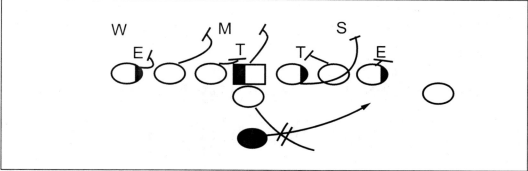

Diagram 10. Outside zone versus 4-3

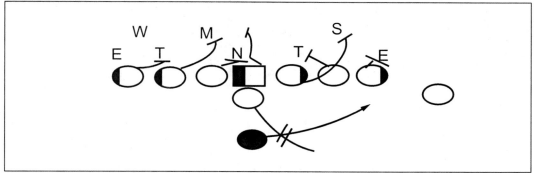

Diagram 11. Outside zone versus 5-2

9

Offensive Line Drills and Techniques

Steve Marshall
UCLA
1996

Every place I've ever been we have been kind of a multiple offense. What I'm going to do today is try to give you what I teach our offensive line when we talk about multiplicity of offense. The offensive coordinator wants to get into a multitude of sets and have a lot of different ways to do it. For the offensive line, it is important to have a simple and direct way to teach a lot of things.

I have not been an option-type coach. What happens to the offensive line when you do not run the option is that you see a lot of defensive fronts, because the defense doesn't have to play option responsibility. I guess some of this is theory, but I like to teach our offensive line a lot of different things and group them into packages.

The biggest thing in coaching the offensive line is to put it into an easy form to learn. The offensive linemen must learn to come up to the ball and get after somebody's tail. They don't need to worry about what to do. They need to focus on how to do it. We don't want those linemen thinking at the line of scrimmage. We want them to have a great attitude about coming off the ball and killing somebody. Offensive line coaches are the worst at this. They spend too much time with perfect footwork, hat placement, and things like that. Those things are not possible on every play. If you give them a base to understand what the play is and what you are trying to accomplish, then you have a chance.

There are three ways that we teach blocking schemes. I break down the plays that we want to run into three categories. The first group is *man blocking*. An example of that would be numbering the defensive players. In an odd front defense, the noseguard is 0, the linebacker is 1, defensive tackle is 2, and so forth. From there, we tell the center to block 0, the guard 1, the tackle 2, and the tight end 3. If I say fan, it means the guard blocks 1 on the line and the tackle blocks 2 on the line. That is how we would block man.

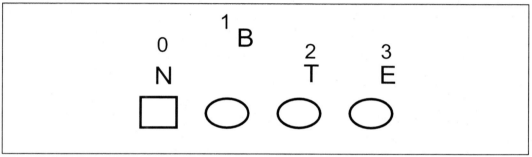

Diagram 1

The second thing we have is a package of *zone plays*. The base rule is an *one down lineman* or an *over linebacker*. This means, if the lineman has a down lineman on him, he blocks him. If he doesn't, he finds the nearest linebacker *over* him. He is blocking an area scheme. There are all kinds of names for these techniques. Scoop blocking is zone blocking. The power slip is zone blocking. Linemen must have the concept of what they are doing.

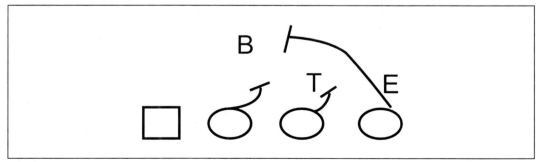

Diagram 2

The third one I want to get into is my favorite. This is the *combination block*. It is a combination of man and zone blocking. The counter gap play is an example of this. We have some guys blocking zone and others are blocking man. Everybody has his own terms. What I'm going to use are the terms I know. The callside guard and tackle are blocking area. But, they are blocking the man within the area. The callside tackle's rule is 5, 4, 3, and 2 technique to the backside linebacker. The callside guard's rule is 3 and 2 technique to the backside linebacker. The callside guard and tackle step with their inside foot and take anything that comes all the way to the backside linebacker. I call it *pop and turn*.

The callside guard steps inside protecting the A gap area. The callside tackle does the same thing to the B gap. On the callside on a combination block, the guard and tackle know they are working in tandem. In this defense, there is no 5 technique, but there is a 3 technique. They come off, and the 3 technique goes outside. The tackle and guard pick that man up in tandem. The guard knows he is going to the backside linebacker at the proper time. This is an example of *combination blocking*.

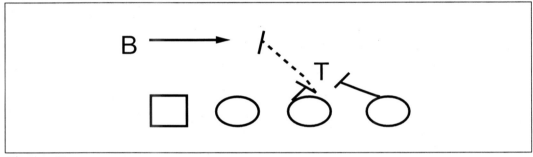

Diagram 3

The offensive linemen within these three concepts should know how to handle everything we do. This does not include option blocking, because that is a different set of rules. You could do some of these things in the option scheme, but there are different rules for most of it. There are different blocking techniques, but the base rules come from these three packages.

What I want to do is take one play step by step, the way we do it and how we teach it. The play that I want to use, because I think it is the ultimate smash-mouth play, is the counter trap. The Washington Redskins ran it and made it popular. This is the NCAA run. Everybody has this play with the pass and naked play off it. It is kind of like a package within itself. In a single season, we will run this play out of 10 to 15 different formations and 10 to 15 different ways. The concept for the big, old meatheads up front never changes. I'll put up three different defenses and three different offensive sets.

I'm going to take you through our base rules of *down and around*. I'll draw this first one up against a 40 defensive look from a pro set weak for the offense. The tight end has three different things he could do. We sometimes go into a game with three different ways to block the same play. The defense gets pretty smart and reacts to the way an offense blocks. You can't do the same thing over and over again and expect the play to go consistently. For the teaching, I'll go through the different ways for you. The tight end's base rule is 7, 5, 4, 3, 2, to the backside linebacker. In this defense he has no 7, 5, or 4 technique, he goes to the backside linebacker. This is called a *cram it* technique. That means he is going inside regardless of alignment. He steps with his inside foot and forces his outside shoulder across the 6 technique. If the 6 technique comes inside, he takes him down with his zone principle. He gets his inside foot on the ground and blows through the outside hip of the tackle straight up the field for the backside linebacker. We tell him as he passes level one he gets vertical, but his eyes are on the backside. The coaching point is to never let anything cross his face. If anything crosses his face, he eats it up.

The defensive end will adjust to the inside move of the tight end and not let him inside. If he does that, the play is gone. We go to an influence scheme next for the tight end. We can *slam influence* or just *release*. I like the slam influence. The tight end steps and targets the outside number of the defensive end as a landmark. The goal of the tight end is to make the defensive end widen. The ball is going inside the end. The tight end slam releases to the strong safety, outside linebacker, or whoever is out there, by blocking the defensive end for a moment and releasing him. The tight end can also free release and block number 4 on the outside. The number one goal of the tailback is to cram the ball in the C gap area.

The tackle's rule is 5, 4, 3, 2, to backside linebacker. There is no 5 or 4 technique in this defense. But, there is a 3 technique. The onside guard has a 3, 2, 1, 0, to backside linebacker. The tackle and guard know they are working in combination on the 3 technique to the backside linebacker on level two. A key coaching point here is to always take care of level one. We want to take the 3 technique for the ride of his life. When I was at the University of Louisville, we said knock his butt off the ball. Now that I'm at UCLA, an academic school, it is called a vertical push.

We want the 3 technique going backward, not down the line. The technique depends on whether you are the tackle or the guard. We recruit linemen. We don't recruit a left tackle. We recruit linemen, and they play all the positions. The guard knows he has the 3 technique. We want the guard to step with his inside foot, but he has to step relative to his technique.

The guard makes a call to the tackle. We use calls to communicate. You can use anything that you want as a call. Sometimes, it is just as easy to say, "Partner, me and you are going to block the crap out of this guy." Whatever fits for you is the best way to do it. At some other places, I've had to have a call for everything.

We tell the lineman to take a *punch step*. That means stick the foot into the ground so you have a base. The tackle has to step inside relative to the 3 technique. That means he has to step hard inside, or what we call a *lateral punch step*. They are sticking their feet in the ground to block the 3 technique, but their eyes are backside on the linebacker. The guard is stepping and sticking the 3 technique on the inside half. The tackle sticks the 3 technique, and he knows, since he is outside, he has the leverage on the 3 technique and linebacker. He has to maintain that leverage, because the ball is going outside him in the C gap. Since the tackle has leverage already, he uses both his hands to control the tackle. The guard has to see the backside linebacker and see his alignment. If the guard and tackle take the 3 technique for the ride of his life and let the linebacker run underneath them, we haven't accomplished a thing. The guard has to look at the alignment of the linebacker to see if he is normal or less than normal. Normal at Tennessee is six yards deep, running downhill. Normal at Washington is two yards deep. For the sake of this lecture, let's say the linebacker is shallow or less than normal. If that is the case, the guard is a one-hand player. All we are telling the guard is not to stick the inside hand into the 3 technique. We are 2-on-1 with the tackle, so we have to win. If the linebacker comes inside the guard, he cannot physically turn his shoulder if he has stuck his inside hand into the 3 technique's body. If he sticks only his outside hand on the 3 technique, he has the ability to come off for the linebacker, if he should run under the double-team. If the linebacker plays the play normal and comes over the top of the double-team, the guard gets his second hand on the 3 technique, takes him, and the tackle comes off for the linebacker. The guard has to have the feet of a burglar to hang on with one hand until that linebacker has committed to going across the double-team. This technique could be the tight end-tackle, as well as the guard-tackle. The technique is the same for any two linemen who do it.

The center's block is the hardest block on this play. The center's rule is to block the first defensive lineman away from the call. Your center has to be better than the 1 or 2 technique he is blocking, because this block is tough. He is going to *angle drive* the back-side. We call it that because it is a drive block that has to be executed at an angle. People think it is easy. I've got four centers still playing in the NFL, and it was tough for all of them. The center has to step relative to the technique of the 2 technique. All I tell him is to get to the area where the landmark is supposed to be. The center has the reader, who cross face the center when they see his step. You have other guys that simply blow their butt upfield. The game plan will dictate the technique the center is going to use.

We keep our center in a two-point stance for this purpose. I feel he can step better that way. He steps with his onside foot and tries to get his head across the bow of the defender. What we try to do is step with our left foot, get the head across, and try to pin the hip of the 2 technique with his right hand. He probably can't pin that hip, but it gives him a surface to block so he can hold onto his butt, because that is what he is trying to do. We try to pin the hip and take him away from the call. If you don't have a good center, you can use the reverse block using the same target. On contact the center flips his hips into the hole. Defensive linemen don't like this type of block. This is the answer we give our guys when they are having trouble cutting off the 2 technique. That is the down part of the down and around blocking scheme.

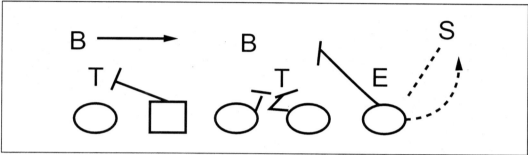

Diagram 4

Now, let's talk about the around part of this play. Line coaches are the ultimate schemers. They are always trying to come up with ways to block. But, you have to keep it simple for the guys who have to do the blocking. Your schemes are not worth anything if your meatheads can't perform it. We want to *revisit creativity*. How can we keep this play the same, but help them at the same time? It is all about finding the things that your guys do best. If it ain't simple, I don't want to do it. There is no such thing as a complicated play. If it's complicated, it ain't worth anything. The fun part of this play is the guard and tackle pull. The backside guard is going to pull and trap the 6 technique area. All we tell him is he is to go a hundred miles an hour. He is going to blow up the 6 technique area.

There are a lot of different ways to pull. Here is what we teach. We rip our elbow out, drop-step, and target. We don't want to get too deep. We target relative to the technique we have to block. A coaching point for the guard is not to get too tight to the center. If they do, when they rip their arm, they could hit the ball and cause a fumble. When we run these types of plays, we widen our splits a little. The extra width gives the blocker a momentary advantage to see what he has to find. He pulls, targets, sprints hard, and blows up the 6 technique area. We have to be lower than the defensive end and create horizontal movement. If the defensive end wrong arms him, he plays football with a nasty attitude. He doesn't have time to key anything. If the end wrong arms him, we still try to blow him up.

The tackle pulls for the first callside linebacker. I tell him to pull and trap the callside linebacker. I don't know where he is going to be and neither does that tackle. The tackle has to widen so he can get his spacing with the guard. If the guard does his job, the tackle has to be able to see the hole to get up on that linebacker. A tackle who gets too close to his guard can't get inside or outside. The only thing he can do is stack up the play. It is not the depth of the tackle, it is the width of his split. If the tackle reads the wrong arm technique by the defensive end on the guard, he goes outside and looks back inside for the linebacker. Nothing has changed for him.

The fullback, or motion man, or whoever it is, blocks the picket fence on the backside. They block the backside C gap area. The tailback takes his steps to the backside, takes the ball, and runs downhill to cram the ball in the C gap. He is running on the hip of the tackle. He is reading the tackle's block. We can run this play from two backs, one back, or any amount of formations, and from motion. What we have done is created a whole offense from one scheme.

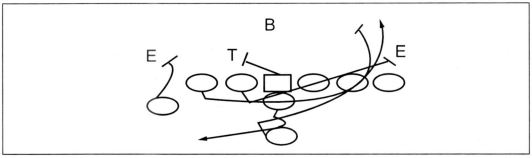

Diagram 5

We can block this by pulling one guard. We take the fullback and replace the guard. The guard replaces the tackle. This is not a counter, but it is the same play for the linemen. The guard takes his split, pulls down the line, and tracks the callside linebacker. The tackle now becomes the picket man to the backside. He steps inside and protects the B gap. If nothing shows, he steps out on anything coming outside.

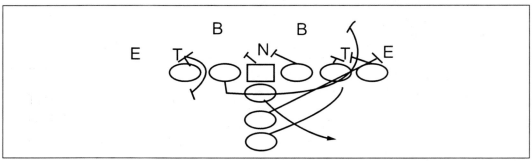

Diagram 6

Those are two plays and two base ways to run to a tight end or an open end side. The good thing is both of these plays are taught exactly the same way. They are not the same play but are in the same premise. If a team tries to stop these two plays, our first answer is play-action pass. You can't be hard headed and run the play when the defense is effectively stopping it. If you still want to run the play, adjust it.

If the guard is getting stoned by the wrong arm technique of the defensive end and the tackle can't catch the linebacker, we adjust the play. We can add a term; in our case, we add *sweep*. The play becomes a counter sweep. The play looks the same. The guard gets a little depth in his pull. He logs the defensive end this time, instead of trapping him. We want him to get depth, so he can get outside leverage. We want him to cut the defensive end's outside leg. The tackle pulls. As he gets to the center, he gets depth to about three yards. It is an automatic log by the guard, and he is going around the corner. The first two steps look exactly like the counter trap. The coaching point we tell the tailback is to get his shoulders toward the sideline. That is an answer when you are having trouble with the counter trap. We haven't changed a thing except our coaching points.

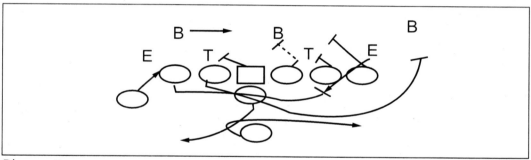

Diagram 7

To run this play, you have to drill it. To run this play, the linemen have to react to what they see. You can start drilling this during the winter program. It teaches the short pull and long pull. We line up two lines of guys. You can go one at a time or two at a time. That's up to you. We want them to pull, react to what they see, and change direction. That is extremely important for an offensive lineman. If a lineman cannot redirect, I don't want him. The guard pulls and targets the cone. He sprints to the cone and turns up. As soon as he turns up, there is a coach right there that gives him a direction. He reacts to the coach and redirects in the direction the coach has pointed. What this teaches the tackle is this: as he comes up in the hole, the linebacker is not going to be standing still, waiting for him. That linebacker is going to be on the move. The tackle has to find him, redirect his path to get to him, and then block him. We set one cone at eight yards and one at four yards. That lets them practice the long and short pulls. We check their running form to make sure they are running over their pads. If they get too high, they lose their leverage. Everything in offensive line blocking is leverage.

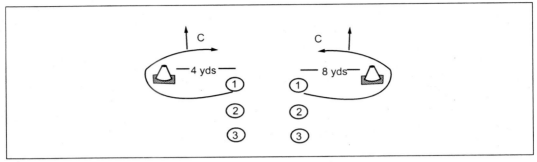

Diagram 8

The next thing we do is put in a manager in the place of the coach. We put a towel behind his back tucked into his pants. We give the manager a little box drawn on the ground. The managers hate this drill because they get beat up. As the tackle comes around the cone, he has to go get the towel from the manager. The manager can run around in that box to avoid the lineman. It is a fun drill, and it teaches the lineman to stick his foot in the ground as he rounds the cone. Once the lineman gets in the box, he has to chase the towel until he gets it. We make the box small, so that it is one move by the manager and then they get him.

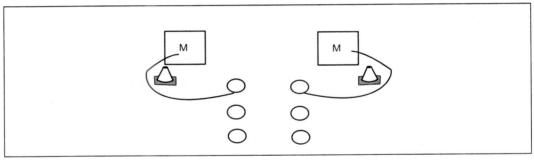

Diagram 9

Don't do a drill just to do a drill. That is worthless. When I do a drill, I want it to be completely applicable to what we do. In this drill, we are using a slide pull technique like a sweep play. The guard has a 1-on-1 block with a linebacker. We are trying to teach eye read and angle to the block. The tackle is blocking down, and the guard is pulling for the linebacker. He keeps his shoulders parallel to the line of scrimmage as he pulls. We set up cones to represent the tackle and tight end gaps. They have to have their eyes on the linebacker, but they have to feel where the tackle and tight end gaps are. The coach stands behind the guard and signals the defender where to go. The defender has flags on like a flag football belt. The defender blows the hole where the guard pulled from, or runs through the tackle gap, or runs through the end gap, or just runs outside the end gap. The guard pulls and grabs the flag or towel or whatever you are using. We don't let the linemen touch the cones. They have to weave their way through the cones and grab the towel. We work them both ways, going two at a time.

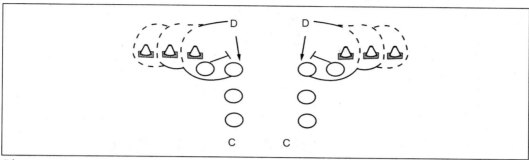

Diagram 10

This next drill is for the guard and tackle, working their pulls in the counter trap. We set up the spacing for the play. We have the right side pulling left and the left side pulling right. We have a dummy holder in the 6 technique area. I give them directions for what I want them to do. They go upfield with the bag, come down, or come down inside. The guard has to read the target and get his path relative. The tackle is reading the guard's path and reacting accordingly. It is a rapid-fire drill with four guys going at once. You can do the same drill with the fullback and the guard.

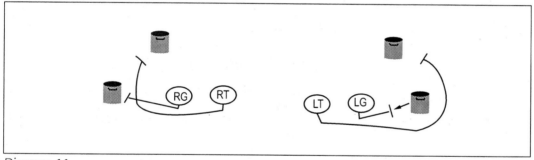

Diagram 11

Those are three drills to work on pulls. The key coaching points, as I go through these drills, are, one, chest on the knee, two, head up and targeting, three, bent knees, and, four, run through the block with great explosion. The only thing that gets me concerned is that they get to the block on time. I don't worry so much if their footwork is not exactly right. If they are hustling and giving good effort, I'm not too concerned about trivial things.

10

Pass Protection in the Five-Step Drop Game

Mark McHale
Marshall University
2002

When I go to clinics, I like a lot of mini-clinics like this one because you can learn in this setting. If I am searching for something I am interested in, I try to find the best person in the field for that particular phase of the game. I try to set up an appointment and meet with that person. This year, I will visit four or five coaches. These are not only NFL coaches, but also college coaches. Also, I visit high school coaches during the recruiting season. I ask them what they are doing in some area of the game I am interested in. If they work our camp, it is the same thing. I want to know what they are doing. If it is a junior high school coach, I ask them what they are working on. Football is an area where you can always learn. There is a wide scope as far as learning football is concerned. If someone knows something that I do not know about the subject I am working on, I want to know about it.

I took the opportunity to listen to Steve Stripling of the University of Louisville speak here today. If you are coaching the offensive line, you can learn how to coach them better if you know what the defensive line is doing. Steve gave an excellent lecture. It is important for the offensive line coach to know what the defensive players they have to block are being taught. My point is, you must learn from the best because modeling is important. I want to learn how the defense is taught so we can teach our linemen how to block them.

I think it is very important to understand what the speaker is going to talk about. I am going to talk about the five-step drop passing game pass protection. If I were coaching in high school, would I use the five-step drop passing game? You bet I would. There are two reasons why. One reason is because everybody is playing the box game. Steve Stripling started his talk discussing six or seven men in the box. You may have five or six men in the box. You can do the numbers any way you want. The defense is set up to stop the run first with the numbers in the box. The second reason is this: If you have trouble running the ball, it is your job to get them out of the box. To do that, you must be able to throw the football.

We have a high school coach in the state of West Virginia who won his fifth state championship with the five-step drop passing game. He comes to visit us every year. He uses a lot of what we do in high school. Can you use this system in high school? We think you can. I have used this passing game at the high school level. I have coached at a lot of places. I have visited with a lot of good coaches over the years. I think I have something very good to share with you. You can take it or leave it as you go out the door. But, I have something I believe in. I will make an effort to get it across to you. It is hard to give all of this to you in one hour and 25 minutes. I will try to get this across to you as best I can. I will talk to you just like I would talk to the players I am coaching at Marshall University. That is the way I will approach this lecture.

Last year, statistically, we threw for 4,200 yards in the regular season. We did have an extra game in the MAC. In the GMAC Bowl in Mobile, we threw for 570 yards. In order to do that, the quarterback cannot get sacked, pressured, or hurried. My job is to protect the quarterback so we can throw the ball.

We use the passing game on first down, on long-yardage plays, short-yardage plays, and other situations to mix up the plays. We approach the game with the idea that we are going to run the ball first. We will do that. If you are not going to try to stop the run by numbers in the box, we will run the ball until you do stop us. That is our philosophy.

In the GMAC bowl game, we had 108 plays on offense. How many of you saw the GMAC bowl game? How many of you saw the first half and turned the game off? A lot of others did the same thing. The score at halftime was 38 to 8 in favor of East Carolina. We scored 56 points in the second half. We ran 108 plays and threw the ball 70 times. On 90 percent of the times we threw the ball, it was the five-step drop passing game. I am going to cover the pass protection we use on our passing game scheme.

Steve Stripling talked about the University of Louisville defense leading the nation in sacks with 48. If I gave up 48 sacks, Bob Pruett, the head coach, would fire me. It is the responsibility of the offensive line to pick up the stunts, hot blitzes, and all of those things. In the regular season, our offensive line gave up *eight sacks*. We are very proud of that record.

A lot of that record is due to the fact that the offensive line coach got with the rest of the offensive staff and coordinated the passing game. It is very important, as a line coach, to get with the other coaches, and decide how we want to work out the protection schemes. We must be very involved in the running game. We must meet with the running back coach, the quarterback coach, and the tight end coach. You have to get together with all of the coaches and everyone has to be together as a one set mind. You must be cohesive with the staff. You must visit as a staff in discussing techniques. You need to meet with the coaches on individual techniques.

I went down to visit with Florida State this past month. They want to put in the five-step drop game. I could not teach the Florida State staff by drawing up a play and showing them where everyone goes on the play. I have a playbook that our offensive line uses. How many of you have a bible? I call it my bible. I use the bible for basic fundamentals in life. If I want to find out something about the basic fundamentals of life, I can find it in that bible. We tell our linemen their playbook is their bible. If they want to know something about the passing game we are covering, they have a book. This week, our players are picking up their booklet, getting ready for spring training. They turned it in after the bowl game. We have been working on it all winter, to get ready for the spring. I am going to teach you in the same manner as I teach the players.

When I visited at Florida State, the entire offensive staff was in the meetings. The entire offensive staff must be on the same page. They must understand the terms used in the passing game that will be utilized. They need to know what we are talking about when we talk about buckets, angle buckets, numbers, clusters, timing of the backs, and the entire terminology used with the offense. It is important for the line coach, if you are not the head coach, to understand the total picture of the plays. You must be on the same page.

You may have some questions as I move through the lecture. That happened at Florida State. I told them to be patient. When I put the next overhead on, the questions were answered. We should get to your answer. When I finish, it may be someone asking me to review one of the points.

In a nutshell, I am going to talk to you about the things an offensive lineman has to do fundamentally in the five-step drop passing game. I will try to get it across to you how the coach gets this across to the players to protect the quarterback. First, it is with fundamentals with a coach and the players. We must be able to communicate. As fast as we can, I want everyone in here to raise their right hand on my command. Hut! Good. We communicated. I already knew that you knew which hand was your right hand. If some raised the left hand, we would have a problem. But, everyone here was able to communicate. Football is the same way. To be a coach or a teacher, you must be able to communicate and get all of the players to do the simple things. You must have a system so you can talk to the players. When you leave here, you should be able to say that you know the four major pass rushes by a defense, and you should know how to count them.

Coach Steve Stripling talked about the things he liked to teach in a one-on-one pass drill. I am going to do just the opposite. I am going to show you how to counter the moves the defensive linemen use. This will enable you to have a fewer number of sacks and pressures when you go to throw the football. I have a drill tape that I use to teach the moves to defeat the four basic moves by the defensive lineman. I will show you how to set the drill up so you can work on it in practice. Then, I will show you that the drill applies in the game. What you teach the players in practice, they are going to do in the game.

I learned a lot from Joe Bugel when he was coaching with the Washington Redskins. He had a lot of coaches visit the Redskins because they were winning a lot of games, and they had won a Super Bowl. He asked me to show him what we taught our linemen. He said, "Mark, I have a lot of coaches come in and use the chalkboard to tell me what they teach their linemen. But, when they get the films on the linemen, they are not doing what the coach said they did on the chalkboard." He told me the players are not taking the steps in the game that the coaches said they took.

You are a coach. "Coach" means you are a teacher. If you are a teacher, you must communicate and get your worst players to execute as well as your best players. If I can get the worst player to execute as well as the best player, I am a good teacher. I have five positions that I must work with. I have to rank them one through five. You have your worst one and the best one. That worst player had better be doing what you are teaching the best player to do.

Everything must tie in with what you teach. For example, I will go over one simple thing—line splits. Everyone has a rule. Basically, we teach two-foot splits. Those are horizontal splits. I go one step beyond this and talk about vertical splits. Vertical splits are like this: If you bought a ticket to see us play and you were sitting on the 50 yard line looking down on us on offense, you would see that there is a space between the offensive and defensive line. You can see how our linemen are lined up.

You should know how long the football is if you are a line coach. The center will tilt the ball somewhat. But, the space is still between the two lines. The little space that no one can enter except the center is called the neutral zone. No one can be in that area except the center's hat. No one on offense can have their helmet break the imaginary line of the belt line of the center, or they will be considered in the backfield. If they are lined up with their hat beyond that belt line, they are illegal. I am talking to you to teach you about vertical splits.

We are talking about being *on* or *off* the ball. If we want our line *on* the ball, we are as close to the ball as we can be without being offsides with our fingertips. That is level one for us. If we are *off* the ball, we are as far off the ball as we can be. We have the helmet back toward the center's belt. To us, that is level three. The area between level one and level three is level two.

If I have one lineman who is 6'6" and another lineman who is 6'2", I can't tell those two players to have their feet in the same spot on the center. It has to be the headgear of each player on the center's belt or number. That is the level for them. On some occasions, the guard may be at level one, and the tackle could be on level three. We could have that type of alignment. This is called the spine or line posture to us.

I have what I call a tool bag. I use the tool bag to coach the offensive line. One of my tools is used on line splits. If the defense is rushing us to get us out of position, we want to line up at level three. We want to gain as much time as we can to pick up that defensive lineman or linebacker on the stunt. If I have a slower man, he is deeper to the line. If I have a man who is faster, he is closer to the line.

If we are down on the goal line, we want to line up at level one. If we are in short-yardage situations, we are on level one. If we are running the quarterback sneak, we are on level one. If we want to jump a bull rusher, we get up on level one. There are some tools you can use to help those big linemen who may not have good feet.

Again, as a base, we split our guards two feet, our tackles two feet, and the tight end three feet. On the goal line, we are split two feet. We are on level two for base teaching. When we zone block, we are at level two. We do not want contact on the first step. We want to use the second step down to beat the defensive lineman.

Let me get into the meat of the lecture. I am going to give you the pass protection techniques for the five-step drop passing game.
- Our dropback passes consist mainly of the quarterback taking a five-step drop straight back from the center or in the shotgun.
- The quarterback's depth is seven yards.

- Our job is to give him a pocket where he can set, step up, and throw.
- Our routes are timing routes, and if the quarterback has to move, then the timing is off.
- A "hurry" is just as bad as a sack.
- Take pride in having a perfect pocket every time.

I was from the old school. I used to teach pass protection by telling the line they had two yards wide of real estate and a depth of five yards. We do not teach it that way anymore. We have introduced a new term in our protection. I talk about the "dish" in pass protection for the linemen.

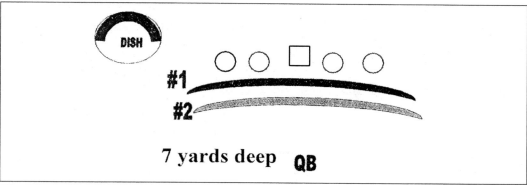

Diagram 1. The dish

- A dish is just what it says: a plate you eat off of.
- In the diagram above, you are looking at the shape of part of the dish.
- The #1 dish is where you take the defender on at contact.
- The #2 dish is two yards behind dish #1. This is where you work a defender if he gets inside of you or outside of you after contact (i.e., a right guard drops his post foot vs. a 3 position, and he has to catch up to him).
- Rule for pass protection: You attempt to work the #1 dish every time, but if you can't, then you cannot get past the #2 dish.

The phrase "work the dish, work the dish" will be used a lot by your coach. This is what he is referring to when he says this.

Now, I can communicate with the offensive line. How do we work the dish? We talk to them in terms of sets. We talk to them about taking a "set." If we are zone blocking, I talk about the first step and then the second step. It does not matter if it is a square zone or an angle zone. I do the same thing in pass protection. You must have a set foot and a post foot.

Now, we look at the fundamentals and techniques that will help you maintain the dish. We said we must have a set for the linemen. When they are set, they must know where the defender is lining up on them. We said the key to the passing game is protection. The key to protection is the set. This is the way we communicate to our players about the defender who lines up in his area.

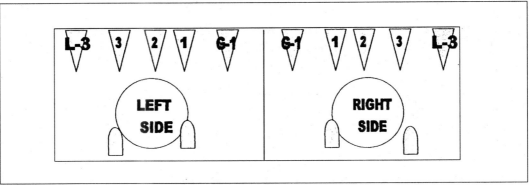

Diagram 2. Sets (left side, right side)

The diagram on the left side is for a left guard or left tackle. The center is a left guard or tackle, depending on which way he works.
- L-3 = loose 3 position (in the gap to his outside)
- 3 = 3 position (outside shade)
- 2 = 2 position (head up)
- 1 = 1 position (inside shade)
- G-1 = gap 1 position (in the gap to his inside)

The diagram on the right side is for a right guard, or tackle. The center is a right guard or tackle, depending on which way he works.
- L-3 = loose 3 position (in the gap to his outside)
- 3 = 3 position (outside shade)
- 2 = 2 position (head up)
- 1 = 1 position (inside shade)
- G-1 = gap 1 position (in the gap to his inside)
- These are the positions that a defender can line up on the line of scrimmage for a pass rush.
- His position will determine which set you will take in order to best protect the quarterback.
- Sets will change from this theory if you have help.
- We use numbers to define our sets.

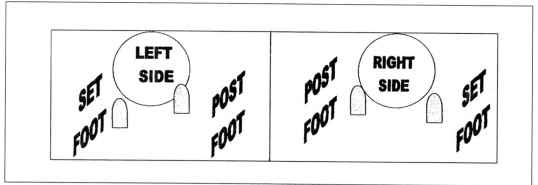

Diagram 3. Set foot (left and right side)

- Sets will start with the post foot or set foot.
- Sets are determined by what "position" the defender is in.
- Always know if you have "help" (i.e., another blocker or body presence or not).

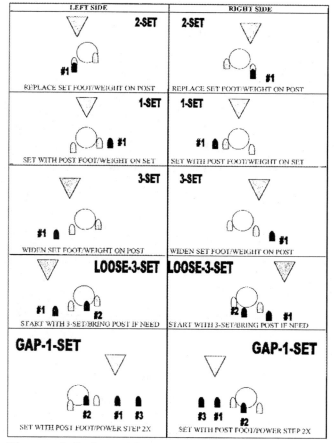

Diagram 4. Basic sets, 2-set

A clown's foot is a player who feels comfortable versus a long set. It is a pre-kick, and they lose the 3-set. You will see this on the film.

Now, I have a tool bag. I can communicate to them where the dish is, tell them what level to get on. I know their stance, and I can communicate post foot or set foot. I can communicate with them in working in practice. I can tell them how I want them to start the drill or the play in practice. I must be able to communicate with them somehow. This is the best method of communicating for me. You may call it something else. I researched the situation, and this is the best for me.

Diagram 5. Tackle sets

If we use play-action protection, we call it a jump set. A jump set involves the following actions:
- Use an angle-bucket with the set foot.
- Advance at the same angle with the post foot.
- Bring the set foot again and get under control.

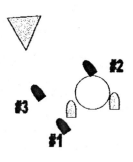 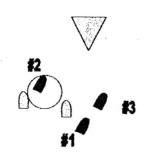

➤ USE AN **ANGLE-BUCKET** WITH THE SET FOOT	➤ USE AN **ANGLE-BUCKET** WITH THE SET FOOT
➤ ADVANCE AT THE SAME ANGLE WITH THE POST FOOT	➤ ADVANCE AT THE SAME ANGLE WITH THE POST FOOT
➤ BRING THE SET FOOT AGAIN AND GET UNDER CONTROL	➤ BRING THE SET FOOT AGAIN AND GET UNDER CONTROL

Diagram 6. Jump sets

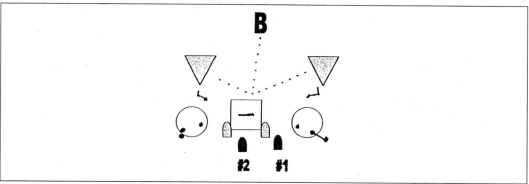

Diagram 7. Spider sets

A spider set can be used by the center, guard, or tackle. He is uncovered. A spider set involves the following actions:

- The left guard takes a 2-set.
- The right guard takes a 3-set.
- The center sets off the ball with depth, starting with the foot that will put him in the midpoint between the guards.
- This invites the two down defenders to rush inside where the center now can help. All three eye the linebacker to bump off a dog.
- The center also looks for the T-T twist.

Spider sets are also used by guards and tackles when they are uncovered and have the linebacker over them. The same set is used.

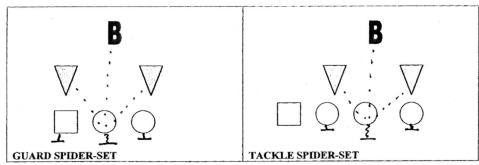

GUARD SPIDER-SET   **TACKLE SPIDER-SET**

Diagram 8. Guard and tackle spider sets

We have dual-read sets. A dual-read set is similar to the spider set. The uncovered man must read two defenders. We use terms with these sets to indicate what we want them to do. We call Polly for the center, Molly for the guard, and Trolly for the tackle. It tells the man to check the linebacker and then to check outside. He may or may not do that. We may just get a piece of the man, but that is all we need to keep him from getting the quarterback.

Then, we use tandem sets. We may have three offensive men responsible for two down linemen and a linebacker on defense. The three blockers watch for any games coming from the three defenders.

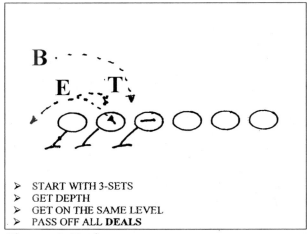

➢ START WITH 3-SETS
➢ GET DEPTH
➢ GET ON THE SAME LEVEL
➢ PASS OFF ALL DEALS

Diagram 9. Tandem sets

The three blockers start with 3-sets. They must get depth. We want them to get off on the same level. They pass off all deals by the defenders.

We use the term *sifting* to describe safety blitzes. We get all kinds of blitzes in the A gap by defenders trying to get to our quarterback. We check for those stunts and pick those up by the linemen. The key is to get the head up and get it out of the defender and look for those blitzing secondary men.

You must have rules to handle zone blitzes. We call them "zone fires." Again, the key is to look for the stunts. We talk about three zone blitzes. We set to block and look for the blitz.

Let me get into the fundamentals and techniques of blocking in pass protection. We said the key to the passing game is protection. The key to protection is the set. Now that we have gone over the various sets, we must cover the techniques once the proper set has been taken. This is the tool that I teach all of the time. *What is a target?* If you are going to make a successful block, you must have a pre-snap bull's-eye target. It is one of the most critical points of pass blocking.

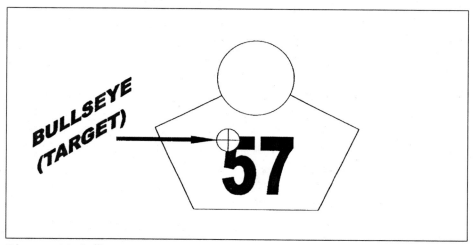

Diagram 10. Bull's-eye target

The following guidelines apply concerning targeting:
- On the dropback pass protection, you must have a "target" on the defender you are blocking.
- The target will tell you the direction he is always going.
- Most linemen get beat by watching the defender's head, and they get faked out.
- In the diagram illustrating the bull's-eye target, the inside tip of the number 5 would be the target for a right guard who has a defender in a 3 position, or it could be a right tackle who is blocking a defensive end.
- You must know the defender's jersey number and have a target pre-snap.
- A left guard or left tackle would use the inside tip of the number 7.
- The center uses the same target concept on his defender.

Here are the coaching points. The target (bull's-eye) is one of the most critical fundamentals of pass blocking. Here is a tip. The faster the athlete is, the tighter the target. The slower the athlete, the wider the target. Look at your target when you are in your stance. It is hard to get a target if you are looking straight ahead in your stance and have to find the target on your set.

Next, we look at the invisible line. There is a line that represents the closest path for the defender to get to the quarterback on a dropback pass. The objective of the offensive linemen is to take a proper pass set that will have you straddle this line. You must get to this set point as fast as you can. Setting on this line will allow you to dictate to the defender that he has a limited pass rush.

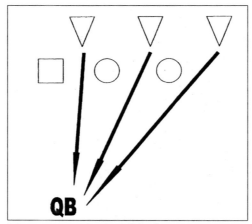

Diagram 11. The invisible line

- You must know your line pre-snap. Take the proper set that allows you to straddle the line.
- As a rule, your outside knee should be in the defender's crotch.
- Your shoulders should be square to the line of scrimmage when you straddle the line.
- You must get depth and width to get to the line.

Here are the coaching points. There are generally two mistakes that all linemen make dealing with the line. First, they turn their body and shoulders to the sideline on the set. Subconsciously, they think they can block them better this way. Second, they lean into the set, thinking that this will get them to the line faster. In reality, it makes it easier for the defender to come underneath.

Now that we have covered set and the line, we must talk about your pass posture. It is just like teaching the power play. You must have proper posture. Let me show you what we mean by pass-blocking posture. These points are critical.

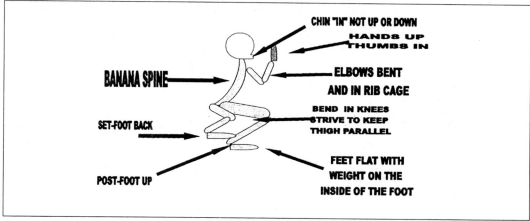

Diagram 12. Pass-blocking posture

You must keep the chin in as you roll to the target. We all know what a banana is. That is what we want. You will get some players that God built just the opposite of what we want. They may be humpbacked. We have to teach them to power-cling to a banana spine. That is what we are talking about for power and pass blocking. We talk about the elbows being bent when we set. You must have a bend in the knees. The feet must be set flat with the weight on the inside of the foot. We always want to keep our stagger. That is what you have to teach for power. You must have power to pass block. This is what I teach over and over.

When the defender gives us his chest, we are going to take it. The jersey is made so the numbers will be on his chest. We want our thumbs up, and we take on the defender. When we take the chest, it is over for that defender. The important part of the block is the jam to the chest. It is the punch or the jam. You can call it what you want. They have to learn how to jam the man and lock out.

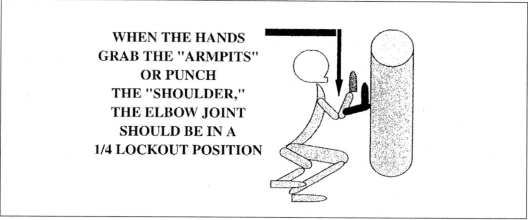

Diagram 13. Punch or jam

- You have maximum power in the punch at the one-fourth lockout position.
- You have to time the jam. It can only be done through repetitions.
- You have your strongest bench press the last one-fourth of your lift.
- This also keeps the defender off you. So, you can see your target and look for dogs, freaks, zone fires, and twist.

When I finish with that section, I give the players a quiz. At the end of the playbook, they have a copy of the quiz. We call it our "Pass Pro Time-Out Quiz." Now, I realize those players do not carry that playbook to class with them, and I know they do not look at it all the time. This is what I tell them. If they are used to taking a magazine to read while they are in the bathroom, I want them to substitute the playbook for that magazine. That is when I want them to read that playbook. They will tell me, "Coach, I read the playbook this morning when I went to the bathroom." So, I know this works. I want them to be ready to take that quiz.

Pass Pro Time-Out Quiz
1. How deep is the quarterback on our dropback pass?
2. A _____ is just as bad as a _____.
3. How many dishes are there?
4. Where is the first dish?
5. Where is the second dish?
6. What is the rule concerning the dish in pass pro?
7. Draw up the different positions and number them according to the position you play.

This is just a sample of what we have on the quiz. We go on and on with questions that make them aware of their assignments and the techniques they must use to be an effective pass protector.

Most defenders rise up out of their stance when they pass rush and, in doing so, they will give you their chest. When that happens, we want to take the chest every time.

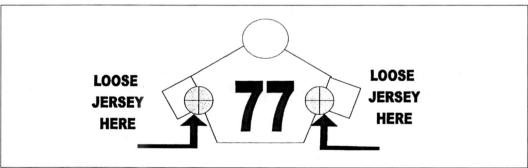

Diagram 14. Taking the chest

Taking the chest involves the following factors:
- After taking your set, shoot the hands for the armpits.
- Time the jam with the one-fourth lockout.
- Keep the thumbs in and grab cloth.
- The only place where there is loose cloth on a game jersey is right in the armpits so a player is able to raise his arms.
- Squeeze the hands and grab cloth, locking out as you do.
- This will enable you to control the defender wherever he goes, and you can also control all of his moves, such as "spinning."
- If you miss the grab, you can re-punch.

When a defender does not give you his chest, then he will come at you turning his shoulders. When he does this, you must treat him like he is a cylinder. You can now place one or two hands on his shoulder. With him coming at you with a shoulder, that means he plans on using several moves. We must be alert for these moves when we get the shoulder: hand smack on your hands to knock them down, rip, and swim.

Diagram 15

Let me cover the different rushes. The first rush we see is the bull rush. The defender can bull rush us and get the blocker off balance. So, we have a counter to the bull rush.

Bull rush — When the defender runs through you, attempting to knock you back to the quarterback (to disrupt his timing or flush him from the pocket), if you can take him on with your jam and keep your head out, that is great. Most of the time, it does not happen that way. You will most likely get your head into him. Get it out as soon as you can.

Hop-hop — Drop both feet back at the same time. This will slow his hop-hop.

Hop-hop-drive — When a defender bull rushes you and you slow him down or stop him, his next move will be to grab you and pull you forward. To counter his move, use the hop-hop-drive technique. As you feel the defender pull you forward after you have used the hop-hop, then counter it by going with him. You will use a drive technique by widening your feet and following him in the pull direction. As you follow him with a wide base, make sure you are under control and grab him with your hands.

Spinner — One of the moves a defender will use when he gives you a shoulder is the spin move. He will generally give you a quick bull move and spin to one side or the other. To counter the spin, use your hands as though you were rolling a barrel. Roll him in the direction he is spinning, while placing your hands on his shoulder. You may have to give ground and match him in the direction he is spinning. His objective is to get by your shoulders on the initial spin so you end up trailing him.

Rip — The defender grabs one of your shoulders and rips underneath to the opposite shoulder. When the defender lowers his shoulder to rip, then punch him forcefully on the rip shoulder. Follow him in that direction. Keep your base as you match him.

Swim — Another move is for the defender to grab one of your shoulders and swim his other arm over the top of that same shoulder. When the defender's arm is in the air on the swim, shoot your hand for his armpit. When your hand gets to the armpit, grab all of the hair in his armpit. Press and bring your body with you in the direction of his armpit. This will knock him to the ground.

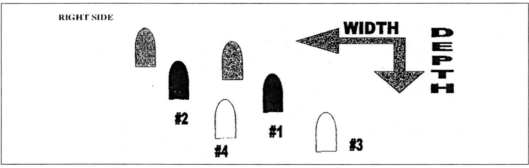

Diagram 16. Kick-slide

A kick-slide is the movement you make when going to your set-foot side (your outside). There are two kinds of kick slides: one, when you are setting to the defender, and two, when you have engaged with the defender.
- When you kick, you get width and depth, keeping the toe and knee straight to the line of scrimmage.

- When you slide, you keep most of your weight on your post leg, which will keep you from leaning to the outside and better prepare you for an inside move.
- The second kick and slide (#3 and #4) distance depends on your target. You kick-slide if the target gets wider. You are trying to gain width and depth.
- If your target comes toward you, you settle with a shorter kick-slide.

Here is a coaching point. Adjust your kick-slide to the side of the original alignment of the defender (the imaginary line), and to his path to the quarterback.

The kick-slide when engaged is the next point we must look at. We must teach the linemen how to react now that we have the defender engaged.

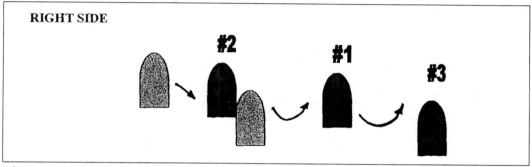

Diagram 17. Kick-slide when engaged

You are a right-handed stance player, and you have jammed your defender. He has worked to your outside. The following points apply:
- You will be using a kick-slide step, but you will be forcing power with your set foot and outside arm.
- You will gain some width and depth. As you do so, you are not concentrating on slowing the defender down when he rushes to your outside.
- This is different than the kick-slide used for setting on a line.

The power steps are used when a defender is rushing to your inside (i.e., the post-foot side). You take lateral steps with the post foot to the inside, attempting to step on an imaginary line. You force the post foot over and up as you force with your inside arm.

The coaching point is this: Once you keep the defender on the dish to your inside, he has no choice but to try to spin to your outside. You counter this by either grabbing his jersey with your inside hand, or rolling the barrel while giving some ground to the outside.

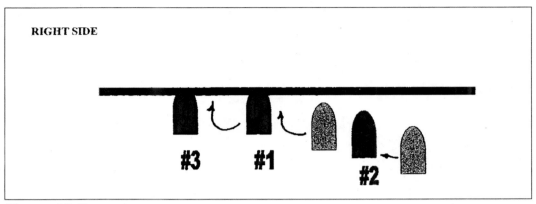

RIGHT SIDE

#3   #1   #2

Diagram 18. Power step

I will now review the dropback protection techniques. Let me list them for you:

- Take a pre-snap look.
- Work your stance (weight shift).
- Look at your target.
- Take the proper set quickly.
- Time your jam.
- Take the chest or place your hands on his shoulder.
- Keep your head out.
- Power-kick-slide to the outside.
- Power-step to the inside.
- Work the dish or second dish.
- Counter all moves.

The hand slapper — You have a defender who likes to knock your hands down when you take your set and start to throw your jam. First, use your outside hand only. Second, jab it forward just one inch and bring it back. The defender will react immediately to the short jab and smack at the hand that took the short jab. He will miss (if you keep the jab short and quick). When he misses, then take the chest. This works every time.

Now that we have covered the dropback fundamentals, we must cover what we are looking for when we get our head out of the defender. We look for the following: twists (like stunts); dogs (linebackers shooting gaps); blitzes (defensive backs shooting gaps); combos (line stunts plus dogs plus blitzes); and fire zones.

The following factors give away twists and the man who penetrates (he goes first) and who the looper is (he goes second).

- Take a pre-snap look.
- Many defensive linemen change up their stagger when they are going to stunt or twist. The foot that is staggered back usually tells the direction he is going. He will go to the back-foot side.
- The two adjacent defensive linemen will work different levels. One will be deeper than the other.
- Sometimes, they will give it away with their calls.
- Some defensive tackles only twist when they get in a loose 3 position on the guard.
- Some defensive ends only run an E-T twist when they get in a 3 position on the tackle.

Always take a pre-snap look. Communicate to your buddy.

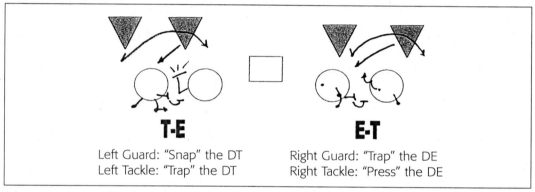

T-E

Left Guard: "Snap" the DT
Left Tackle: "Trap" the DT

E-T

Right Guard: "Trap" the DE
Right Tackle: "Press" the DE

Diagram 19. Trapping the twist

Here are our rules for trapping the twist. The guard must snap the defensive tackle on a T-E in order to help the tackle from being picked. The trapper must get his head in front of the man penetrating and knock the "dog stew" out of him. He must immediately square up on him. The tackle on an E-T must power-step up into the man penetrating to help the guard. You must do this to avoid getting on different levels and getting picked.

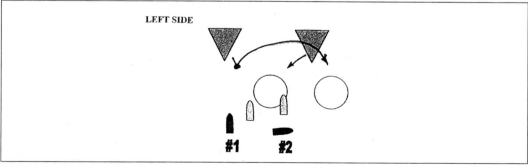

Diagram 20. Techniques vs. the looper

Take your normal set (leaving your weight on your post foot). When you see the looper, follow him with your head, drop your post foot, and air your foot to get your head in front of him. Follow up with your set foot and knock the "dog stew" out of him. Once you trap him with your head in front, square up immediately and get your head out. Getting your head out will allow you to look for a super twist or a linebacker dog coming off the edge.

When you recognize the twist, then verbally communicate to your buddy by yelling "switch, switch." He will now know to expect the twist stunt.

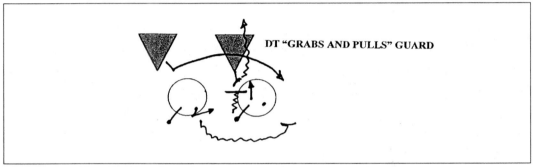

Diagram 21. Man blocking the twist

This seldom happens in a game. But it might, with us using the hop-hop-drive technique against pullers. It happens more in a 2-on-2 drill against our defense.

Centers: Take warning of this twist. This is a twist stunt. It can hurt you.

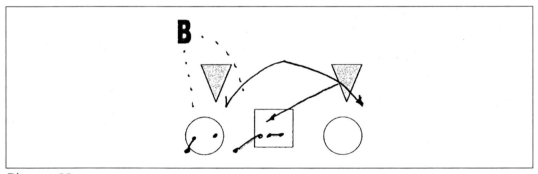

Diagram 22

Your assignment calls for you to set to your left with the guard. You are concentrating on the linebacker. The defensive tackle from your right rams you right in the ribs to execute a T-T twist. Coaching point: Keep your head on a swivel. Look, look, look."

Here is the super twist. This is why you must get your head up and *look*.

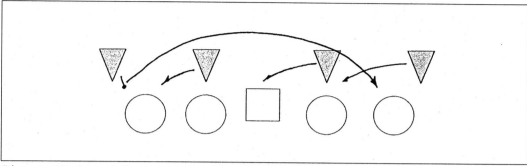

Diagram 23. Super twist

Let me cover the linebacker blitz. For communication purposes, we talk about linebackers dogging in a gap. These are the gaps they can come through. We could also refer to strong A, B, C, and D gaps, and weak A, B, C, and D gaps by formation strength.

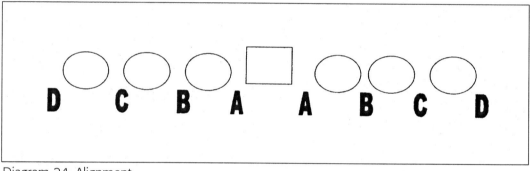

Diagram 24. Alignment

With a four-down and three-linebacker defense, we refer to the linebackers with the following names:

S = Sam — the linebacker to the strongside.

M = Mike — the linebacker to the middle.

W = Will — the linebacker to the weakside.

The following dogs are illustrated in Diagram 25:

Sam strong - B

Mike strong - A

Will weak - B

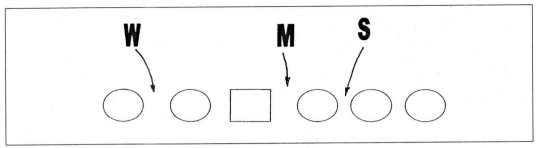

Diagram 25

In a three-down and four-linebacker defense, we have Sam linebacker strong, Mike linebacker strong, PEG linebacker weak, and Will linebacker weak.

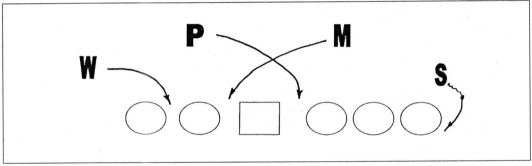

Diagram 26

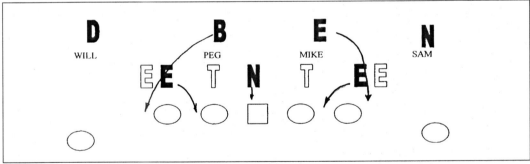

Diagram 27. Defense stems from a four-down defense to a three-down defense

We will still have the same names for the four linebackers even though one is a nickel back, one a dime back, and one a defensive end.

This would be a combo (line stunts and dogs combined). For the most part in pass protection, the quarterback will identify who we will treat as the Mike linebacker anyway. But for communication purposes, like in the running game, we will use these names.

You block linebackers the same way you block down linemen with regard to techniques. You may have to lead with the head on a linebacker who is charging from four or five yards depth, but again, you must get your head out of there to look. You may have to keep switching even after you pick up your linebacker. The key is to look, look, look!

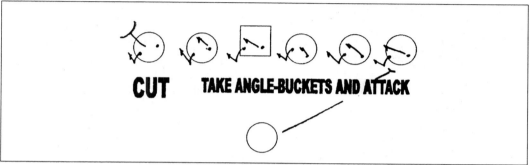

Diagram 28. Three-step drop technique

The quarterback takes three steps. This is a gap protection. Your technique is an aggressive technique. You attack the defender who shows or ends up in your gap. You break down into a pass-pro posture after making contact with the defender. The lineman blocking the end man on the line of scrimmage cuts his man. All other linemen can cut, but there are many dogs, combos, etc. with this protection when we check to it. It is used a lot against the blitz look.

This is how we would block on sprint protection. The backside guard and tackle take gap-1 sets and backpedal. They are making a swinging gate. They must be on the same plane. The center and frontside use the jump technique. They must check the backside.

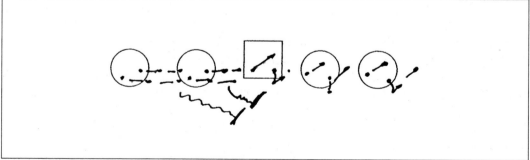

Diagram 29. Sprint protection technique

11

Tight End Blocking Techniques

Greg Meyer
Northwestern University
1996

The first thing I want to share with you is my impression of what I thought a tight end was. When I started coaching at Arizona State, I felt the tight end was a pass receiver first and a blocker second. That was what I liked doing and what I liked to see happening. My experience had been with quarterbacks and tight ends. Then, I had the chance to go with coach Gary Barnett to Northwestern. When he gave me the chance to coordinate the offense, I became much more knowledgeable about the running game because of my experience with tight ends. I don't think we have all the answers, but our offensive line coach was very patient with me. There was a lot of teaching I had to get involved with between the tight ends and tackles. What I found out was that I became much more excited about the running game and about the blocking techniques than I ever knew existed at Arizona State.

I think, as a coach, the greatest way to teach a young man what his responsibilities are is to have great communication. We give the athlete a word for every single technique that he has to utilize to execute his block. You will hear these terms. We not only identify the technique of the defender, but we identify the technique the tight end has to use to execute that block.

The other thing we use is called muscle memory. For your players to make the correct steps into a block, they must take training through muscle memory. The other part of the training is for them to do it without tipping the defense as to which way they are going. Stance and steps are things we do every day. We want our players to get into a stance so they can take the steps they need without taking false or cheat steps. Once they know the stance we want them in, they have to work to get the weight mentally transferred so they can take the correct step without the cheat or false steps.

This is critical. They have to be able to transfer the weight consciously. The next thing they have to do is transfer the weight subconsciously. They have to get the feel so that the move is natural where they can do it without thinking. When that tight end comes to the line of scrimmage, he has to look at the defensive front, listen for the line call, listen for any automatic the quarterback may make, and think about the block. The last thing you want in his head is what foot he is going to step with and how he is going to do it. We have guys that have been in our program for three years and still have a hard time stepping. Our tight ends get into left- and right-handed stances depending on the side they are lined up on. We do this so they are more effective executing the blocks. To get comfortable in a left-handed stance takes time away from practice. The ends must work on their own away from the practice field to get that natural feeling. We don't have time to work as long as it takes to get that attitude done. For some, it comes naturally, but, if it doesn't, they have to put in the extra time.

Because the defense wants to put pressure on the passer, they widen the outside end and use a speed rush. The offensive line coach counters that move by putting the tight end to that side. That makes the tight end a pass blocker. His stance helps him in that respect.

The next thing I'll talk about is power angles. Power angles are proven facts from physics. The first thing in the power angle is to work hard to keep your feet moving. Work on flexibility with your players. The better and more flexible your players are in their ankles, the better chance they have of having good power angles with a good solid base. Some guys have to get back on their heels to stay low in a good football position. That is the last thing you want. You want them on the balls of their feet, but you want the entire shoe on the ground. To do this, you have to bend your knees and have good flexibility in your ankles. We want the knees, feet, and back going straight down the field with the foot in total contact with the ground. We do this in a drill. We call it a duck walk or power strut. All we want them to do is get their toes going forward and step in that position, planting their foot every time for about five yards. If they are on the balls of their feet and meet resistance, they fall back on their heels. But, if their feet are solid on the ground, they have a good solid base. If the knees move outside, that destroys the power of physics, because the power is going in two different directions. An example of creating a good power angle and losing it is a common tendency for most blockers. If the tight end is on a frontside block or cutoff block, he gets inside-out leverage. That puts him in a good power position, but the first thing he wants to do is turn his hips into the hole. As soon as the tight end puts his hips in the hole or turns his shoulders, he has destroyed his power angles. All the good work we have done to get the power going in one direction is lost. Now, the defender squeezes him right back into the hole.

The line of force includes the alignment of feet, hips, and shoulders parallel to our desired line of force. The forearm, head, and shoulders are our blocking surface. The hips and legs are the power source. The feet are the wheels. When the blocker strikes his initial blow at a point, he must be low enough and close enough, and he must continue to make the block work. He has to be low enough to create a lifting force on the defender. He has to be close enough to neutralize his charge. The force must be continued to get the defender on his heels so he is unable to make a counter move.

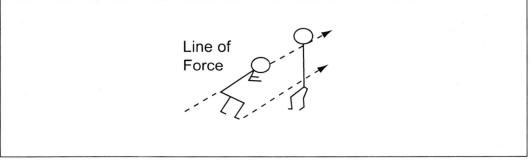

Diagram 1

I am starting to believe that a bunched stance is better for our tight ends. It does not look good. It looks goofy. In the bunched stance, we look like a frog in our stance. I don't care as long as we are able to execute and do the things a tight end has to do. The reason I like the bunched stance is better balance after the first step, it is good for power angles on contact, and it gives us better vision. We ask the tight end to alert blockers to secondary backs in blitz modes. They have to see coverages and secondary alignments. We can better do that from a bunched stance.

We feel, regardless of the technique, once the end knows what his assignment is, his step is going to take him directly to his aiming point. The only exception would be a defender playing heavy on the tight end. In that case, we might false key with the head. We are going to step normally in the direction of our aiming point. The only difference will be the length of the step. The length of the step will depend on the type of block he's trying to execute. The defender is going to react as soon as the end moves. The longer the end has his foot off the ground, the less chance he has of getting a good base. We want them stepping with the correct foot in the right direction, but we want the foot picked up and put down as quickly as they can do it. We want to keep a good center of balance within the framework of their body when they block a base scheme. A base scheme to us is the inside and outside zone play. His rule is man on or man on outside, if we were running the outside zone play.

In the base scheme, the end aims one inch outside the sternum. The end picks up the outside foot and short steps. This gives the defender the impression we are trying to hook him. It is not a long step. It is a short influence step. We want the blocker to picture a rod running down the center of his body when he is in the stance. The weight is mentally transferred to the inside foot. If the defender is a head reader, the end can turn his head to add to the influence. When we execute the base block, we stretch the defender by the outside step and maybe the head turn. But, the second step has to start pressuring back inside to get the inside out leverage. If he has physically transferred his weight to the outside, he has to physically transfer it back to the inside on the next step. If too much weight flows outside, the end has to bring it all back. We want the defender to flow outside and pressure him inside.

The next part of blocking is the punch and hip roll. We used to teach on the first step to get the arms back and cocked for the punch. In the NFL, our kids are telling us they are not looking for that big cocking motion any more. Even though offensive line coaches were stressing it, it is almost impossible to do. Most coaches can't tell whether contact is made on the first or second step. We tell our players to be ready to punch as quickly as they can. During the first step, the hands have to come up into the cocked position. We don't want our players just getting their hands on the defender and pushing. We want to punch through the defender, not to him. If you are working on bags to teach the punch, don't let them stop on the second step and punch. Make them punch and go on to the third and fourth step. We call it punch and go. We want to use the entire surface of the feet when possible. That allows them to stay in balance and maintain a wide base for the power angles. We teach the bunched stance, but, once they come out of the stance, their base widens.

The cutoff scheme is the next thing I want to cover. In this scheme, we step with the foot that we are cutting off with. The distance and angle of the cutoff block is determined by the alignment of the defense. The first step has to make up distance without overextending the base. If the end has to cut off a man who is over our tackle, he knows he can't take a big enough step without overextending the base. The further inside the cutoff, the flatter the inside step must be. If the end is cutting off a 9 technique, he wouldn't take a flat step. He takes an angle step, unless the defender is doing an awful lot of veering inside. The aiming point is to get the opposite cheek on the inside hip of the defender. If the cutoff can't be made, the end continues to push the defender with his shoulders square across the hole, so when the cutback comes, it goes outside of him.

In the second step, our goal is to create inside-out leverage without losing our base. He maintains his power angles and keeps his shoulders square. He wants to avoid turning his hips and shoulder too soon.

A lot of coaches tell their players they have to be mean and aggressive all the time. We use a butt block. This occurs when the end has gone for the inside hip and feels the defender coming off his backside. It has the appearance of an overreached cutoff block. All we want from our end is to screen the defender from the play. He uses his butt to screen him off the play. We don't want him to try to turn around and block him. If he does that, the defender will be around him and have a chance to make the play. We don't tell our people to work for the butt block, but we don't discourage them from using it. If you tell your ends they have to be physical and not use the butt block, they will start to hesitate and get beat across their faces.

We fight pressure with pressure. Some of the biggest plays in the zone play come off the backside cutoff block. Once the end gets his cheek to the inside hip, he fights pressure to the outside. He doesn't try to turn his hips, but keeps his shoulders square and works outside. If the defender gets across his head, he still fights the pressure, but takes him down inside.

In the cutoff block, maintaining contact for as long as possible is critical. Just getting to the cutoff position is not enough. The end has to stay on his block and continue to keep his feet moving because the play has a chance of cutting back to his block. The last thing that could happen is for the end to have stepped inside and the defender is rushing outside. If that occurs, the end pushes him on by the hole. That makes the end's job easy, because he has run himself out of the play.

To communicate to the tight end the defensive alignment of the defender, we use numbers. We call a defender aligned head-up on the tight end a 6 technique. Defenders on the inside shade or eye of the tight end are in a 7 technique. A defender on the outside shoulder or eye of the tight end is in a 9 technique.

Our offensive plays are called even-numbered plays toward the tight end and odd-numbered plays away from him. The tight end moves from side to side according to the formation, and with him comes the even-numbered plays. I'm not saying that is good or bad. In our system, it works. Our tight end knows if he hears 38 or 32 it is a playside run. That is regardless of whether he is on the left or right side of the formation. The tackle knows the same thing. If there is an odd call, they know they are in some kind of cutoff mode. When we run the inside zone play, if the tight end is covered, his assignment is base. The term base is also a technique. If we are running the outside zone play, 38, and the end and tackle are covered, his assignment is Mo. The term Mo is his technique. Mo stands for man on outside. The end takes a six-inch step to stretch the defender. The back can either cut up or go outside.

On the inside zone play, 32, with the tackle uncovered and the end with a 7, 6, or 9 technique on him, the rule is ace. That is an uncovered rule for us. Ace tells the tackle and end they are in a combination scheme from down linemen to the linebacker. The ball is going inside. If the tackle is uncovered and the ball is going outside, the rule, scheme, and technique is called uno. That puts the tackle and tight end on a combination block down linemen to the linebacker.

When the ball goes away from the tight end, the tight end has some kind of cutoff scheme. We name the cutoff so the tight end knows what type of technique he has to use. In our normal inside zone play, our scheme is a wall or base cutoff, depending on if the tackle is covered or uncovered. The wall is used when the tackle and tight end are both covered. They simply wall the defender to the outside. Their blocks are extremely important because the ball could come back on a cutback. The base cutoff is used when the tackle is uncovered. With the wall, the tight end takes an outside step to set up the cutoff. On the base cutoff, the tight end takes an inside step to the cutoff. By using the terms wall and base cutoff, I know the tight end has recognized the front and knows what type of technique to use.

Teams will try to stunt off the backside to stop the inside zone play. If we are playing a stunting team, we have to make an adjustment. The tight end and the tackle have a combination scheme called power Ed. If the defensive tackle and Sam linebacker are running crossing stunts, this call handles that. The tight end comes hard to the inside. If the Sam linebacker veers inside, the tight end is on him. The tackle reads his man going away and combines with the tight end on the Sam linebacker. If the defense runs the stunt the opposite way, which is more effective, the tight end comes hard inside and takes the looping tackle coming outside. The tackle reads his man going away and takes the Sam linebacker as he comes into the hole.

When we run the outside zone play away from the tight end, we use a scramble cutoff and a reach. The scramble cutoff is used when the end has to cut off a 7 technique defender. The ball is not going to cut back. All the end wants to do is keep the defender out of the pursuit lanes. The reach is used to come down on a 5 technique with the ball going away.

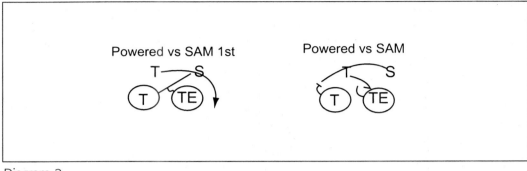

Diagram 2

Let me go back and talk about the ace block. This is the tackle and tight end working in combination on a down lineman and a linebacker. The first thing we tell our tight end and tackle is, "Feel the down man and see the linebacker." We do that more so on the outside zone than the inside zone. Most of the time in the inside zone play, the tackle ends up on the linebacker. The only time that wouldn't happen is if the down man veered to the inside. The tackle would end up on the down man, and the tight end would pick up the linebacker scraping over the top. The linebacker is seeing the same thing from the back on the inside or outside zone play.

For the linebacker to be effective on the outside zone play, he has to go in a hurry. If the linebacker is going to be a penetrator on this stunt, he has to go hard with the flow. That makes him an easy target for the tight end. The tight end against a 6 or 9 technique steps with his outside foot to try to influence the defender. The tackle takes his feel step toward the tight end, looking for the inside veer stunt. If there is a 7 technique on the tight end, he steps off with his inside foot. There will be no influence on the 7 technique defender. The tackle comes off to take away the inside veer by the 7 technique. He feels the down man and sees the linebacker. As long as the linebacker keeps his depth, the tackle will continue to help the tight end on the down man. The tight end knows he has the down man by himself when the tackle goes up on the linebacker.

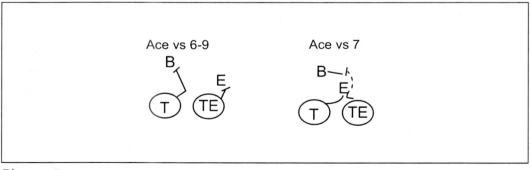

Diagram 3

Here are the main points in the inside zone play. With the tackle and end covered, they block the base blocking scheme. The tight end steps with his outside foot to his aiming point, which is one inch outside the defender's sternum. He keeps his steps short and quick and tries to stretch the technique. He wants to keep his power angle in mind and center of gravity a little inside. He must be ready to work back inside after the first step. The idea is to stretch and then maintain inside-out leverage.

With the tackle uncovered and a 9, 6, or 7 technique on the tight end, we use the combination block. The tight end and tackle secure the down man first to the linebacker. Against a 9 technique, the end will turn into a base block. The first step of the tight end is determined by the technique of the defender. Any stunts between the linebacker and down lineman must be handled by the tight end and tackle. Always maintain inside-out leverage, fight pressure, and continue to stress power angle principles.

On the outside zone play where the tackle and tight end are covered, we use a Mo block scheme. The tight end takes a six-inch lateral step to the outside hip of the defender. The wider the technique, the wider the angle of departure, but don't overstep. The tight end keeps his power angle in mind and his center of gravity as close to the center as possible. If he gets the inside veer by the defender, he has to handle that. The tight end continues to stretch the defender until the defender's momentum takes him too wide, then he turns out and runs the defender to the sideline.

If the tackle is uncovered, he works his uno combo block with the tackle. He works with the tackle to block the down lineman to the frontside linebacker. The tackle has to feel the down man and see the linebacker. The tight end's first step depends on the alignment of the defender. If the defender is head up, the tight end steps with his outside foot. He takes a six-inch power step to make contact on the first step, if possible. He tries to keep his shoulders as square as possible. The tackle wants to cover the linebacker up. It is not always necessary or best to wall the linebacker off. If the tight end or tackle covers up the linebacker, the back will make his cut. If the tight end has a 9 technique on him, the blocking scheme becomes the Mo scheme. If the defender is in a 7 technique and veers, the tight end cannot leave his tackle out on an island. Penetration kills this play. If the veer stunt comes too quickly for the tackle, the tight end has to punch hard to slow down the defender and give the tackle a chance to get on him. He does not turn and chase him down inside. He has to punch, keep his shoulders square, and run the linebacker outside, if he has to.

12

Fundamentals of Line Blocking

Joe Moore
University of Notre Dame
1994

Anytime I have been around a coach, I always wanted to know what he is thinking and what he is teaching. First of all, if you are going to be a line coach, you must believe that your tackle can block their defensive tackle, or that your guard can block their guard or linebacker. You must believe that your players can block someone. If you think you must have a scheme to move the ball, then you have a serious problem, because no matter how much you work with a player he will know if you do not believe in him. They know what you believe. You must actually believe in what you are teaching. You have to believe you can block a man.

It is a proven fact if a team can't run the football, then you can't win unless you have a great defense. I have been around a lot of passing game experts, and I have been at schools where passing game experts have come in. Anytime we have adopted the passing game, we have had to depend on our defense to win football games. If you can't run the football and you do not believe your men can block the men up front, you have to depend on your defense. I am not trying to tell you that you do not have to have a scheme, but, if you think you can throw the ball and win, you are better than I am.

There is one thing I have found since I have been in college coaching. When we find players from high school that have been taught to block when they get to us in college, that high school coach has a winning record. Almost always. I can't think of any lineman that we have gotten that was ready to play where the high school coach was not a winning coach. There must be some correlation between offensive line play and winning. We see a lot of big linemen. I must have turned down 30 players that were 6'6" to 6'7" that weighed 270 to 280 pounds. They could not block a pea off a pea pod. We took some kids that were 6'3" and 6'4" from those schools that were winning and playing for championships that were better blockers. It has been that way ever since I have been in college coaching. Teams that know how to run the ball and know how to block to win. You have to teach them how to play the positions, and you must get the athletes.

It is important to talk to the best people in football. I never took a job where I could not take one of my assistants with me and go visit for one week in the off-season. If I take a job, I want one week where I can go observe football. I never asked for anything else. I never asked how much money I was making, but I made sure I got one week to go visit other schools. I always want a chance to improve myself. Right now at Notre Dame, I plan to go visit other schools. It is so important. You do not need to just sit and listen; you need to go watch people coach. I never talked to a line coach in my life that was not just knocking the crap out of people. Watch them coach, I do not care who they are.

I used to drive by a school that was always working on a seven-man sled. I figured we had a chance to beat that team. I went to visit with them one day and asked the coach why he used the sled so much. He told me the sled helped them get off the ball at the same time. I am not too smart, but I do know this. If they all got off the ball at the same time, they are not getting off as the fastest man, but they are getting off together with the slowest man. If you can watch seven men at the same time, you are better than I am. I have trouble watching a man's left arm. I have trouble watching seven at one time. If you can watch seven men at one time, you should be on *Saturday Night Live*. I am not against the seven-man sled for conditioning. If you want to condition kids after practice, you can. If you start coaching them when they are working on conditioning, you are wasting your time.

I do not believe in using the boards to teach blocking. I have talked to coaches that said they used boards to teach the players to keep their feet apart. If you can't teach them to keep their feet apart without using boards, you need to look at what you are doing. When I have seen coaches using boards, I see two things: the head is down and the butt is up in the air.

One thing I do believe in is strength. The number one area where you need strength is in the legs. Kids like to work with the arms because it makes them look better in T-shirts.

I talk to a lot of good football coaches about strength in the legs. They all stress the squat for the legs. If you get nothing else out of this, get the kids doing the squat to build their leg strength. You can't play football unless you can bend in the knees and hips. Squats are very important. These are things I have always wanted to know when I talked to other coaches. I never once asked another coach for a play. I never asked anyone how he ran a play. If you ever watched us on offense, you would know that, because my offense never was that good. We played good defense and ran the ball off-tackle. One reason I never wanted to get a play from another coach was because I did not want to end up calling him to ask him what we should do when the defense did something different. I have always been sold on fundamentals and defense. Once in a while, we could get the ball in the end zone. I think you can win with one play if everyone plays his position as opposed to 100 plays and no one knows what they are doing. I am a basic fundamentals coach. I like pure and simple. At Notre Dame, coach Holtz likes to run a lot of different plays. I have been there six years now. Slowly, coach Holtz is coming over to my way because I can't learn his way. We are limited on what we do on offense. You win on fundamentals.

The first thing you have to learn to do is to learn how to be a coach. If I see someone teaching something that I think is wrong or if I think he is teaching it wrong, it makes me a better coach. Always challenge your mind and your thoughts. Always try to get better. Always associate with winners. Now, we are always going to have champions. Someone is going to win the Super Bowl next year, the Big Ten, the SEC, the Rose Bowl, and all other championships. That does not mean they are good coaches. Someone has to win the championship. If a team is winning consistently, I will guarantee you are going to find consistent play in fundamentals.

I want to list the things I teach in fundamentals. The number one thing is stance. People ask what is stance? The number one thing when you put them in a stance is this: they must be able to move in any direction that the offense requires without any false movement. It is that simple. If they have to take a false step or a false movement, then you need to change the stance. I have had some kids that never became fluid in their stance. If they are a good athlete, it is impossible for them not to have a stance where they can accomplish what you ask them to do. You must take the time to teach them. Stance is this. A man has to perform whatever you ask him to do without making any false movement. If a player does not have a good stance, he is going to struggle as a football player. The only way you will know if they have a good stance is by studying the film. Look for false movement. We all have VCR's. You can get films of practice, if you really want them. Don't just take team films. Take individual shots of the linemen. Look at their stance. See if they are making any false moves.

A basic rule would be that your feet can never be too wide in your stance. We know you could be too wide, but, most of the time in the stance, the feet are too close together. So, we start with this premise: most people have their feet too close together on the stance. We like for the toes to be turned out and the heels turned inside slightly. I know a lot of teams like to teach the heels out and the toes pointed inside. If you are teaching that, it is fine. I have looked at film after film, and I can't find anyone who plays with the toes turned inside.

We stagger the feet on the stance. It all depends on what you want to teach. If it hinders his movement, then it is wrong. I like the hand directly down under the chin. The more you put your hand out in front of you, the more off balance you are. It makes it hard to block down, and hard to pull, and hard to pass block. You can almost play without the hand on the ground. It all comes back to this one thing. Can he do all the things he needs to do without any false movement? I like the hand down on the ground under his chin. This is true even with the center. They want to call us offside because the center has his hand past the ball.

The first step is to get you into position to make a block. If a man is playing head-up and you are going to base block him, you do not have to worry much because the first step is right there. If the man is in the position you want him in, the first step is there. The first step is almost always with the near foot. Our rule is to step with the near foot first. Very seldom do we have to correct a kid on this. If the blocker has to block with someone on the backside, then we may use the far foot. We do not step with the back foot unless we are using the combo block.

The next most important point is to have an aiming point. The near foot leads to that aiming point. Now, I favor the three-point stance. I would rather have a two-point stance than a four-point stance. So, we want to get in a good stance and then find the aiming point. After that, we must get pad under pad. It is a *leverage game*. If the two players are equal, the man with leverage will win every time. If you are not equal, the leverage man will win most of the time. If the blocker stinks and the defensive man is great, leverage will not matter.

The sole purpose of the block is to get to the man's chest. His whole purpose is to keep the blocker away from his body. Try to get to his chest. I do not believe in blocking with the face mask. I never have. You must get the shoulder pad under his pad. If you can get to his chest and get your pad under his pad, you have a great chance to block him. The elbows must be kept inside. I try to coach the lineman from two different positions. I try never to get to the side of the blockers. I like to coach from behind or from the front. The main thing I look for are the elbows. If I can see the elbows from behind, he is not blocking properly. I do not teach him a lot of things with the hands. I teach him to get on the man with the pads, and keep the feet moving, and to keep the elbows in. If you start stressing the hands too much, you lose the other key points. We do teach them to use their hands, but we stress the other things much more. We feel the hands will take care of themselves. Don't get me wrong, the hands are important. I am not saying that our kids don't hold. We do not teach them to hold and tackle on offense.

The blocker must lead with his eyes and not his face mask. He must lead with his eyes. That is when the coach must get in front of the blocker to make sure he is leading with his eyes. You are better off coaching from the front than any other position. He must look his block in.

I do not believe in any windup. Your feet must be under the blocker. We want to keep the knees up under us. I never mention the word feet except to tell them to get them wide on their stance. Their legs must go with the blocker. That is where the strength is. If the feet are not up under the blocker, the first thing that happens is he loses contact. He must get on and stay on the defender. The blocker must be able to bend naturally. If you can't bend, you can't be a football player.

When I am talking to coaches that have not studied films, I know that person does not know what he is talking about. I have talked to coaches that have been in the game 30 to 40 years. They have watched films, but they have never studied the films. I know they do not study the films when they tell me they roll the hips. We do not roll the hips. People will roll the hips, but they will do it naturally. You cannot teach something that happens naturally. We want movement. We start down low and come up. If we roll our hips as we come up, we lose our strength.

We want to keep the helmet to the playside. We will have 1-on-1 drills to teach all of these points. We have drills where they must keep their helmet to the playside. This is where the elbows and hands come into play. The strength is inside with the arms and hands. We do not want them to turn the defender. We want to get movement on the defender. If we get leverage on them, we want to take them straight back. We do not want the defender to cross the helmet to the playside. If the blocker has his feet up under him and the elbows are in, it is more difficult for the defender to cross the helmet. When the feet stop, you lose your leverage. We like to film as much as we can so the kids can watch and learn what they are doing on their blocks. One other thing I have learned about coaching. Defensive coaches are nice people, but you can't trust them. They will lie to you. They will lie, cheat, and do everything to look good in practice. So, I do not even bother with them. I never ask our defensive coaches what they are doing. I have no idea what front they are running in practice, and I don't care. All I know is this: anytime they ever told me they were using a front, it was the one they were using yesterday. Don't get involved with all of that crap. You can get a defensive coach who will allow you to base block against and do the fundamentals against.

Let me review real fast. First is stance. The kids are going to do what you tell them to do without any false steps. Teach them the importance of leverage. We want movement, and we want to keep our body under us. If they feel the man is disengaging, we want them to accelerate. We want movement. We want them to bust their rear ends to stay after the man when we feel them getting off the block.

I want to show you our run blocking. I want you to see our trap blocking. Everyone knows we are going to run the trap, but we still average close to seven yards on it. Let me cover the running part real quick. Anytime we do a run drill, we go 10 yards. We want them to run through the 10 yards on any drill we use. We trap the 3 technique so much we limit what he is going to do.

I am not big on X's and O's. I really don't like X's and O's. I am not saying you do not have to have them. I know you can't win without them. We came up with something that we feel is good, and we are willing to share what we do.

Does anyone want to know what we do down on the goal line? When we get down deep, we want to get at least three points. We like to run the bootleg on the goal line. I know the blocking schemes, but I do not get involved in the pass patterns. When they start talking about pass patterns, I leave the room.

If you are good enough to run the ball and you get real good at it, this is what you are going to see. We are going to see the eight-man front with a safety playing on the tight end. They have a corner on each side playing man-to-man. That is basically what we see when we start moving the ball on the run. We see this on first down all of the time. We have more than 150 pass patterns. When we get moving the ball on the run and people know they can't stop us, they will go to a nine-man front with the strong safety playing the run. They are not playing man free; they are man-to-man on the corners. They lock on the receivers, with the free safety running. Now, how much imagination does it take to take a man out of the backfield to get him open? They have been drawing up pass patterns for 150 years. Do you know why? Because they can't run the football. They have a coverage for every pass pattern.

I could be a defensive coordinator because all you have to do is assign someone to play man-to-man on the pass receivers. That is all you have to do. If you will show me a passing coach, I will show you that they will not win unless they play great defense. If you want to win, you run the ball. Teach discipline and run the ball, and you will win. Run the ball effectively, and you will get single-man coverage.

This is another thing that gets me about passing the football. The offensive linemen are told to defeat the defender in front of them in a small area about four feet by four feet. The receivers can split outside, and now they have 10 yards to beat the man covering him. Now, you tell me about passing the football. All of you are passing coaches. Run the ball first, and then it is easy to pass.

Another thing we like to do on the passing game is to use motion. We like to take those little guys and bring them in motion and then run the patterns. That is effective against man coverage.

I want to talk about the zone play. If you are going to run the zone play, you should use motion. This gives the defense a different look. If you can run the ball, you will get man coverage. The receivers should be able to get open against one defender. I am not a passing man, but I do believe in the passing game. You cannot win unless you can throw the football. If you can run the football, the defense can only run certain things against you. If you cannot run the football, you will see every defense that has ever been designed by man. They are drawing some of them up now. If you can run the football, the defense is limited down to almost nothing. What most teams have started doing is this. They will go to the nine-man fronts and play man. "They ain't going to beat us with the run. If they beat us, they must do it with the passing game." If you can make them say this, then you throw the ball. If you can't throw the ball, you are wasting your time. You must be able to throw the football to go against all of those men up on the line of scrimmage. Run the ball; the rest comes easy.

13

Developing Offensive Linemen

Guy Morriss
Baylor University
2003

The thing I want to talk about today will not be related to schemes, but more about techniques and some thoughts about weightlifting that are beneficial to offensive linemen. What we talk about may not be for you. By the time you leave here you may think I am crazy. But if you can leave with just one little idea that will help you, then the time will be well spent. That is what these clinics are all about. It is sharing ideas and seeing old friends and talking football.

I want to give the young offensive line coaches some advice. The older coaches will know what I am talking about. In the old days when the coaching staff started dividing the players up, this is the way it was done. "Old Billy Bob is not much of an athlete. He can't do this and he can't do that. We will just make an offensive lineman out of him." Those days are gone. So when you get into those staff meetings and you start dividing up the players, the offensive line coaches need to get in there and battle for some of the athletes. At times the offensive line coaches get stuck with less talent than the other positions. That attitude is still prevalent. So it is up to you to get in there and fight for the players. It is going to be you who will get the criticism when you can't get a first down, or you can't knock teams off the ball. Defenses have just gotten too good not to have good players on the offensive line. We have to catch up athletically to our defensive linemen.

I enjoy going to clinics and other practices. I like to check out other coach's offensive line drills. That is what I go look for today. We all have our schemes. We all know what we want to run on offense. I am always looking for new ideas for drills. The safeguard is this: You go out and start looking at drills and you see a drill and you think it is just what you are looking for. The thing you must ask yourself is this: Will that drill help your players get the job done on Friday night? The drill must fit into your plan. If you do not watch out, you will end up with a lot of drills that do not help you teach the players what they need to do on Friday night.

It is important to stay on an *even keel*. This is true for all positions, and not just offensive linemen. I think players will survive in a predictable environment. I do not like to be around moody people. I do not know about you, but I just do not like them. If a coach is moody and not on an even keel, it will rub off on the players. Again, if you do not watch out, the players will become the same way. They will be higher than a kite one Friday and be on a low mood the next Friday. Do you know whose fault that is? It is your fault. That is because the players are up and down the roller coaster. We feel it is important to stay on an even keel.

Be very *positive* with the players. I think kids need that, especially nowadays. The thing of it is you must coach your butt off every day. You must coach as hard on the 20th day as you do on the first day. You must coach as hard the last game as you did on the first game. If you can be the same every day, the kids will appreciate that very much. Be the same guy every day. Another point that is important is to *leave your ego at the door*. An ego will take you down quicker than anything. It just becomes excess baggage you are toting around with you. It will rise up and get you.

To me, one word has become very prevalent in coaching circles. You hear it a lot at coaching clinics. That word is *philosophy*. Everyone has a *philosophy of this and a philosophy of that*. This is where I want to start as far as teaching offensive line play.

I will tell you a story that happened to me. I was interviewing for a high school coaching job in Paris, Texas. It was with the Paris High School Wildcats, home of Raymond Berry. It is the same Raymond Berry that I played for at New England in the NFL. I grew up near Paris, Texas. I always knew I wanted to be a coach. Coach Berry recruited me into the coaching ranks. He gave me a job at New England. That is where I started my coaching career. Later Raymond got cross with the owners and we all got fired. So I went back to Paris to see if I could get the head coaching job there. I was excited about the prospects of becoming a Texas High School Head Coach. I got an interview with the Paris School Board. This little lady was the school superintendent. I ended up in an all-day interview ordeal. I was just knocking the board dead. I was giving the right response to all of the questions and covering everything the superintendent wanted to know about. Everything was going great. I was thinking, "This job is mine. I just have to last another 10 minutes with the board." I just knew she could not go much longer with the questions. She went over and sat down at the table across from me. She said, "Coach, I just have one more question for you. Tell me your *philosophy of life.*" I thought for a minute and responded. "Lady, I am just happy my feet hit the floor every day." I could not see what my philosophy of life had to do with football. Needless to say, I did not get the job. I decided from that point on that I had better come up with ideas that I could say were my philosophy. I put several things down that I could refer to from time to time.

My philosophy for *offensive line play* could be used for any position on the field. I have used it for several years. It includes the things I believe in. This is what we talk about to our offensive line. These points are things I have learned through the years from my coaches and from others. I have revised it into my own words that make a little more sense to me. It is nothing new. Most of you may have the same ideas in your notebook. Hopefully this will reinforce your thinking.

You must have a hunger to succeed. If you want to be good at something, you must work at it. You must want to be good at what you are doing. One word we use a lot is passion. We have a passion for football. I have a *passion* for offensive linemen. That passion should drive you to be the very best you can be. You must do the same thing as your players. You must make up you mind what you want. Decide what you want and then go after it. You must give it everything you have. If you can convey that passion down to your players, they are going to have it. They are going to emulate the line coach. You are going to be their role model and you are going to spend more time with them than anyone. You must have that passion and hunger to succeed.

Be positive. Being positive is nothing but an attitude and how you see things. This is true not only in football but in everyday life. I am a *the- glass-is-half-full guy.* Some coaches work as if the glass is half empty. I do not like to be around those people that see things as half empty.

When you talk to your kids, tell them to be honest with themselves. If they do a good job, tell them they did a good job. Let them pat themselves on the back once in a while. If they make a mistake, let them know and make them accountable, but hug their neck and let them know you love them. I can assure you they will run through a wall for you. If they trust in you and know you care about them. Players do not care about how much the coach knows. To them it is *how much a coach cares.* Right! Fuss at them hard and be consistent. But you have to love them and pat them on the back.

Tell them not to get too upset over mistakes. Everyone makes mistakes and they will make their share of them. It is a fact of life. Don't beat yourself up too bad on making mistakes. Take pride in your effort.

Coach with a blue-collar work ethic. I got credit for three extra years of coaching in my introduction. Thank you! I actually played 15 years in the NFL. The only reason I was able to stay in the NFL that long was because I had developed a work ethic early in my life. I thank God for my father. He instilled that characteristic in me. Ha, Ha! He used to kick my rear end regularly. But you know, I was glad I had that kind of work ethic when I went to the NFL in Philadelphia.

I was drafted in 1973. When I went to Philadelphia it was the first time I had been east of the Mississippi River. I was in culture shock when I got to Philadelphia. I think the people of Philadelphia were in culture shock after being around me for a day or two. I ended up living in a little Italian neighborhood in South Philly. I lived on Packer Avenue that was a small street that had row houses on it. It had one little house connected to another little house all the way down the street. It went for a block and a half. The houses were not big, but there were a lot of them in a row. It was right in the heart of Little Italy.

The Italian people are very resilient and they are very happy people. I had neighbors on each side of me. They would come out on the stoop each morning. The little guy would have a baloney sandwich in a brown bag. He would have the baloney sandwich and some fried onions or something like that for his lunch. The kids would come out and kiss their father good-bye and he would go off to work. When he came home in the evening, the kids and his wife would rush out to the front to meet him. Everyone was just happy. Those men were just happy to have a job. He was happy he could provide food for his kids. The kids were healthy and his wife was not bothering him. He was a happy man. I thought this was a neat approach.

I would walk out to my stoop. I did not have to worry about lunch because I knew the Eagles would fix lunch. I could walk to the Vet Stadium. I would walk over there into the locker room. I would look around and I would see the total opposite of what I saw with my neighbors. This was back in 1973. The Eagles had just come off a 2-12 season. They were not worth a crap. When I walked into that locker room, I saw nothing but spoiled, rich, and overpaid football players. I should not use the term overpaid, but they did not appreciate anything. They had their hand out looking for someone to give them something. They did not understand how to work.

I thought about the situation and decided that my dad did not raise me that way. I stepped back from that situation and said, "This is not the type of person I want to be." I wanted to be like my little Italy neighbors. I have always been appreciative of what

I have. I have a wonderful family. I think this is what really put the finishing touch on my work ethic. This is something you can control. How hard you want to work is up to you. This game is all about hard work.

You must be dedicated and committed to a purpose. All of the effort is not going to do any good if you do not have a purpose. Whatever you are doing give 100 percent to it. If you are in class, be a great student — be into it. If you are a football player it is the same deal. You must be into it 100 percent. If you are having knee surgery and you have a doctor standing over you and he is worrying about the stock market, you would be concerned. "Hey Dr., be 100 percent into fixing my leg." You must be dedicated and committed to a purpose.

You must have self-discipline. You cannot ask your kids to be disciplined if you do not have it. The kids feed off the coach. I have been very fortunate. I was in Philadelphia in 1980. We went to Super Bowl XV. During that year and a half, the Eagles were in Super Bowl XV. The Flyers won the Stanley Cup. The 76ers won the NBA. The Philadelphia Phillies won the World Series. It was a great time to be a professional athlete in Philadelphia. All four of those teams had discipline. It does not matter which sport it is, there is one common thread — *that is discipline*. If you do not have discipline, you are not going to win.

This is especially true today. We are a *reset society* today. The kids get on the *Play Station* and if things are not going like they want them to go, they just hit the reset button. They just start all over. With one little punch of the button, they have a clean slate. In today's world you must have discipline.

You must keep your emotional cool. We do not ask our players to do anything extra. We want them to do the same thing in a game that they do on the practice field. This is why we get on them about having great practices. We try to create as much game tempo as possible on the practice field.

We are only on the field one-and-a-half hours. We may go for one hour and 45 minutes at the most. But everything we do on the practice field is at high speed. We are moving from the time we step on the field. We do not walk from drill to drill. We try to get in as many reps as we can. Coach Goodner will have his defense set up and we will run two offensive teams at his defense, just one play after another. We go as fast as we can go. We want the kids to get a lot of reps. We do not coach a lot on the field. We go inside and coach off the tape. We try to show them as many looks as we can in practice.

You must be resilient. Everyone has problems. We win games and we lose games. We tell our kids we are not going to win them all, not necessarily, not all of the time.

You are going to get beat, but you have to get over it. You cannot reverse the loss, but you can get yourself ready for the next game. As a coach you cannot spend too much time crying in your beer. If you do that, the next thing you know you will lose two games in a row. Then two games become three games. Hell, get over the loss and move on. You can't do anything about the loss after it happens. Do something about the next game.

You must have stoicism. You must know the difference in being hurt and being injured. A lot of the kids do not understand that thinking today. Most kids today have been pampered. After the first practice everyone is hurting. Everybody is going to hurt in football. You have to know the difference in being hurt and being injured.

Don't let early failure discourage you and never, ever, let early success satisfy you. Does that make sense?

Never assume the kids know or understand something you are teaching them. Take it for granted that you are starting from scratch. When you introduce a new play, or a new idea, or a new philosophy, do not assume the players know what you are talking about. Kids have a lot of distractions to deal with today. If you make an assumption that a player knows what you are talking about, you may find out he does not have a clue what you are talking about.

Try to put it all together on game day. You must play the game with great emotion. That is what this game is all about. I think kids today are afraid to show emotion. They are concerned their peers are going to make fun of them. Heck with that attitude. Emotion is what this game is all about. That is what the game was invented for.

You must keep focused. I got a chance to play for Coach Raymond Berry. He would draw a bull's-eye upon the wall and ask us what is that? "It is a bull's-eye." Then he would ask us what we had to do to win. We would say, "We must put the arrow inside the bull's-eye." He would reply, "No! You have to hit the center of the bull's-eye." That is what we are talking about when we discuss focus. Try to hit the center of the bull's-eye.

We believe in great effort. That is the one thing the kids can control. They can control their effort. If you demand it from them, they will give it to you. They are going to give you what you ask for. We demand a lot of effort from our kids.

The last point along this line is the fact *you must go out on the field game day and execute.* You must take care of the details.

This is about as close to a philosophy as I can come. I think it is important to set goals for your kids. Most kids like to have something to shoot for. You must make the goals tough, but make them so they can obtain their goals. It is obvious that you want short-term goals and long- term goals. You need to put those goals up on the wall and let the players go past it and see it day in and day out. You have to talk about the goals with the players over and over. An example of a short-term goal would be to average four yards per carry. A long-term goal would to be able to bench press 400 pounds by the time the player graduates. I think it is important to post those goals and go over them as much as possible at least once a week.

Next I want to talk about *strength training and conditioning*. Back when I was young, we did not lift a lot of weights. Coaches thought weight training would make you muscle bound. When I went to the Philadelphia Eagles as a rookie, I started on the offensive line. I weighed 217 pounds. Then about 1976, all of a sudden defensive teams started using the 50 defense or the 3-4 defensive schemes. Let me tell you, it is difficult to block Ernie Holmes at 217 pounds. That is when I started lifting weights and adding pounds to my body. Everyone realized there was something to the weight lifting. It has really boomed and started to take off today.

Today *we feed* our kids better than ever. We have more information about *nutrition and supplements*. There is no reason why there should not be great weight programs today.

Our whole deal is this: *We want to train the complete athlete*. I know sometimes strength coaches get carried away. Trust me, I love strength coaches. The thing we must keep in mind is the fact we are trying to train football players. This is where you as an offensive line coach must come in sometimes and let the strength coach know you are training the complete athlete or the football player. You must not lose sight of this.

We are going to *lift weights. Flexibility training* is also important. We have found out it is important to stretch. Most of you are doing conditioning during this time of the year. Off-season work is very important to offensive linemen.

We have talked about how important nutrition is to football players. There is no reason today that kids cannot learn to eat properly.

The *agility drills* that we do are specific drills to help us improve on the things we do on Saturday, which is to play the game of football. We lift free weights. I think this is important especially for offensive linemen.

Our philosophy of weight training came from a gentleman up in Columbus, Ohio named Louie Simmons. He is fantastic. He is training about 85 percent of the world-class power lifters and world record holders. He also understands how to train football players.

What he does is to use chains and the big, thick rubber bands with the athletes. If you get a chance to hear Louie Simmons talk, it would be worth your time. I can tell you the amount of weights the players can lift is going up and up. In the two years we were at Kentucky, all of our players improved on this system. We are going to use the same set-up at Baylor.

Let me see if I can explain how the system works. When you bench press and push the weight up off your chest and you go through the full range of motion, the weight never actually changes from the time it leaves the chest until you get it to the top of the lift. What Louie has done is this. He has a big rubber band mounted into the floor that is attached to the ends of the bar. The athletes sit on boxes when they do these lifts. The boxes are easy to make. The rubber band attaches to the cleat on the box and to the end of the bar. The principle is that as you go upward through the full range of motion with that bar, the rubber band starts to kick in as you take the slack of it up and you get more resistance at the top end of the movement. You are adding weight as you go through the full range of motion. You can do the lifts with rubber bands on the end of the weights or you can do it with chains. When the bar is sitting on the chest, most of the chain is sitting on the floor. As you start the weight upward the chain moves up off the floor. The weight increases through the full range of motion.

The way they have explained this system to me is that the gain is coming at the top of the lift. As the band starts to stretch, or the chain comes off the floor, the weight becomes heavier. The extra strength is coming through the full range of motion.

I had my doubts in the beginning. I am old-fashioned and I had to see it myself. Men, it works. It is cheap to use this system. You can start out by wrapping the rubber bands around a couple of 45-pound weights to get the tension on the rubber bands.

On our *dynamic days* we are going to do the following lifts. We do the bench, squat, incline, power clean, and snatch. We lift heavy twice a week. We are on a split routine. We lift Monday and Tuesday, take Wednesday off, and work Thursday and Friday. Monday and Tuesday are heavy days; Thursday and Friday are light days. We still use the rubber bands on light days. We just take the plates off the rubber bands. We may use about 50 percent of the mats. Now we are working for speed through the whole range of motion. Course stabilization is a fancy way of saying we do a lot of crunches. We want to build strength in our stomach and midsection.

I want to talk about a few drills and pass protection. We throw the ball quite a bit. We threw it more when I was at Kentucky with Coach Hal Mumme. When I became the head coach, I decided to become more balanced and so we run the ball a little more now. A perfect world for me would be to throw the ball 60 percent of the time and run it 40 percent of the time. Last year, with the SEC Offensive Player of the Year at tailback, we gave him the football a little more often.

As the offensive line coach, you are always in a battle with the quarterback coach. The quarterback coach will tell the line coach, "You must get those sorry-ass linemen blocking. We do not have enough time to throw the ball. My quarterback can not get his reads with the defense on top of him." I know that feeling. I have been there.

The offensive line coach will respond, "Hell coach, the quarterback can't stand back there and take all day to throw the ball. He has over two minutes to throw the ball. He has to get the ball out of there. He is drifting all over the place. How do you expect us to protect him?"

I guess this battle has been going on forever and it will continue to go on forever. However, there are a few things you can do to reach a happy medium. It is good if the line coach is also the head coach, I will tell you that. I know who is going to win that battle.

One thing we did to help both areas at Kentucky was to junk our seven-step passing game. We do not throw the seven-step game anymore. We could not protect the seven-step game. Generally speaking, we have done a good job of protecting our quarterback over the years. We pride ourselves on this. We threw the ball a lot and our sacks ratio was as good as anyone else's in the SEC. We went back and charted our offense and found that most of our sacks were coming on the seven-step game. That is when we dropped the seven- step game. We run the *three-step and five-step game*. We throw the ball in .9 seconds on the three-step drop, and 2.2 seconds on the five-step drop. We do not want to hold the ball any longer than 2.2 seconds. If we do not get the ball away in that time, we are going to find us a new quarterback or a new quarterback coach.

The thing that is important is for the quarterback to become conscious of getting rid of the ball on time. You can use a whistle or horn and have a ball boy blowing the whistle or horn. You can get a horn and set it for a certain time to go off. I did not think it would be effective with our quarterback. But after a few times they start hearing the horn sound and know they had held the ball too long. The horn made the quarterback aware of throwing the ball on rhythm.

On the three-step drop, the quarterback is going to drop 4.0- to 4.5-yards deep. On the five-step drop, he is going to drop to 7.0- or 7.5-yards deep. The offensive line must visualize what that distance is to protect the quarterback. To get this across to the linemen, we have the offensive line drop down on a knee at the distance the quarterback is going to setup at. We have them take a knee. Then we put the quarterback on a chalk line and have him take the snap and take his drop. We want them to see what the distance really is.

We have the quarterback drop three sets on each drop. This helps the offensive linemen to understand what the quarterback is doing on his drop. The linemen get a mental picture of the 4.5 yards, and that is the spot they have to protect. They can understand this point. We did the same thing with the three- and five-step drops. It is important to let the offensive linemen see the landmark you are asking them to protect. You need to make sure the offensive linemen know where the quarterback is setting up.

On any offensive pass play you run, the offensive linemen must know the depth of the quarterback and where he is setting up. Is he going to set up on the inside leg of the tackle on the shotgun snap? Is he going to set up behind the center on the straight dropback pass? The line needs to know this for each play. As coaches, sometimes we assume the players know this. That is not really the case. They must know where the quarterback is going to be and they have to be able to count on the quarterback being there. The quarterback must make sure the he knows where he must be on the set-up.

How do you ask five players to protect a spot when the spot changes on every snap? You cannot do it. It is all a simple matter of geometry. That angle makes a big difference to that offensive tackle. They must know where the quarterback is going to be on the drop. The quarterback must be disciplined to be at the spot designated for each play called. Make sure the quarterback is getting there.

It is okay for the quarterback to have that mental clock because he has to get that ball out on rhythm. The offensive linemen must know they cannot have a mental block. We are striving to block for as long as it takes. The quarterback has to throw the ball in the time period we allot for each play. The linemen block forever, and must not worry about the time factor it takes for the quarterback to get the ball away. They cannot have a mental clock on the time they have to continue to block on pass plays. You have to teach the kids to hang on forever, or as long as it takes for the ball to come out of the quarterback's hand.

The problem linemen face is that they block for a period of time and then they start looking backwards to see if the pass has been made. That is when they get themselves in trouble. We tell them, "The crowd will tell you when the ball is gone. If we have a big completion, the crowd noise will let you know the pass has gone."

When we go out looking for players who can pass protect, we look for *natural knee benders*. We look for players that have a lot of athletic ability. Again, we are trying to catch up with the defensive linemen.

You can drill a player until he is blue in the face, but if he is not a knee bender and the good Lord did not bless him with that trait, you cannot help him a lot. Now, I can go recruit that type of player as a college coach. I understand you inherit the high school players. It all goes back to getting those players that are good knee benders. They need flexibility at the ankles and knees and hips. Go watch them play basketball. See if they can handle the ball and see how they move around the court. If they can do that, they have a good chance of being a good pass protector. This is my personal opinion and that is the kind of kid I look for. I like players with good flexible hips and ankles.

In all of our drills, we base the fact that we want our offensive linemen to be *lateral movers*. We want them to be able to move side to side. We want them to be able to slide their feet. In each drill we teach them not to turn away from the line of scrimmage. We do not want their hips and shoulders to open. We want everything square and in front of the lineman. They have to be like a baseball catcher. If a good catcher gets a pass ball, he does not stick his hand out at the ball. He slides his body over in front of the ball. He must have lateral movement to get over in front of the ball. It is the same for the offensive linemen.

When we decide what drills we want to use, we select drills that teach lateral movement. We go through the *running ropes* everyday. We go down through the ropes straight ahead first as a warm-up drill. We will hit every hole, with high-knee lifts (Diagram 1).

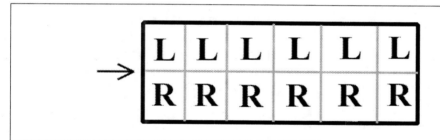

Diagram 1. Running ropes (warm-up drill)

Then we hit every other hole (Diagram 2). We want their hands about chin high. We want their arms flexed like a boxer. We want their hands six to eight inches from their chin so they can still punch. We go down and back, down and back as many times as we think they need that day. We ask them to lift their front foot, step over the hole, and bring their back foot over. This is not a speed drill. Slow them down and make them very deliberate and get out of the drill what you want. We want their hands chin high, six or eight inches from their chin, with their eyes up. The first week of running the drills they are going to look down at their feet. That is natural. The more they run the drills the better they will become and they will not have to look down at their feet.

After they get the drill down pretty well, I will start standing beside the ropes. As they come through the ropes, I will reach out and grab them by the shoulder pads. We are going to distract the lineman. We may slap him in the helmet, hit him in the crotch, or do anything to distract him. I want him to move his feet and keep his eyes on what I am doing. I want him to take his hands and knock my hands down, up, or knock them off his pads. There is no rule in the book that says the offensive linemen cannot use their hands. They can keep the defensive man's hands off them. This will take them a few weeks to get good at it, but this will teach them to pick up their feet.

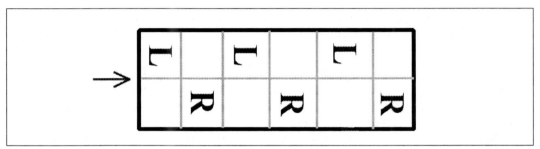

Diagram 2. Running ropes (every other hole drill)

We run a *wave drill*. You have seen those big linebacker standup dummies. They have a cone shape to them and we lay them down long ways (Diagram 3). We put a player in between two dummies. I get in front of him and I give him directions with my hand. I want him to go over the dummy on the right and then come back and go over the dummy on the left. It is a really simple drill. He is going to lead with his front foot and lift his back foot. It teaches him to get that front foot over the dummy and his back foot comes over. Then he goes back the other way. It is a good movement drill.

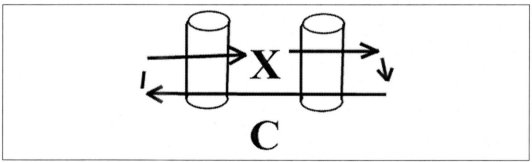

Diagram 3. Wave drill

The wave drill emphasizes *change of direction and lateral movement*. You can have some fun with this drill. You can catch the linemen off balance when they are not concentrating. It is a good drill to teach lateral movement and to keep their shoulders square. They want to be perpendicular to the line of scrimmage.

The next drill we do is the *spin drill* (Diagram 4). Here we stress the fundamentals of keeping the *shoulders square, proper balance,* and *body control.*

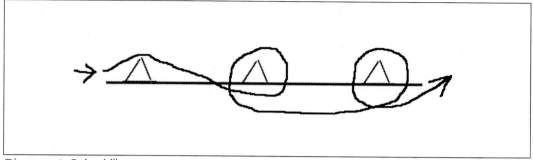

Diagram 4. Spin drill

We have a big bag that holds about 300 pounds of sand. We call it *Big Bertha* (Diagram 5). We bang on that bag every day. It is hung on a swing set apparatus. We have the managers pull it up off the ground so it swings on the swing set. The players bang the bag, keeping their feet open, and their shoulders square. You can put the offensive lineman down in a two- point stance or you can back him off the ball. As soon as the bag swings forward he hits and lifts the bag. You can put him in the three-point stance and snap the ball and then have him take on the bag. We just keep working against that bag for four to five good pops. This teaches the players how to use their hands and how to punch.

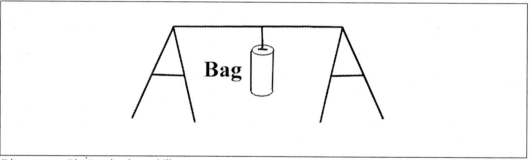

Diagram 5. Big Bertha bag drill

We use another drill we call the *softball toss* (Diagram 6). This drill teaches *lateral movement*. The coach gets in front of the offensive lineman five- to six-yards apart. You take a softball and roll it on the ground to the lineman three to four yards to his right or left. The lineman must slide his feet to get over in front of the softball, field it, and toss it back to you. You go three or four times to each side. This forces him to move his feet. He must slide his feet and shuffle over to get the ball. After he picks the ball up he tosses it back to the coach. Then he shuffles back to the middle of the drill. The one thing you do *not* want him to do is to click his heels. He must keep his feet fairly wide. This is a good hand-eye coordination drill. It is a good conditioning drill as well.

I want to talk a minute about the *offensive lineman's stance*. I am not an etched-in-stone kind of coach. I give our kids a lot of room to experiment with their stance.

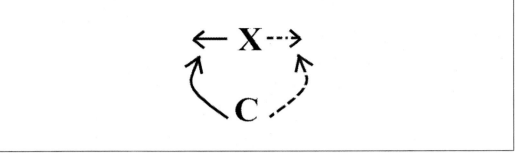

Diagram 6. Softball toss drill

You may have a 6'5" offensive tackle. You may have a 5'8" offensive guard. One year that happened to me when I was coaching in high school. The 6'5" player may be your best athlete. That small player inside may have stiff hips. The center may be okay but he has a certain problem. None of those positions are the same. That is the reason I cannot understand why a coach would want everyone to line up in the same stance. All payers are not made the same. God made everyone of us different. Some of us have more flexibility than others and some of us are a lot stiffer than others. We do not try to make five players look like a bunch of clones.

I am not a big coach on having the right hand down if you are in the right- hand stance on the right side. If you are left-handed, I think you can still play on the right side. You may get the best results with them using the right hand on the right side and the left hand on the left side of the line. But if a kid tells me he cannot get the hang of it by making him put the hand down that he is not comfortable with, then I will allow him to put that other hand down. If you don't allow him to do it, he is going to fight you. It will take you forever to convince him he can do it. Let him be in a left-handed stance. I do not see a big deal about all of that. We let the kids get into a stance they can get into where they feel they can make all of the moves we ask them to do. They must be able to pull, drive block, pass set, and do other blocks. If the player is not comfortable he will start tipping the play off. You are trying to put the player in a stance his body will not allow him to get into. Let him find a stance, as long as it is fairly sound, and he can do the things you ask him to do.

I think *balance* is the key in a stance. You ask them to do a lot of things from that stance so they have to be balanced. I like my linemen to be a little wider with their feet. In conditioning drills, we always tell them to be shoulder-width apart. If you have a player who is 6'5", then shoulder-width apart is not wide enough for him. Let him get his feet a little wider. You want to lower his center of gravity by lowering his hips.

I do not teach traditional *toe-to-instep stagger*. I want a big player to spread his base out. We want his feet wide and we want him to get a little stagger. Give them a day or two to experiment with their stance.

I want them to come up with their arms relaxed and their arms on their knees. I want them to be in a position where they can reach out and touch the ground with their hand. They have very little weight on their hands at all. They must be able to flick the grass and stay in that stance. When they pick the hand up, they do not want to fall forward and they do not fall backwards on their heels. That is what we mean by being balanced. When you first start teaching the stance the players cannot sit in that position for a long time. The quads are not used to this. They can't sit there long because the quads are on fire. They are not used to using those muscles.

On the off hand, or the hand not on the ground, you can put it on the opposite knee or down on the ankle. I do not like the elbow on the knee with the hand up in the air. That is a personal preference. We do not want their shoulders tilted. So it is up to the coach where the off hand goes.

After you get him in a comfortable stance, then you can start working on him on the moves you want him to do. When you start teaching the moves, take it one step at a time. "We are going to take one step with the right foot." The next day we add another step to the drill. Then you build on the drill. Then you go one, then two steps. "One, two, right foot, left foot." You work on this until the players get comfortable coming out of the stance doing what you want them to do. The teaching must be very deliberate. Drill the heck out of them.

The key to *pass protection* is how fast the players can come out of the stance and get them to where they want to be to blocking their defender. It is a matter of how fast the offensive line can go from spot A to spot B. You must get the blocker to the point you want him to be at to block the defender.

On a three-step drop, our players are going to take a six-inch drop at the most. That is as deep as we want them when we are throwing the three-step drop pass. The blocker must be really firm. It is almost a matter of replacing their feet, now that we have them understanding how deep they have to be to block the defender.

Most defensive teams offset the defensive linemen. To help the other offensive linemen is to teach them how to *set up on an angle*. Most offensive linemen will jump and turn when they are trying to block the 3 technique. That is old school. If you open the hips and shoulders, you give that defender a two-way run at the quarterback. I want my linemen to set and drop straight back off the line of scrimmage. It does not matter how fast the defender is, you do not have to drift more than six inches outside to take care of the speed rusher. If you will take that six-inch step and back up, the defender must cross the line to get to the quarterback. I want the tackle to sit in there as square as he can be. As soon as the defender makes a move toward the quarterback, now he starts to open. He is just reading the defensive end. When he turns to come to the quarterback, that is when the tackle starts to open. He should be fronted up and it should put him right down the middle of the defensive end. The big mistake I see is the offensive linemen opening up too soon. We want to take the defender deep before we open. The key is to get some depth and get them back off the ball, but not at a big angle. We want them to stay square. When the defender comes to the quarterback the blocker must open, drop his hips, and work his body down low. This is where all of the drills we teach come into play.

When the defender comes to the blocker, we want to be heavy with the inside hand. When we first start teaching these techniques, we make the offensive lineman bury his outside hand. We make him use one hand on the drill. If you only had one hand as an offensive lineman, which hand would you want to use? The *inside hand* unless you are the center. We make them stick the outside hand in their shorts when we start teaching the drill. He must stick his inside hand under the defender's breastplate and grab him. To the official it looks like he has a closed fist. When the defensive lineman gets up the day after a game, his chest should be black and blue from the number of times the blocker pinched him in that area. If you bring the hand outside you are going to get called for holding. The key is to get those handles on the breast. That is what they made those breastplates for as far as I am concerned. If I can get him by those breastplates, I can steer him around. He is not going anywhere. If he wants to go outside, we can stretch him with the outside foot and push him with the inside arm all the way to the sideline. We can let his momentum carry him outside the quarterback.

If he wants to come back inside, I must square back up. I am going to take my outside arm and take him down inside and push him over the pile of players inside. We have help down inside. We do not want to try to redirect the defender. Take him the way he wants to go. The same is true for the inside blockers as well.

Against zone stunts, you want to have the five offensive linemen set up at the same depth. Against *man stunts*, you have room to adjust with individual moves. But against the *zone blitz*, you must draw the line two- to three-yards deep all across the line so they can pick up the stunts at the same plane.

14

Offensive Line Techniques

Don Riley
University of Kentucky
1993

If I gave my talk a topic, it would be transferring the Oklahoma drill to run to daylight. It is important for us to remember what we are attempting to do when we set up our drills. We do not want to set the dummies up so they are only one yard apart on the Oklahoma drill the first time we teach the drill. We want to show the players what we are trying to accomplish. We want to show up the holes so the back can run to daylight. Move the dummies two yards apart so we can give the offensive linemen an advantage to start out with. I think you have to be honest with the players you deal with. Trust is the most important ingredient for success. They trust you, and you trust them. This is the way I approach the players I work with.

I tell the players that I know that somewhere along the way they had other ideas about being a linebacker, fullback, or some other football player other than an offensive lineman. Somewhere along the way, someone told them they were not good enough to play another position, so they moved them to the offensive line. I tell them this, "If you were as good as the player you are blocking, I would not be coaching you. We want you to understand our view. We want to give you all the tools that we can that will allow you to be successful." We tell them we are not going to put them into a situation where they cannot be successful. We are going to put them in a position where they can be a winner.

We all have been to clinics and listened to talks on stance. It all comes down to what you believe in as a coach. I am convinced after several years of coaching that we had to widen our stance because of pass protection. We used to say get the feet as wide as the armpits. Now, we say get the feet as wide as the shoulders' width. If you have a narrow base, you can be turned easier. We want to make sure we start with a slightly wider stance.

The next thing we want to tell our young people is this: you block with your hips. You must learn how to use your hips. Next, we tell them to drive with the eyes. They have to focus with their eyes. I can remember going to hear Blanton Collier lecture when I first started coaching. He made things so simple. He talked about how important the eyes were in playing football. He stressed where their eyes go on everything they do in football.

Sometimes, we overemphasize hip extension. We throw our hips, and, at times, we throw the hips down. When they go down so far, it causes us to arch our backs. All the defender has to do is to get his hands under us and lift us up to get rid of us. When you drive off, you have to drive your knees down. When you start lifting, you bring your knees up because your hips are following through. You want to explode your hands and forearms up under the defender's pads.

I do not know how many of you ever saw a mule-pulling contest. Being from the coal mining country, I saw the mules pulling coal out of the mines. When a mule is in a pulling contest, they hook up big sleds for the mules to pull. They really bend their knees and work with their backs. They keep their feet close to the ground. They do this so they can have power and balance. They keep their feet really wide. This is the way it is with the offensive linemen. On contact, he must widen his feet. If the feet are wide when the defensive blow is made, you have a chance to keep your balance. One of the real key ingredients for an offensive lineman is to have balance. You can't have balance with a narrow base. Now, you want your feet wide, drive off, and lock up. What happens a lot of the time is the blocker tries to finish the job before it is necessary. You must learn that the defender that you are blocking has been told by his coach to make the tackle. What you have to do is to lock up with the defender with your feet wide. You have to use powerful steps with the knees down. Once you feel the defender trying to disengage and get off the block, you must react. To get off the block, the defender is trying to get his hands away from you. That is the time you must accelerate your feet and then bring them together. That is the time you lift, climb him, and climb him. If you are climbing the defender and the back is running hard, his momentum will carry him forward and you will gain positive yardage. Those are selling points and are very important to use when he is teaching offensive blocking to his players.

The next point that is important for the offensive linemen to know is this: after studying the game of football for 30-plus years, it seems to me that if I had kept stats, more offensive linemen make tackles than defensive linemen. How many times have you seen offensive linemen making a block where they do not get their butts out of the hole and the back runs into the block. You have to get your butt out of the hole as a blocker. I think this next point is true for a blocker or tackler, regardless of the position you play. You must always block and/or tackle with the opposite hip. If you are blocking with the right shoulder, you must accelerate the left hip to get your feet to move in front of the man. That is a very important point a player must learn to be a good lineman.

We believe this. For you to be a good offensive football team, you must give the game to your quarterback. You must find a way to make it simple so you can gain an advantage on the defensive structures that you are going to be facing each game. What we are saying is something like this. If you are going to run the football, we do not want to give the lineman an uphill block. We want to give him a downhill block. This is what I tell my players: if the funnel is wider, more water can go through it. If the funnel is small, less water can go through it. There are certain defenses that align themselves where we call plays and just hope they work. When we call a pass play, we call a protection and hope it works. They have to understand how defenses play. The most important thing an offensive coach can learn is not offense, but defense. *How do they play*? They are trying to stop you. As Patton said to Rommel, "I am going to read your book so I will know what you are trying to do to me." This is very important.

How does the defense play? We need a system for communication to discuss how they play. They are going to align somewhere. Now, I know everyone has his own system to communicate with the players. I was able to coach on the west coast for 12 years. That was a great experience. I went to visit the four pro teams in the area and learned a great deal. I found there was something different about all four of them. That was good. I know that there is not *one way* to do a lot of things in football. It comes down to this. It is what you can teach your players that really counts. I will go over our techniques that we use at the University of Kentucky.

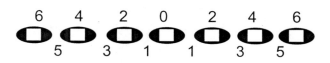

Diagram 1. Offensive techniques

Techniques

The techniques indicate the defensive lineman alignment in relationship to the offensive lineman. The middle of the center is our 0 technique. Head-up are even techniques. The gaps are odd techniques. If the defender is on the outside of where the play is going, we say he is in a shade technique. If he is on the backside of the center, we call that an I technique.

- Head-up—even numbers
- Gaps—odd numbers
- Outside—shade
- Inside—I

Our players will call out the techniques. They call out, "Shade," or, "I." These things mean something. This means there are certain things that we must understand in gap control as to whom we anticipate to be covering a certain area. Our blocking designs are set to block the defensive structures. If the linemen are lined up in the gaps between the center–guard, guard–tackle, and tackle–end gap, we say they are in the 1, 3, and 5 gap. That may be contrary to what many of you are teaching today. If someone is threatening us, we can refer to the A, B, C, and D gaps.

The quarterback can read the defense and tell the type of defense they are playing. We want to build a package to attack the defense. The number one package in America was what was started by Bud Wilkinson many years ago. It is a three-man front with four linebackers—the Oklahoma 5-4 defense. We all know what that is. At the university, we call this look the LSU defense. We play LSU, and they play this defense. All of my life, I have been calling it the Oklahoma defense. I am at Kentucky now, and I have to call it what they call it. That is one of the standard defensive fronts that we know exist in football. We have three down linemen and four linebackers.

The other standard defensive front that we know about is with four down linemen and three linebackers. That is the standard 4-3 defense. From these two fronts can come a multitude of alignments. I want to share some of the common fronts with you. Let me show you how it works. This is what I call America's seven-man fronts. We take the LSU defense and take the tackle and move him down on the strong guard. That is what we call a strong eagle defense. On the other side, if they take the weakside tackle and move him down on the guard, we call it the weak eagle. If they move the nose guard to the weakside, we call it a slide weak. If the nose guard moves to the strongside, we call it slide strong. We teach them compensation. When one man moves, then another man must move with him. When the linemen move in one direction, the secondary will move in the other direction. That is the way defenses work. They can anticipate the pass rush, so they can get the right blocking angle on the defender.

We call a stack defense the Auburn stack, because they run this look. They can have a three-man front or a four-man front. We see a stack 'Bama defense. They run their stack a little different. We see a stack diamond and a double eagle. We see a college 4-3 and a pro 4-3 defense. That is all of the defenses we see. That is all we can see in terms of gap control.

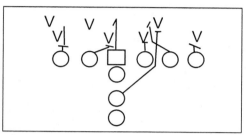

Diagram 2. Strong eagle

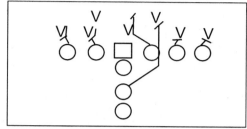

Diagram 3. Weak eagle

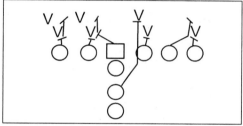

Diagram 4. Slide weak

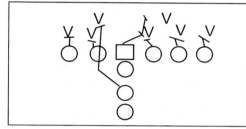

Diagram 5. Slide strong

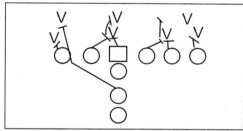

Diagram 6. Stack Auburn

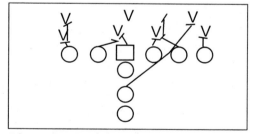

Diagram 7. Stack 'Bama

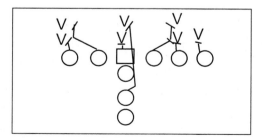

Diagram 8. Stack diamond

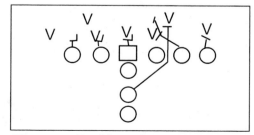

Diagram 9. Double eagle

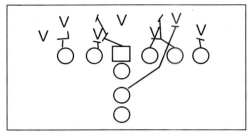

Diagram 10. College 4-3

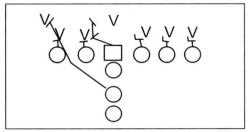

Diagram 11. Pro 4-3

We want to understand the defense so we can plan our attack to run to daylight. Those who know Kentucky football know that we ran a new offense last year. I was fortunate to have coached at UCLA, where we had some good tailbacks. We gave them the ball and let them run to daylight. We tried to isolate the defense and give them a base block and then let them run where fewer people were. Our plan at Kentucky is to have a plan from our stack I alignment to run what we call the blast play. You can call it the isolation or blast play. The blocking design is lead blocking. The play concert is the daylight play.

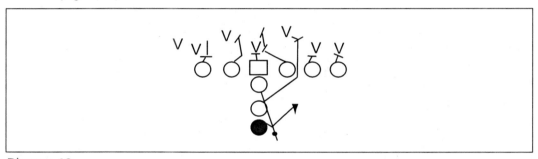

Diagram 12

The tailback runs off the block of the first down lineman on the playside. It is run off the first down lineman the quarterback designates. The play can be run to the split end or the tight end. We allow our tailback to aim at the hip of the tackle. He can run the 500-pound bear; he can run where he wants to run. Our job is to stay off the ground and lock up on the blockers. When the defender tries to get off the block, we want to accelerate our feet and get our butt out of the hole.

What are the *big musts* on the play? We list the things that we must do on the play. You can block it two ways. You can block it hard or soft. This is the hard blocking design.

Big Musts

- Hard ball play.
- Inside leg of tackle landmark.

- Ballcarrier runs through daylight.
- Blockers provide daylight.
- Must have play-action pass that simulates onside blocking design.

It is important that you understand the concept and not the plays. You want to develop your offensive attack so the defenders see a picture that sometimes is false. He does not know whether to come up or go back. What happens on the sideline? The coach wants to know why he was dropping back instead of coming up. He yells, "I thought it was a pass." He becomes disoriented. It is important to have play-action passes with your running game.

Let me go over the clocking assignments on this isolation play. We do not write a lot of things up. We say we clock defenses. We have a theory behind blocking defenses. We clock defenses or techniques. Our quarterback will call out who has the base block. If the tackle is in a 4 technique, the quarterback calls, "Ringo 4." These are ideas and are not specific. He might call, "Ringo 2," "Ringo 6," "Lucky 4," or "Lucky 2." He is telling the man who has the base block. The general rule we give our line is this: if you are the first blocker inside the base clock, you are to clock away from the play. If we call Ringo right–4, then the right guard will block down inside on the nose man. He will seal the defense. We are trying to run to daylight with a wider hole, seal the defense, put our fullback on the linebacker. We do not want to go right at the linebacker. We want it to look like a pass. He wants to run at the inside hip of the base block. The tailback is seven yards deep, and he knows where the base block will be. He is in no hurry. He will run to daylight.

Assignments

Position—Assignment—Calls
OSWR—
BSY—Base block
OST—Base or seal
OSG—Base or seal
C—Base, seal, or scoop—Game plan
BSG—Seal or scoop
BST—Seal
BSWR—
FB—Block first linebacker, being aware of technique call
TB—Run off block on the first playside defensive lineman (technique call)
QB—Deep exchange; fake pass action—Ringo, Lucky, opposite, number

One thing we are always working on is blocking schemes. We have certain calls. We always ask ourselves this question. *How do you block an eagle defense*? People on one side of the line cannot see the eagle look. We make sure our tackle calls out the eagle defense so we all know the defense they are in on his side. We slip block against the eagle. We use the offside guard and center to wall off the defense. A pro call means we face a middle linebacker. We have a call that we use called away. This means we are going to seal away from the play. If the call is Ringo 4 and I am the right guard and I am uncovered, I am going to slip block away from the play.

I have been hearing this statement since I was a little boy. "Knock him off the ball!" If you can do that, you are going to win the ball game. "Put him on his back!" Do you know when you put the defender on his back? When he is reaching to make the tackle and you accelerate your feet. That is when you can knock him on his back. What they are trying to say is this. *Come off the ball*. If you have players that can knock them off the ball and knock them on their backs, then I want you to send them to UK, because they are hard to find. I love to coach those type players.

The college 4-3 is a defense that you need to take a long look at. In theory, most teams who play a pro middle linebacker do not give him two gaps to defend, one on each side of the center. They will not give him A and A gap; they give him A and B gap on the same side of the line. Most of the time, if you have the tight end in the game, they will have a man in the 2 shade on that side. If you start running the sweep play and cut the middle linebacker off with the slip block, they will find a way to move them outside. In most cases, he will be in a 2 Shade. If this is true, then you can say that the middle linebacker rarely ever has both A gaps. He may have the A gap on one side on the flow and the B gap on the other side on flow. It is important that we understand this structurally.

When you are blocking with young people, it is important for them to believe that the technique you are teaching is going to allow them to execute during the game. I went to UCLA in 1976 after 20 years of coaching. Terry Donahue was in his first year at UCLA. He was only 32 years old. Like all coaches, he wanted us to gain more wisdom to make us better coaches. Terry brought in people to help us learn more about people. He brought in a professor from the physical education department to talk with us. Basically, what he told us was this. "Do you know what running ropes will do for you? It will make you a good rope runner!" Let's transfer that to our situation here. "Do you know what the Oklahoma drill will do for you? It makes you a better blocking team." The thing about it is this. You must have an aptitude to make use of the Oklahoma drill in your offensive system. If you can do that, the players will gain confidence in themselves, because it will give them more success. They need all the success you can give them. You have to let them become successful. Make sure the drills you put your players in are applicable to the real game. If you can do that, I think it will improve your football game.

It is important to learn the fundamentals of the game. By learning this, it will allow your people a chance to have success. Don't forget this important point. The man under the center is the man that can make a difference in widening the hole in the Oklahoma drill. If he can make the calls for the offensive line, they will open the holes. Our rules for the quarterback to learn to call the defenses are not hard. We teach it in a systematic way and help him understand the all-American defenses.

I want to close with this one aspect of coaching. I feel we have lost in athletics in the fact that the coach-player relationship has become less and less because of the demands that we have as coaches today. On the college level, we have to recruit. We have to do a lot of paper work. We have to make sure we are complying with all of the rules. We have to record every telephone call we make. It is amazing what we have to go through. In high school, you have to teach class and have lunchroom duty. The kids go home, and they may or may not have a parent at home when they get there. A lot of people have both parents working today. We do not get to know the players like we did a few years back. A philosophy that we have at Kentucky is this. "You are what the players make you. You do not make anything out of them." I spent 30 minutes with each of the players I work with this week. I coach the offensive line as well as the kickers. Players want to know where they stand with you as a coach. I had a friend that did a study on what it takes to be a college lineman. He came up with a chart to measure the offensive linemen. I will put this up so you can see how we rate our linemen (see next page).

When you come to visit at the University of Kentucky, we want to share things like this with you. As Bill Arnsparger said in 1956, "People in Kentucky—boy, do they like good football." We want you to know we appreciate being able to visit with you. Thank you.

Offensive Linemen Evaluation

Name_____

Ranking—Bench Press
Superior 100%—420-up
Excellent 90%—415-400
Very Good 80%—395-375
Good 70%—370-350
Average 60%—345-320
Marginal 50%—325-280

Ranking—Power Clean
Superior 100%—330-up
Excellent 90%—325-315
Very Good 80%—310-295
Good 70%—290-270
Average 60%—265-240
Marginal 50%—235-220

Ranking—Parallel Squat
Superior 100%—540-up
Excellent 90%—535-520
Very Good 80%—515-500
Good 70%—495-470
Average 60%—465-430
Marginal 50%—425-380

Ranking—Vertical Jump
Superior 100%—30"-up
Excellent 90%—29.5-29.0
Very Good 80%—28.5-27.5
Good 70%—27.0-26.0
Average 60%—25.5-24.0
Marginal 50%—23.5-21.0

Ranking—Stand Jump
Superior 100%—9'4"-UP
Excellent 90%—9'3"-8'10"
Very Good 80%—8'9"-8'6"
Good 70%—8'5"-8'2"
Average 60%—8'1"-7'10"
Marginal 50%—7'9"-7'3"

Ranking—40-Yard Sprint
Superior 100%—4.80-less
Excellent 90%—4.81-4.90
Very Good 80%—4.91-5.00
Good 70%—5.01-5.10
Average 60%—5.11-5.25
Marginal 50%—5.26-5.35

Anthropometric
Spring Score-Fall Goal
Height _____
Weight _____ - _____
% fat _____ - _____

Strength
Spring Score-% Value-Fall Goal
Bench _____ - _____ - _____
Clean _____ - _____ - _____
Squat _____ - _____ - _____
Avg. _____ - _____ - _____

Power/Speed
Spring Score-% Value-Fall Goal
V/Jump _____ - _____ - _____
S/Jump _____ - _____ - _____
40 Yds _____ - _____ - _____
Avg. _____ - _____ - _____

Strengths
1. _____
2. _____
3. _____

Weakness Areas
1. _____
2. _____
3. _____

Limitations
1. _____
2. _____
3. _____

Areas to Improve
1. _____
2. _____
3. _____

15

The Five- And Six-Man Pass Protection Package

Chris Scelfo
Tulane University
2004

It is good to be here this morning, and I am going to talk about our five- and six-man pass protections. When I first got to Tulane, I found a type of offensive linemen like I have never coached before. I had just come from the University of Georgia, and the five guys I coached there are in the NFL. I came into a situation at Tulane where we didn't have five guys who would be in backup positions at Georgia. I struggled with that for a little while.

I decided I was going to call every contact I knew and ask them what the most important aspect in college football was today. I talked to NFL guys all the way down to high school coaches. I talked to everyone in between those two groups that I possibly could. The common denominator in all that conversation was protection. That topic existed in every successful coach's agenda. That is where I have set my focus the past couple of years.

I am going to give some credit to myself, our University, and our program. I know you don't hear a lot about Tulane up here. Two years ago, we had a first-round draft choice at quarterback who signed with the Washington Redskins. This year we will have another first- or second-round pick, depending on how well he does at the combines. That is coming from a school which is not known for putting out NFL players. Tulane is known for putting out graduates in the professions.

As coaches, we spend too much time trying to find the magic play. We spend too much time trying to out-scheme and outsmart the opponent instead of working on the fundamentals of the game. My philosophy in the passing game goes back to protection. If you can protect the quarterback when you have to throw the ball, you are going to be successful.

When you listen to coaches talking about playing the Super Bowl, they all have one thing in common. They all talk about getting to the quarterback with the pass rush. I am not going to talk about mismatches today. I'm not going to talk about the defender coming off the edge that no one can block. I am going to talk about match-ups. I am going to tell you how to get five- and six-man protection done. It is very simple to do.

When we started to build our offensive line, we took our best player and put him at left tackle. We took the worst of our five offensive linemen and put him at center. From there, we filled in between the best and the worst with players of varying skills.

In our protection schemes, we are always trying to build the scheme so we will have a free player. I know most of you in here coach both offense and defense. You know the offensive line is the last stop before the bus stop. If you can't play in the offensive line, there is no place to play. The best players on the team are on the other side of the ball. As offensive coaches we are asking the worst athletes on the team to block the best athletes on the team. How smart are we as offensive coaches?

We are asking these guys to block the best players on the team and they can't do it. They couldn't block them in a phone booth. But we ask them to do it and then get mad at them when they can't. What we have to do is give them some help. What we try to do is free someone up to help in the mismatches on the line.

In our rules for the offensive line, we have two basic formulas. We tell our offensive linemen that the defensive front is either even or odd. People think there is more to the offensive line than that. Well, there is, but there really isn't. The defense can only put eleven players on the field. They can only line up in an even or odd front.

The first question people ask is, what about the shade defenses that are so predominant in college football today? They look even and odd at the same time. If our guards are covered, the defense is even. If the guards are uncovered, the defense is odd. The offensive linemen have a problem when one guard is covered and one is uncovered. Is that defense an even/odd defense?

The answer to that question is no. We split the offensive line and talk about even and odd to each side. When we apply the rules for five- and six-man protection, we are going to apply it to the right side of the line and the left side of the line. Two calls will be made for the offensive line. If the right guard is covered by a lineman or walked up linebacker, he calls even. The right guard and right tackle block even rules. If he calls even, we block even rules although the defensive line stems to another position. His call has nothing to do with the scheme that the left guard and tackle are working. If the defense is aligned in a 3 technique and 5 technique to the right side and a 5 technique and 9 technique to the left side, the right side will block even rules and the left side will block odd rules.

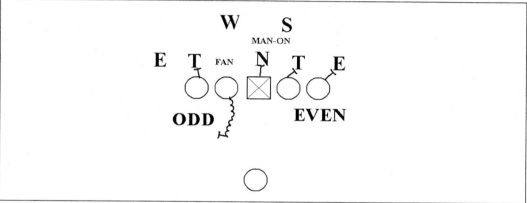

Diagram 1. Odd and even

I don't have time to coach my offensive linemen to block all the defenses there are in football today. We can't teach them to block a 4-3 defense on first down, an under front on second down, and a 4-6 front on third down. They block rules, not defenses.

The center has his set of rules. He is the worst player, but he is the smartest player. He has some additional things to know in a protection scheme. The center's rules are the same in the five- and six-man protection. If it is an odd defense, he blocks the man that is covering him, which we call man on. If it is an even defense, he blocks to the call side. The call side is the formation call made in the huddle. The call side means he blocks the linebacker to that side. In the 4-3 defense, he is not covered, but has a linebacker aligned on him. His rule is man on.

The center's rule is not a constant rule. If the defense changes, so does his rule. If he has a noseguard, he is blocking an odd rule. However, if the nose stems to the guard, his rule becomes even. His rule is not hard and fast because he is the only one affected by the rule. The hardest thing the center has to do is apply the rule to the direction call he heard in the huddle. If the call is right in the huddle, he has to apply that rule when the defense is jumping all over the place.

We play teams that move or stem their fronts. If the guard comes to the line of scrimmage, he has to make his call as to where the defender aligns. If the defensive tackle aligns in a 2 technique on him, he makes an even call. The offensive guard knows the snap count and has the advantage of knowing how much time he has before the ball is snapped. If the defensive tackle stems to a shade technique on the center, the guard knows whether he can change the call or not. If he can change his call to odd, he does. If he doesn't have enough time, he lives with the even call.

When you are watching a game and you see a defender come clean with no one attempting to block him, that is a communication problem. If we can't change the call, we live with it. That is not the way we want the play to come off, but at least we are not turning a defender loose unblocked. The scheme is still sound, but the angles are different and harder to execute.

When you have an experienced offensive line, you can handle the stems of the defense and not make too many mistakes in calls. This will be the third year we have had our offensive line together. We think this spring we will be able to handle stems and twists of the defensive line. It takes continuity of coaching to build a cohesive line. When defensive changes occur that quickly and we can still protect, we have come a long way. If we can protect the quarterback, the receiver will beat the defensive back. The stemming defense is one advantage the defense has on the offensive line. If we can hold up against that, we can protect.

Let's look at the odd front to start with. We have five offensive linemen and the quarterback aligned in the shotgun. There are seven defenders in the box. That means I have five receivers aligned somewhere in an offensive formation. The defense is going to have to cover them with some kind of scheme. This is how we begin to coach our quarterback. If we have five receivers, the defense is going to commit at least five defenders to cover them. If we have six-man protection, the defense has to have at least four defenders committed to coverage.

When we protect with five men, we want the quarterback in the shotgun set. We don't want him under the center. In the shotgun, the quarterback can get the ball off when he sees the defense blitzing more defenders than we can protect. Never put him under the center in a five-man protection if you can prevent it. You can show your quarterback in practice that he has time to get off the throw with an unblocked blitzer coming off the edge. He may get hit, but he will not be sacked.

In the true odd front, where the center has a noseguard and both of the offensive guards are uncovered, the entire offensive line will be blocking odd rules. In our five-man protection, we want to block the five most dangerous defenders. That sounds good, but the five most dangerous defenders can change as quickly as I talked about them.

We want to figure out who the defense wants to get to the quarterback. We have to know who the cover defenders are in the defense and who the rushers are. The defender who leads them in sacks is obviously a blitzer. We want to know all we can about their defense. With the ability of the linebackers to play half in the box and half out and the ability of the defensive outside linebacker to drop in coverage, it is hard to figure out who the five most dangerous defenders are.

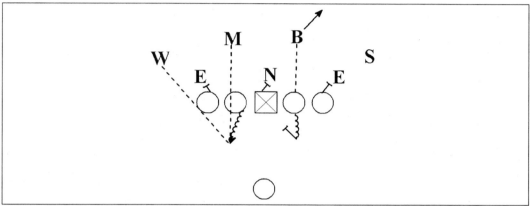

Diagram 2. Odd defense

If everything is balanced in the defense, we are going to start with our rules taking care of the quarterback's blind side. If you have a right-handed quarterback, it is the left side, and just the opposite for a left-handed quarterback. That being the case, we are going to declare the three down linemen, the Mike linebacker, and the Will linebacker as the five most dangerous defenders. We will double fan and protect the left side of the defense. The center blocks the noseguard, and the tackles block the defensive tackles. The left guard is double reading the Mike and Will linebackers. If the Mike linebacker drops and the Will linebacker runs a blitz, the left guard steps out on the Will linebacker.

The quick throw by the quarterback is tied into our five-man protection. We run a series of quick patterns with a designated hot receiver as part of our protection. The quarterback has someone that he can get the ball to. The defense can always bring one more defender than the offense can block. We can block ten, but the defense can bring eleven. The designated wide receiver must have a quick read and quick route. The quarterback has to know who that receiver is and how to find him.

The next question we have to answer is, how are we going to help the center in five-man protection? He is the worst lineman, and has to snap the ball and block a nose guard. When Buddy Ryan was the defensive coordinator for the Chicago Bears, he created havoc in the league with his defense. He did it by covering both the guards and making the center block 1-on-1 with a nose guard. That created a mismatch with the center, and the guards could not help him. The center is on an island. We try to give our center help on every play (Diagram 3). The guard that is double reading is the one who is designated to help the center. He is reading linebackers. If nothing happens, he helps the center. The guards are getting depth off the line of scrimmage already. He is falling back inside to help the center if his linebacker doesn't come.

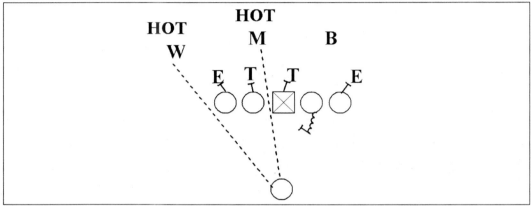

Diagram 3. Help the center

The uncovered lineman or one covered by a linebacker has to get depth off the line of scrimmage as quickly as he can. If the linebacker walks up on him, he still is retreating and getting depth off the line. If the offensive lineman can only get a piece of the defenders, we have five receivers who are going to beat the defense. All we need is a little time to find them. We ran 26 plays last year in five-man protection that went for 35 yards or more.

In the six-man protection everything is the same for the offensive line. We still have the quick throw for the quarterback, and we are still protecting his blind side. The most important thing is having the receiver and quarterback on the same page on the quick throws. We don't throw to a position. We designate a certain receiver to be the hot receiver. He is the one who has to see the blitzes and break off the right pattern. The quarterback is going to throw the ball to him regardless of where he lines up. He could be the inside receiver or the outside receiver. He could be by himself or a middle receiver. That keeps the defense from getting a fix on him.

In the six-man protection, I will set up the defense with an even side and an odd side. On the even side, the guard calls even and he and the tackle block the number one and number two men on the line of scrimmage. On the odd side we have to decide what we are going to do. We have to decide who is going to be the most dangerous men to this side. We have to know the personnel and what they do in the defense. If the man outside the tackle is the rush end, we are going to fan the protection to him and block the first down defender on the line of scrimmage with the guard, and the second defender on the line of scrimmage with the tackle. But blocking that situation in that manner causes me a problem. That leaves the center on that island blocking a nose tackle, and I don't like to do that. The even side rules are the same as the odd side rules on five- or six-man protection.

The next question we have to answer in the six-man protection is where to put the sixth protector. That is the same situation as your receiver's routes. You can run any routes that you want as long as you have the hot route for the quarterback. The same thing holds true for the sixth protector. You can put him anywhere you want. You can put him anywhere you want within the box and not affect any of the other protectors in their scheme or the quarterback.

We insert the sixth protector according to the scouting report (Diagram 4). I don't like to fan the front, and I want to give the center help. The sixth protector for a given week could be an additional tight end to the left side of the formation. That allows the guard to help the center. We may not use a tight end in that position. We could put another tackle in that position and still run our offense. Of course, that tackle would not be eligible as a pass receiver, but I can still run all my running game toward him or away from him without a problem. I could line that tackle up on the wing if I wanted to. I could line him up in the backfield if I wanted. We do not limit ourselves in relationship to the sixth protector.

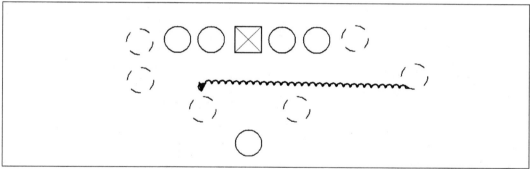

Diagram 4. Alignment of the sixth man

When you put the sixth protector into the protection scheme, the five core linemen's rules don't change. They block their odd or even rules on the five- and six-man protection. When we put the sixth protector in the scheme, we tell him who to block. We assign him a man to block on each scheme. The sixth protector could be a tight end, a fullback, a running back, an extra lineman, or a wide receiver that motions into the box to block the edge. We are not limited by who we choice to use.

We see different variations of defense, but the defenses are either odd or even. The defense can overload the offense with additional defenders in the box, but we are still counting odd or even alignments, and the quarterback is taking care of the overloads. If my sixth-best offensive lineman is my replacement at right guard, and my tenth-best lineman is my replacement at left guard, when the left guard goes down with an injury, I am going to replace him with my sixth-best lineman. Even though he has been practicing at right guard, I can get him ready to play left guard because the rules do not change from the right side to the left side. I have the ability to interchange linemen without confusing them as to their pass protection. When you start moving linemen around in your offense line, protection is the area of concern. It is not a problem for our group. One thing about offensive linemen that is constant. They are the smartest people on the football field.

In our huddle call for each of our formation, we have a right and left call. That is telling the center which way he blocks on the even fronts. When we come to the line of scrimmage and the center reads an even front, he knows he is blocking to the right side because that was the huddle call. The sixth protector will always go opposite the call side. His alignment doesn't matter. We will tell him where we want him to align, but that point is not important. When we face a 40 defense, the center, right guard, and right tackle are assigned to block the defensive tackle, end, and linebacker to the right (Diagram 5). The left guard, left tackle, and the sixth protector are assigned to block the defensive end, tackle, and linebacker to the left.

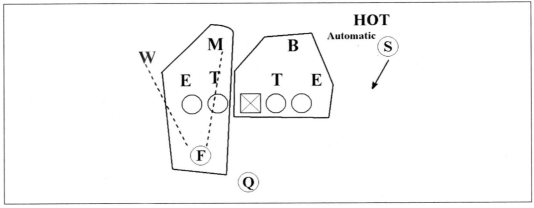

Diagram 5. Six-man protection vs. forty

In the six-man protection the sixth protector double reads the inside and outside linebackers to his side. The quarterback knows what his protection is doing. If both linebackers come off the backside, the quarterback knows he is throwing hot. If they bring one linebacker off the backside, he is protected. If neither linebacker comes, we have an extra blocker on that side.

On the call side, if the fourth man comes, the quarterback is throwing hot. If no one else on the call side rushes except the fourth rusher, the quarterback is throwing hot. He is going to the hot throw without hesitation. He knows we can only protect against six, and the fourth rusher from that side makes seven.

We know through our scouting report what the defense is trying to do. If we feel they are going to attack us from the backside, we have the ability to put the center on the weak side (Diagram 6). We can do it in the course of a game if we feel we need to.

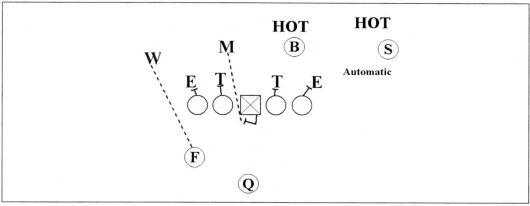

Diagram 6. Center adjustment

In closing, there are five things that you should remember from this lecture:
- Get help for your center.
- Block odd or even rules.
- Have a hot read and a hot route.
- Plug your sixth protector anywhere you need him.
- Run any combination pass routes you want.

If you can do those things and train the quarterback to see the blitzes, you will be able to throw the ball when you have to throw it. Remember not to be too critical of the offensive linemen in pass protection. They are inferior talents trying to block the most talented players on the opponent's team.

16

Offensive Line Drills

Jimmy Ray Stephens
University of Florida
1998

We have the reputation of being a passing team, but I think the running game gives us the balance to be successful. Keeping that balance in the offense is important. We try to keep it simple in the running game. We have to spend so much time with pass protection that the running game has to be simple.

The offensive line is based on a lot of repetition. Repetition is the mother of learning. We repeat things so many times that we try to reduce things down to habit. We want to be able to execute without having to think so much. When the offensive lineman is thinking a lot, it slows down his aggressiveness.

I try to go to the pro camps in the areas to stay on top of the new techniques and drills. The fundamentals generally stay the same, but I like to keep abreast of what is going on. Sometimes, you have to be creative and come up with your own drills. Most drills are borrowed from people who have done them for years and years.

What I'm going to show you is an offensive line teaching progression. This is where I start out every year in the spring and fall. Never assume that your guys already know what you want them to know. We have guys who are fifth-year seniors and have been in this program for four years. We still start from scratch every year. The progression is split, stance, approach, contact, and follow-through. That goes for run blocking as well as pass blocking. Everything we do is pretty much a three-step approach, and, after that, it is effort. There are different types of contact. If we are at the point of attack, we are using punch and hand blocking. There are times when we use the flipper in the contact. When we are the post man on a double-team, we use the flipper. We use the flipper or forearm on the backside in the scoop block. We use a rip upper cut when the lineman is farther removed from the play. That would be like a sweep moving away from the lineman. That requires a flatter angle coming down inside.

Follow-through is nothing but effort. We try to finish every drill with a shove. It might be that little extra shove that gets the defender off balance and causes him to stumble or arm tackle the runner. We teach our 1-on-1 run blocks first. Everything else works off of that. We have playside zone blocks and backside zone blocks. We work at every position about the same as far as technique. We work our guys in 2-on-2 situations as much as possible. We have the double-team block both playside and backside and, finally, the fold block. We don't fold block much. Because of the shades and slants that we are getting now, most everything is zone blocking.

We have our pattern blocking, which is the counter gap and trap blocking. That is zone and pattern blocking all rolled into one.

In pass blocking, we have 1-on-1 blocking. We have the position and contact phases. We have counter moves for various pass-rush moves, in that we have 2-on-2 blocking, which involves the switching games. The last thing is our pass protection schemes.

Real quickly, let me talk about our practice schedule. I'll show you an example of a Tuesday and Wednesday schedule when we are in full gear. On Monday and Thursday, we have a 50-minute block for special teams. Fortunately for me, none of my guys are in those groups except for field goal and extra point. That gives me a 50-minute block that I can go back over fundamentals of the 1-on-1 block and things I need to work on.

This is a typical schedule. After stretching, we kick point after touchdowns and field goals. We have a team takeoff period and then go to an individual period. It usually lasts about 25 to 30 minutes. During this time, I try to do run-blocking fundamentals. After the individual period, we go into a 7-on-7 period. That is an inside run period live against the defense. It is a full-speed contact drill. That is about the only full-speed drill we get during the week after the season starts. After that period, we take a break.

From the break, the rest of the squad goes to some form of the kicking game. I go by myself and work on pass-blocking techniques and fundamentals. Next is when coach Spurrier goes to his pass skeleton drill. As you can see, there is more time allotted to the passing game than there is in the running game. During that time, I work 1-on-1, 2-on-2, and 5-on-4 pass protection. We work that full speed against the defense. After that, we go into a team drill. That is the way we do things on Tuesday and Wednesday.

Thursday is a review day. We spend a lot of time on special teams. During that time, I review all the blocking we expect to see during the coming week.

What I would like to do now is get into the drill tape. As we go along, I'll point out some coaching techniques and points. The first thing we do is to go through the low ropes. These are four inches high. We are trying to keep our feet as close to the ground as possible. We want the body lean and have our feet and arms working together. We want as fast a turnover as possible.

The next thing we do is go to an agility period. We use the carioca drill. That is where we turn sideways and work our feet in front and behind one another. We try to stay low and use rapid movement. We don't want to cover ground. We want to see how many we can get in within the 10 yards we work. That is a loosening-up drill.

The next drill we do is called the *demeanor drill*. Basically, all it is is a two-point wave drill. We are working on wide base, straight back, head up, and good foot movement. What we are looking for are feet close to the ground, retaining the wide base, and good ground coverage. They never want their heels to click together in this movement. If the right foot moves six inches, the left foot should move six inches. The closer the feet are to the ground the quicker he can redirect his movement. We move them forward, backward, and sideways. We want them to feel like they have a steel rod right down their spine. We want the weight balanced. We don't want it on the outside of the feet, back on their heels, or up on the balls of the feet. We try to balance with the whole foot on the ground. We want the weight on the insteps.

The next thing we go to in the fundamental work is the first step. We take very little first steps. We make contact on the second step. We work the lateral or bucket step as a first step. The first step depends upon the alignment of the defender. The 45-degree angle step is called a lead step. The elbows come to the rib cage on the takeoff. The hands must come up quickly. We don't want to bring our hands back to the hips.

On the offensive line field, we have painted on the ground five-yard squares. We have seven squares across the field and about four squares deep. We do our drills in these five-yard squares. They have space to work without running over each other, and we can work them all at one time. There is nothing that irritates me more than having one guy working and everyone else standing there watching. We try to keep them all moving at the same time. We try to do everything off a line. The center is the only guy who will have someone right on him. Everyone else will have about a foot and a half of the neutral zone between him and the defense. We try to get off the ball so we can recognize slants and stunts up front. Also, it helps us get our second step on the ground. We want the second step on the ground when contact is made.

Let's go through these first steps. The bucket step is a drop step with width. We are trying to gain width, depth, and to open the hips up. We want our hips and shoulders open to the target. Sometimes, you have to lose ground to gain position. One thing that we never want to do is move to move. That means adding a false step.

In this drill, we lay hand shields down on the ground to indicate alignments of defenders. The offensive line is going to work on footwork for our inside zone play. The hand shields can be head-up, inside eye, or outside eye. Those are the only places a defender can be. The first step for the playside people is a slide step. The second step goes just inside the near foot of the defender. We try not to cross over so we don't lose our base. The third step is a width step or position step.

The backside people are working on backside scoop angles and steps. The backside guard's angle is tighter than the backside tackle's. The guard is using a flipper and trying to get his eyes on the inside armpit of the defender. He uses the same flipper and foot so he has his foot on the ground as he delivers the punch. The tackle is going to cross over into the gap and try to get a rip up in the pit position, just like a defensive lineman pass rushing. On the backside, contact is made on the second step, also. Most of the time, unless the defender is really slow, the backside cutoff block will end up in a drive block on a 45-degree angle inside. That lets the back cut all the way back if he has to. Remember, you may have to lose ground to gain position. If I am a backside tackle trying to cut off a 3 technique, my first step can't be upfield. If it is, the next step will be farther upfield or he will have to cross over. If he does that, he loses his base. He uses a bucket step to open his hips and loses a little ground. The next step allows him to get his head in front of the 3 technique.

On a double-team block, the post man has to step with his inside foot to protect the inside gap. This is the counter gap play. Basically, everyone is blocking down. But, it doesn't make sense for the man who is covered to take off inside to block a backside linebacker. He posts on the double-team and comes off for the linebacker when the double-team gets to linebacker depth. The first step for a head-up to 4i defender is inside. If the defender is in an outside shade, the step is more upfield. That is to keep the defender from splitting the double-team. The first step is inside, the second step is upfield for the contact, and the third step is the width step.

The drive man on the double-team first step is an open step. That opens his hips toward the target. There are three types of down blocks. It is important to know that because the defender is going to read differently on them and the target or landmark will change. Most defenders are going to read on the run and attack through the V of the offensive blocker's neck. On the down block on the double-team, the landmark is farther upfield. The landmark is the near hip of the defender. If there is a down block without a double-team, the down block has to be a flatter angle, because the defender is going down with the offensive linemen as he goes inside. The landmark becomes the defender's inside armpit or far hip. If the down block comes with a guard pull, there is a different reaction by the defender. The defender will work lateral with the pulling guard, and the landmark becomes the defender's near armpit. The angle a down blocker takes depends on the assignment of the offensive linemen inside the down block.

The other thing the down blocker must consider is how the defender is playing. He has to find out if the defender is penetrating or reading. We feel that our people play better if they have their outside foot back in their stances. That is particularly true in pass protection. Therefore, we teach right- and left-handed stances. People on the right will have their right hand down and right foot back. People on the left will have their left hand down and their left foot back.

The next thing we work on is a five-yard pull technique. We drop step and pull around the bags. The coaching point is coming around the bag. As the player turns upfield, he drives the inside arm down. That keeps the center of gravity low as they turn upfield.

The next thing you'll see is the one-step punch. We teach the punch. We hit the bottom three knuckles on the hand punching up and through. After the punch, we get our hands in the fit position under the breastplate of the pads. We punch, arch the back, and roll the hips.

The next drill you will see is the fit drill. We take the offensive blocker and defender and lock them into a fitted block. We put the hairline where it is supposed to be on contact. Then, we try to get the good demeanor. The back is arched; the weight is flat-footed, rolled to the inside on the insteps; and the hands are behind the back. We do this without using our hands. If the blocker gets his weight on the balls of his feet, he gets more horizontal and lower in the blocking scheme. In high school, I'm sure people use more of a horizontal thrust. In college and the pro level, there is a lot more vertical thrust. We are blocking up higher, because of the pass protection. The main thing is to get the hat on a defender and stick on him. Don't lose your block. When you get up on the balls of the feet, you are getting overextended with a flat back. If the defender steps right or left, the blocker will fall forward and lose his block. We feel the days of knocking guys off the ball are over. The guy across from you will be on scholarship, too.

What we are looking for is a stalemate. We are coming off and moving our feet like crazy. At some point in time, the defender has to drop step to try to get off the block and make the tackle. That is when the offensive lineman finishes the block and puts the defender on his back.

In the no-hands drill, we want the defender to move right and left so the blocker has to keep his feet moving and maintain contact. After we go with no hands, we use the hands. We still fit in, but now the hands are fitted into position. The defensive man tries to completely stalemate the offensive blocker. That forces the offensive blocker to push out of the stalemate and accelerate his feet at contact, while maintaining a wide base. We want the defense to take a right or left movement, so the blocker can practice staying with his block and finishing.

After we do that, we put it all together. We slide step, second step and punch, widen step and drive, and finish the block. Most of our drive blocks are up in drive angle blocks. Very seldom will someone drive someone straight back off the ball. Everyone lines up at angles, and that is the way we drive them.

Now, we put them in a linebacker drill and go over their foot movement. When everyone was covered, they used the slide step as their first step. With linebacker coverage, they use a bucket step. The lineman gets a one-handed read to the down man who is one hole over. He keeps his eyes on the linebacker. The lineman takes a bucket step, and his second step is a crossover step. His crossover step has to be kept underneath the lineman's body. If it isn't, his pads turn too flat to the sideline and he will never get them square to go up on the linebacker. If the linebacker fast flows and the down man slants inside, the offensive lineman goes from a one-handed read to two hands on the down man. On the third step, the lineman has to make a decision. He is either locking on to the slanting down man or climbing up to the linebacker. After

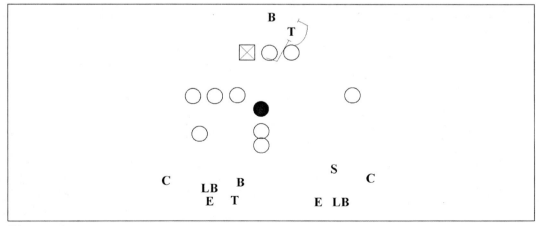

Diagram 1

he gets to the second level with the linebacker, his technique goes back to what he did if he were covered. He punches, locks on, arches his back, rolls his hips, and accelerates his feet. The finish is the last thing he does.

The covered man starts off with a two-handed punch. If the defender locks him and works outside, he continues to block him. If the defender starts to move inside on the slant, the guard inside has one hand on him. The covered man has two hands on him. They end up in a double-team on the slanting tackle. The guard goes from a one-handed feel to a two-handed drive block on the slanting tackle. The offensive tackle goes from a two-handed punch and drive to a one-handed press-off to go to the linebacker who is flowing across the top. All zone plays start out as an inside-out double-team. Try to stay away from long steps. We want short steps all the time. The harder the punch the more the hips will roll up underneath. If you don't get a punch with the upper body, you end up leaning on one another with no power.

Their techniques are done by all linemen and tight ends on the zone play. If the uncovered man was the tackle and the covered man was the tight end, they would do the drill just like a guard and tackle. The tackle would bucket set, half cross step, and take a wide step with the one-handed read on the man over the end. The end would use the slide step, two-hand punch on the second step, and widen on the third step. If the man over the tight end slanted, the tackle would go from one to two hands and get into an angle drive block. The tight end would go from a two-handed punch to a one-handed press-off up to linebacker depth. If the defensive end locked the tight end's block and started to work outside, the tight end would continue his angle drive block. The tackle on his third step would release the down man and climb up to linebacker depth to take the linebacker.

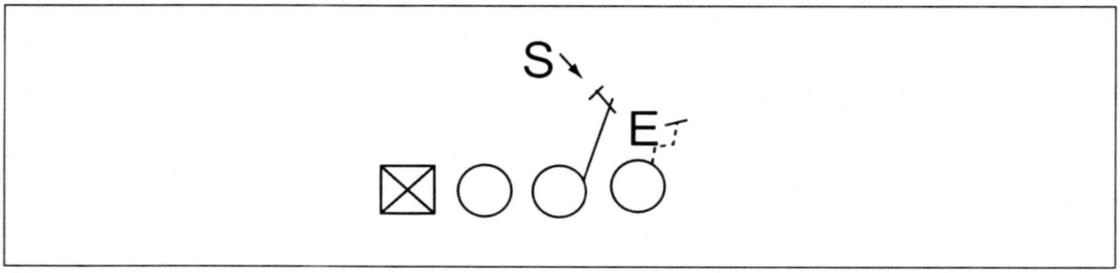

Diagram 2

In our drill, we line the defender outside and lock on or slant. When we line the defender inside, we do both. On Monday, we do all of our 1-on-1 drills. On Tuesday and Wednesday is when we do these 2-on-1 zone blocks. The center is the only man who makes contact on the first step. If he is in a double-team situation with his right guard, he steps off with his near foot to the guard. His flipper and head remain on the backside number of the defender. If the post man on a double-team sets the post with his hands, he will never get them off to pick up a run through by the linebacker. His eyes are on the linebacker. The guard steps off with a slide step to the inside. If the linebacker runs through on the backside, the center comes off and blocks him. If the linebacker flows over the top, the center has to helmet adjust and slip to the playside to get his head across the block. The guard is coming off for the linebacker.

Let's get into our pass sets. If the guard has a man head-up on him, he is going to take a short inside slide step. That is to protect the inside. If the tackle has a guy head-up on him, he is going to step inside and off the ball a little. If there is an inside shade and that is his responsibility, he has to set heavy down inside and move both feet. That is called a two-step set. He has to get to a frontal position and square the man up. The contact will be off the inside foot. If there is a tight outside shade, we use a one-step set. If there is a loose 3 technique, we use a two-step set. The lineman wants to set so that his body is between the defender and the quarterback's pocket. The center and guard should keep his pads square at all times. The tackle will have a slight turn with his pads toward the sideline, but should never have his pad turned all the way toward the sideline.

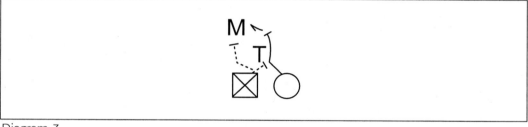

Diagram 3

The thing we emphasize is get set quick, get the hands up quickly, with the head and shoulders back. They always keep their post foot up and the set foot back. They keep that stagger to help them stay low. If the blocker doesn't get his second foot down, he gets too spread out in his base. The defender will beat him upfield, and the only choice the offensive lineman has is to bail out and cross over. We have to be balanced. The more foot you've got on the ground the more balance you have.

During our pass set drill, we also work on our draw set. We inside set, punch him up, pivot, and turn. We incorporate that into this drill.

17

Offensive Line Drills and Techniques

Chris Vagotis
University of Louisville
1990

Let me talk about offensive line play. My philosophy is a lot different now than it was when I was coaching in high school. We can recruit in college, and most of you can't in high school. So, I know where you are coming from. If something fits into my program, I am going to put it in the program. I am not going to give you something that you cannot do. I am not going to talk about running our whole offense, which consists of close to possibly 120 plays against multiple defensive fronts. I want to give you something you can use.

In high school, I would take my best lineman and put him at center. Anyone can learn how to snap the ball. That good lineman may not want to snap, but he can learn to snap the football. We tell the center to take the ball and grip the ball around the right stripe and tell him to squeeze it hard. We want him to lift the ball up to the quarterback's hand with the laces the way you want them.

We want the center to make a natural arc with his arm as he brings the ball straight up. "Set-hike. Set-hike." That is all there is to it. Most centers want to throw the ball back.

A good drill to check to see if the center is getting the ball back is for the quarterback to let the ball hit his top hand and then drop to the turf. If the ball goes forward as it hits the ground, it means the center is too short on the snap. If the ball goes backward, the center is lifting the ball too deep. The ball should drop straight down to the turf.

We teach the center to snap with both hands on the ball. He snaps and moves his feet. He snaps and steps, snaps and steps.

In high school football, the center is the most important position. In college, our openside tackle must be our best athlete because he has to block the outside rusher. If you throw the ball a lot, that is true. It all depends on what you run on offense. If you run the veer, take the big hogs and put them at the guards. If the defense you face covers your guards, you should put your best players at guards.

We do not use any drills that do not correlate with what we do in a game. We do not do up-downs. All drills we do are directly related to what we do in a game. We do incidental drills in our off-season conditioning program, such as the wave drill. To me, those types of drills you use for punishment.

I. Four plastic cones — seven-yard square. We can backpedal, shuffle, and pull right and left on this drill.

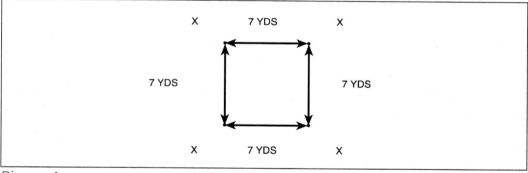

Diagram 1

Cone Drills

- Shuffle to first cone and sprint through next cone.
- Step around—atance step around—touch cone—eyeball coach. Used for pulling guards. Eyeball linebacker.
- Backpedal—pivot—sprint—sprint. We get in a three-point stance. When he starts to backpedal, he wants to punch with his hands. We do not want him to take a hitch step; that is taking a step forward. He is like a boxer punching a bag as he kicks back.
- Scramble stance: sprint to coach, scramble to next cone.

Sled 50 pass pro stance—frontal on sled—lock out hands—head held back.

Diagram 2

Off set right—left—scramble low to knee—aiming points—six inches outside knee, three inches high.

Off set right—left—reach outside breastplate.

Drive—flat back—short, choppy steps—head up.

Low drive to crotch—high drive to V of neck.

II. Bags and boards—six beveled boards 12' x 1'x 2" thick with a T-board 3' x 2" x 2". The boards are painted with lines to represent hands of down man and linebacker.

Diagram 3

Board Drills

- Drive versus down man; linebackers.
- Scramble versus down man.
- Turn versus down man; linebackers.

Bag Drills

- Drive with bags.
- Off set right/left—scramble low to knee.
- Off set right/left—reach to breastplate.
- Trap technique.
- Trap technique—step around first force log.

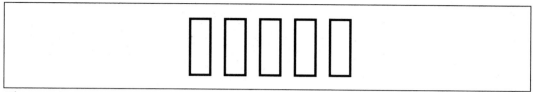

Diagram 4

Chute Drills

- Drive
- Reach right and left
- Scramble right and left
- Trap right and left

The purpose of the drill is to keep the shoulders down, back straight, and all five men coming off the ball simultaneously. I do not believe in using the shoulder block. I think the shoulder block causes more neck, shoulder, and spinal injuries than anything else in football. If you don't do the shoulder block perfectly, you open up the neck area to the defense. I believe in aiming the hat in there and sticking the hands inside and knocking the man off the ball. Take no mercy on the defensive man. He will gore you, if he gets you down. Knock him down. Do it legally, but put him away.

On our alignment and stance, we are no different than most teams. Our offensive line is in a three-point stance with a toe-to-heel relationship. Our halfbacks and fullback shift from the I to a finished position on the command of set. They get to a three-point stance with their feet square, unless the play called is to be run from the I or if the play called is a split play and the snap count is on a first or second count. Our X and Z receivers are in a three-point stance.

On our splits, our guards should have a 24-inch split from the center. Our tackles should have a 36-inch split from the guard. Our tight end is 36 inches split from the tackle on his base alignment. He could also be in a flex set. Here is a very important coaching point. Our guards line up on the *heels* of the center. The tackles line up on the *hand* of the guards. The tight end lines up on the *hands* of the tackles.

Hole Numbering System

- Holes are numbered through offensive linemen.
- All plays ending in an *even* number go to the right.
- All plays ending in an *odd* number go to the left.

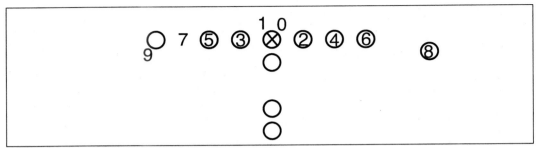

Diagram 5. Pro right

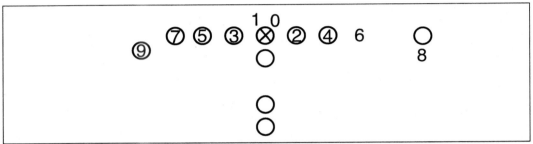

Diagram 6. Pro left

We cut the center in half and give him the 0 and 1 numbers. If we called a 32 play, the 3 back would carry the ball through the 2 hole. We are very simple. We count everyone on defense from the inside to the outside. Against the 50 defense, the linebacker is number 1, the tackle is number 2, the end is number 3, and the rover is number 4.

We have alignments and techniques, so we can communicate with our players. We have three areas for each alignment. If the noseguard is in a 0 technique, he would be in a plus (+) technique, if he shades to the tight end. If he shades away from the tight end, he is in a minus (-) technique. The guard has a 2, 1, and 3 technique. The tackle has a 5 and a 7 technique. Our end has a 6, 8, and 9 technique. We use this to communicate where the defense is playing more than anything else.

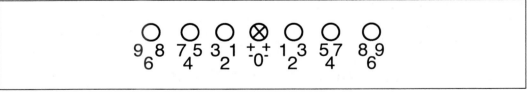

Diagram 7

I want to cover some basic blocks that we use. I will cover the technique, when we use the block, and how we teach the block.

Drive Block

We must have movement on the block.

When: the ball is coming up your butt, and the play is a quick-hitting play.

Examples: 20/21 for the center; 12/13 for the guards.

How: sprint out of stance taking a six-inch step with your playside foot in the direction that puts you square to the defender. Your feet at the point of contact should be exactly square to his. The aiming point for the rivets should be through his crotch; your forearms should make contact on his thigh pads. We must fight to maintain our flat back. After contact, we must maintain a wide base and drive through the defender with quick, short steps. Coaching point: imagine a point five yards behind the defender where your rivets and his butt should land. *Run through defenders*. Drive to and through the defender.

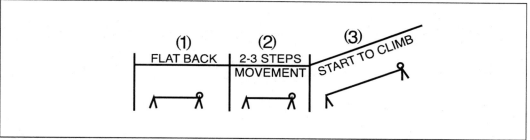

Diagram 8. Points in the driving block

When coaching the drive block and making corrections, make your linemen aware of the mistakes of the blocks. Ask the players watching what the blocker did incorrectly or correctly.

Turn Block

This is basically the same as the drive block, only higher. We must have movement.

When: the ball is being handed off up your butt to the second back on a slow-developing play.

Examples: guard versus 3 technique on 14; tackle versus 5 technique on 34; center versus nose on draw - 0.

How: take a six-inch step with your playside foot in a direction that puts you square to the defender. Your feet at the point of contact should be exactly square to his. The aiming point of your rivets should be the V in his jersey. Your fists should make contact in his breastplate. Even though we are blocking slightly uphill, we still want two steps worth of movement before we try to turn him in either direction we can get him to go.

Scramble Block

When: the ball is going inside or outside of you on a quick-hitting play that has a chance to cut back. Basically, for plays called inside of our guards.

How: sprint out of stance with flat back. Just before contact, dip and explode. Aiming point for the playside should be six inches outside of the defender's playside foot. The flatness of your angle will be determined by the width of the defender's alignment. Aim your rivets six inches outside and three inches above his playside knee. Try and split his crotch with your back and work your butt between him and the ball.

Coaching point: scramble with him at least two steps, then give an upward thrust with the head and body. If you feel you lost the block, get back on your feet and get to the play.

Veer Block

This block is for the guard and tackle. They block through the first man inside.

When: as the rule calls for it. We do not use this block much now. The guard doesn't veer if covered (unless the game plan dictates).

How: First, when veering for a man off the line of scrimmage.

Example: tackle on 20 versus 50. You sprint out of your stance, aiming your inside foot six inches inside of the defender's outside foot. Aim your rivets six inches outside and three inches above his playside knee. Split his crotch with your inside fist and reach for the ground behind his playside foot with your outside fist.

Coaching point: if you miss him, look inside for the next linebacker or lineman in pursuit. If the tackle slants across your face, take him down with you.

Second, when veering through a man on the line of scrimmage.

Example 1: guard on nose

Example 2: tackle on eagle tackle

We aim our inside foot six inches outside of the defender's playside foot, expecting the guard or center to widen him at least that far. We take a zone step (lateral) over and up, driving our inside shoulder through his playside hip, trying to turn him over to the man scrambling him while we work to veer block the next man inside, usually a linebacker. We should only stay with the man we are veering on, if he gains a head-up position on us.

Reach Block

When: same theory as the scramble block except higher. It is used when the second back has the ball on a slow-developing play that has a chance to cut back. So, we must maintain contact a lot longer.

Examples: backside of draw 2 or 3; backside of 34 for tackle; the onside on 38 for tackle.

How: sprint out of stance aiming your playside foot six inches outside of the defender's playside foot. (Try to make him think it is a turn or drive block.) Aim your rivets for his playside breastplate. (Your angle will be determined by the width of his alignment.) Aim your fist for his armpits. Try to make him fight pressure of the drive block, then slip your back shoulder, trying to get outside position on him.

Coaching point: the wider he is the less you can disguise the reach block. If he is too wide, make a fold call or try to scramble him.

Finally, I want to cover our sprint draw play-action passing game. The first question we must answer is this: why the sprint draw play-action pass? We run it for these three reasons: first, to help set up the sprint draw run, second, gives us seven-man protection (can stop all blitzes except a perimeter blitz), and, third, can be thrown against all coverage.

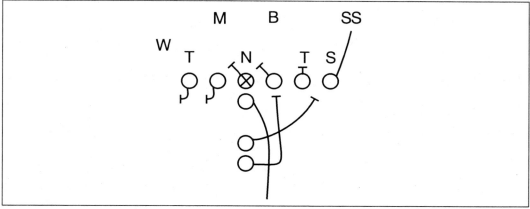

Diagram 9

Sprint Draw Protection

OT—turnback.

OG—turnback: CP—if you and tackle are both covered, block straight.

C—turnback: alert straight call.

BG— turnback: alert straight call.

BT— turnback: alert straight call.

Y—route.

X—route.

Z—route.

FB—Block #3 controlled aggressive.

HG—Sprint draw fake: block playside linebacker. If linebacker is on the line of scrimmage, check Mike to Will. You are responsible for perimeter pressure strong.

QB—Sprint draw fake: play-action technique.

Now, let's look at three passes.

Route 1: Can Be Thrown Versus *Any* Coverage

- This play is designed to vertically stretch the center of the field.
- After play-action fake, the quarterback sets up 9 to 10 yards behind strongside guard.

Versus Three-Deep Strongside Zone Coverage

- The quarterback may look to hit the tight end in front of the weakside end who has taken a straight pass drop underneath number 1 (split end) because number 2 and number 3 (fullback and tailback) have gone strongside. Otherwise:
- The quarterback picks up weak safety after fake. If weak safety has settled down in the middle of the field, the quarterback will look to throw the deep post over the middle of the field to the split end.

- If the weak safety has run to take away the deep post, the quarterback will look to throw the square-in to the flanker or the flat route by the tailback with a high/low distribution off the strong safety. (Hopefully, we have held the strong inside linebacker with the fake long enough, so he is not a factor getting underneath the flanker.)

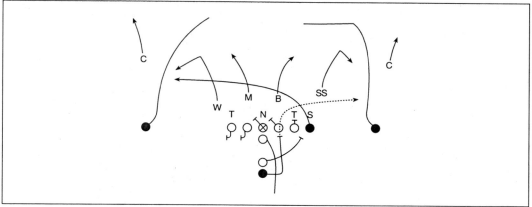

Diagram 10

Versus Two-Deep Zone Coverage

- Most likely, the tight end is not open, because either the weakside corner or linebacker is in the flat waiting on the tight end after the jam on the split end.
- We do not generally think of going to the deep post with the weak safety and strong safety each covering one half of the field.
- Our thinking is to create a vertical stretch on the strongside of the field with the flanker and the tailback. (This time against the strongside outside linebacker who covers the slot in a weakside rotation.)

Versus Man-To-Man Coverage

- Forget play fake; take five-step drop.
- Look to the tight end first being chased.
- Look to the split end on deep post, since the weak safety is out of middle of the field.
- Look to the tailback being chased, if the strongside linebacker does not blitz.

Route 2: Can Be Thrown Versus *Any* Coverage

- This play is designed to vertically stretch the weak corner or weak outside linebacker in the weakside flat area.

- After the play-action fake, the quarterback sets up 9 to 10 yards behind the strongside guard.

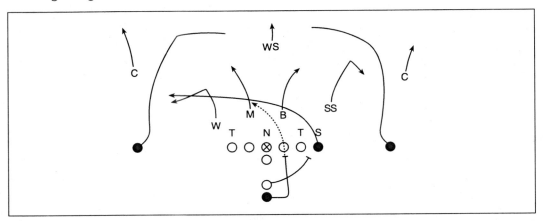

Diagram 11

Versus Three-Deep Strongside Coverage

- The quarterback will look to high-low the weakside linebacker in the weak flat.
- C/P: if the weakside outside linebacker is between the tight end and the split end, the quarterback should look to hit the tight end.
- If the weakside outside linebacker jumps the tight end, the quarterback will look to hit the split end 1-on-1 with the weakside corner.
- If both the tight end and the split end are covered, look to hit the tailback hooked up.

Versus Two-Deep Zone Coverage

- The quarterback will look to high-low the weakside flat occupied by the weakside corner or weakside outside linebacker, who is responsible for jamming the split end.
- If the defender designed to jam and occupy the flat settles back in the deep flat, the quarterback should hit the tight end.
- If the defender designed to jam and occupy the flat (Will or corner) does jam and looks to pick up the tight end as he tries to invade the defender's zone, the quarterback should look to hit the comeback run by the split end off the man defending the deep weakside one half.

Versus Man-To-Man Coverage

- Forget play-action fake.
- Fake five-step drop and look to hit the tight end being chased.

- If the tight end is not going to be open, go seven steps and hit the split end on a comeback.
- Note: may get flanker on post with the weak safety out of the middle of the field.

Route 3: Can Be Thrown Versus *Any* Coverage

- This play is designed to vertically stretch the center of the field.
- After play-action fake, the quarterback sets up 9 to 10 yards behind strongside guard.

Versus Three-Deep Strongside Zone Coverage

- The quarterback may look to hit the tight end in front of the weakside end who has taken a straight pass drop underneath number 1 (split end) because number 2 and number 3 (fullback and tailback) have gone strongside. Otherwise:
- The quarterback will pick up the weak safety after play-action fake, if the weak safety has settled down in the middle of the field to the flanker.
- If the weak safety has run to take away the deep post, the quarterback looks to throw the square-in to the split end or the check-down to the tailback, who has settled approximately six yards deep over the original position of the weak linebacker. (With distribution of the flanker on a square-in and the tailback on a check-down, we hope to get high-low separation off the weak linebacker.)
- We hope the run fake holds the linebacker so he doesn't affect square-in.

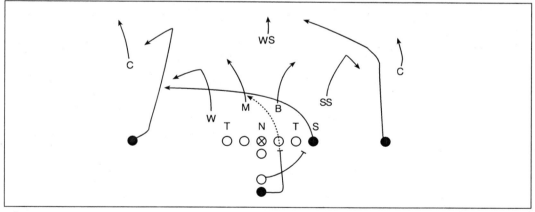

Diagram 12

Versus Two-Deep Zone Coverage

- More than likely, the tight end will not be open; either the weakside corner or the outside linebacker will be in the flat waiting on the tight end after jam on the split end.

- We do not generally think of going to the deep post with the weak safety and the strong safety each covering the deep half of the field.
- Our thinking is to create a vertical stretch on the weakside inside linebacker with the split end and the tailback.

Versus Man-To-Man Coverage

- Forget play fake, take five-step drop.
- Look to the tight end first being chased.
- Look to the flanker on deep post, since the weak safety is out of middle of the field.

18

Coaching the Offensive Line

Art Valero
University of Louisville
1998

I'm not going to talk too much about our basic offense and how we go about doing things and what we look for. We will let anyone who wants to see us come out and watch us on film and see what we are doing. Then, you can figure us out, because it is a very, very complex offense. We are a one-back offense. And, unlike most one-back offenses, they do certain things in terms of protecting the passer and running the football, and that is all they do. They don't have the answers for all of those questions that come up with the receivers.

We have a lot of answers for those problems that always arise for a one-back scheme. Our feeling is this: we will spread you out offensively by formation. We are going to spread you out and make you declare. We make you decide if you are going to play with three true linebackers or if you are going to play a nickel scheme, where you try to change those guys who are too big to be safeties into linebackers. If you are going to get those types of guys, we feel like we have wide receivers who are better than you are in terms of running routes. When we come back into our one-back set, we look for spreading you out. We basically have a rule of thumb. If you have one linebacker in the box, we are going to run the ball. If you have two linebackers in there, we are going to throw the ball. So, the perception may be that we are a throwing football team and we are going to throw every down. Well, that is not true. We are a 50-50 football team. Unlike some coordinator's comments, where they may not be sure if they want to run the ball or they want to throw the ball, we want you to play us one way or the other. Then, our identity will come out in terms of either shortening this football game up and running it at you, or we are going to shorten this football game up and create big plays and throw the ball. We would prefer you play nickel against us. That means you have got your fifth-worst football player on the field in the secondary trying to cover our wideouts. Not only is he your fifth-worst pass defender, like most defensive backs, he is probably your eighth- or ninth-worst running defender. So, that puts it all back into our hands.

When we talk about formations, we will go balance into a two-by-two set that we will get into a majority of the time, although we don't necessarily like it because it doesn't create any unbalanced situations. We like trips, which means we have the tight end into the boundary with three receivers to the one side, or we will go with the tight end to the field with two receivers and a single receiver into the boundary. So, we are going to try to spread you out from a one-back standpoint. To us, blasphemy is when you put more than one guy back there in the backfield. When you put more than one guy back there, what ends up happening is this, he just brings another defender into the box. That is something that we do not want to happen. Because, now, you are asking this: instead of those six guys blocking for that running back, now you are asking for six guys, plus a guy who may not be one of your better blockers to block the extra man. We would rather spread you out and then go about our business.

Our system of football is 50-50 run and pass, and that is our identity. We want to be able to do both. The keys to our success on offense, and, since 1990, this offense has been ranked in the top 10 each of the years, not only by throwing the ball, but by running it. So, we feel like we have got a good system of football. In order for us to win on offense, there are basically five things that we need to adhere to all of the time.

Number one is that we are going to run the ball first and foremost. It is our responsibility as a coaching staff, it is our responsibility as an offensive line, to make sure that we run the football. Number two, we are going to throw the three-step drop or what we call our 90 passing game. Those are our short routes. We let our wideouts make big plays off of that. Our third thing that we are going to do is empty the backfield. So basically, we've got five eligible receivers going out. We put the ball in our quarterback's hands and let him make something happen. Those routes may be three-step drop type routes or five-step drop type routes. We are going to spread you out horizontally so we can stretch you vertically. The fourth thing that we have got to do is make play-action passes work. That is where we get big plays. The fifth thing we do is throw our 80 or our five-step drops. What we want to do when we throw five-step drops is to throw them when we want to, not when we have to. A lot teams want to drop back and go five steps every single time. The one thing from an offensive line standpoint that they seem to forget is that the quarterback doesn't move very often. He sets in the same spot, and that puts extra pressure on your people up front. So, we talk about it as a staff in terms of throwing five-step drop routes; we take the offensive linemen into consideration, and the job that they have to do.

A couple of things I want to talk about real quick just to start this thing out. Again, I'm not going to talk much about our general overall scheme. I want to talk about what I like, and that is the offensive line play. The skills each football player learns throughout his life, in grade school, in high school, college, or the NFL, are skills he has developed over his lifetime. Let me give you an example. Say you are a fourth-grader. You go for recess. What is the first thing you do? You and your buddies split up sides and go play football. You are working on skills as a young person that entire time. You work on throwing the ball. Now, not everyone can be a quarterback, but, nevertheless, you work on those skills of throwing the football. You work on catching the ball. You work on running the ball after the catch. You work on pass coverage. You work on tackling; you work on all of the different things and skills that we all as coaches like out of our athletes. But, there is one major skill development that is never brought into the picture. That is either blocking or, if you are a defensive guy, getting rid of the block and going on to make the tackle. Not too many fourth graders ever go out and say, "Hey Johnny, let's go work on our football techniques. You rush the passer and let me protect the passer today." So, those are things that never ever happen as a young man. Those are skills that you never learn. So, what happens, once you get into junior high or middle school or high school, your coach says, "You are an offensive linemen," or, "You are a center today." What is the kid thinking? "Oh my gosh, what did I do wrong? What did I do to deserve this?" Then, he starts thinking, "All my buddies are catching passes and getting their names in the paper, and here I am, because I'm slightly overweight, and I cannot move very well, and I have very few skills, so what do I get to do?" Well, that happens all of the time. Those fat kids, my heart goes out to them. Once upon a time when I was young, I was a fat kid. So, I got stuck playing with my hand down. Those guys who create that situation that allows everybody else to get into the limelight are the guys who make your offense go. Each of those skills that you have to do are the ones that allow you to have success on offense, whether it be running the football or throwing the football.

What we try to do is this. There are four must things that an offensive line must do. We talk about it in boxing terms. This puts everything into perspective as far as what I am looking for in an offensive linemen and what we try to get out of them. That term is this: "if you kill the body, the head must die." I heard a boxer talk about that one time, and it is perfect for offensive line play. It simply means this: if you can work on a defender's body and you can beat on him, and beat on him, and make it a physical part of the game from the first quarter through the third quarter, then in the fourth quarter, his head will die. He will give up. He will not want it anymore. And, those are things that we are constantly striving to do. When people say, "Yeah, you are 50-50," this is what we say. We are going to make running the football a major emphasis, and we are going to make being physical a part of protecting the passer a major emphasis. Because, we are going to try to work on your body.

The first thing we have got to live and die with is this. I tell them if they do not have an attitude right now, then you've got to go out and find an attitude, right now. Our attitude is this: we take no crap from nobody, no time, nowhere, period. It does not matter if it be on the practice field, whether that is during a game, or whether that is on campus, or downtown. But, unlike other positions, we have to be smart about it. Sure, if we go out and get in a little scuffle during practice, that is just two guys competing. Our job at practice is this, and you may not want your guys to do this: if one of us gets in it, we are all in it, because I have to know somebody covers my back. Now, you may get punished, and you may have to run after practice. It is just like when you were a little kid and mom bakes a brand-new cake. She tells you not to touch it until dinner. You sneak a piece after school. You may get in trouble for it, but it was sweet going down. That is a thing that we make sure we do. We want our offensive linemen to make sure they protect each other and protect the rest of the offense.

The second thing we have to do is technique. My firm belief is that you can win games on technique alone. There is not going to be anybody that you play who is physically just going to grab you, shake you, throw you, and then go make a play. It cannot happen 80 times in a game. If you have breakdowns, it is going to be because somewhere along the line you had a technique error. It could be your first step, your aiming point, your strike position, if you had leverage, or whether you ran your feet or not. Something we really preach on is technique. Now, you can get up here and diagram plays and how you are going to stop plays. Schemes can be great. But, it comes down to the technique and the execution of that technique that allows you to have success or not.

The third thing is that we have to play with intensity. It goes back to the attitude part. No other position on this football field hits somebody every snap. A guy on defense is trying not to get hit so he can make a play. A wide receiver is trying not to get hit, hopefully, so he can score. The quarterback does not want to get hit. You cannot allow that guy to get hit. The only position on the football field who hits somebody every play, or they are not doing their job, are the guys up front.

The fourth thing is we want to make sure we compete. We must compete every down to win. I've got a young son who is 11. As he started to grow up, he was playing T-ball and soccer and all of those youth sports. In the places where we lived, the younger you were, they never kept score. It drove me nuts that they couldn't keep score. In this life, you either win or you lose. Not everyone can win; someone has to lose. You either win, or you lose. Even though you might have won, you might not have given everything you had. Or, even though you lost, you might have played the best you could play. But, it is a team concept, and you have to compete to be the very best you can all of the time. That is what we need to do.

The one thing we will get on our players about more than anything else is the lack of effort in terms of competing and competing to be the very best. I haven't had all-Americans to work with. One thing as an offensive line coach you will find is that you must have kids who are willing to overachieve. They must be better than what they are really capable of being. A lot of that is just how competitive that kid is and how competitive you make your environment. The overachievers are the guys who win games. Those are the musts that we as an offensive line need to adhere to.

We try to make it as simple for our front five guys as we can, both run and pass. In terms of breaking it down, we only want to be good at a few things. We want be good at five good things on running the football and five great things on throwing the football. You put those two things together and form fists, and now you can go to battle.

When we want to run the ball, it all starts with *stance*. It all begins and ends with a great stance. The second most important thing is our *steps*. What is our footwork doing? The third is our *strike*. We want to know how are we going to be able to deliver a blow on the defender and control the defender using our upper body and our hands. The fourth one is the *drive* part of it. How fast can we run our feet? The fifth thing is the *finish*.

Real quickly, I will go through stance. Everybody has different ways of teaching a stance. But, again, we are 50-50, so our stance has to be pretty balanced. When we talk about a stance, we want this, with the exception of the center. With the center, the only thing different is that his feet are parallel and not staggered. We want a good solid base with the feet slightly wider than shoulders' width apart. We want a toe-to-instep relationship in terms of a stagger. So, we have good flex in our ankles, our knees, and our hips. Again, we want our steps to be balanced. So when we go down, we want to be balanced on all three points of our body and our fingertips, on the balls of our feet. So if I was looking to the side, I want all of our players to be balanced with a toe-to-instep relationship. Now again, you've got taller kids with longer cut legs, you have to give them a little bit bigger stagger, probably just a little bit wider in their base. We want their backs flat and their eyes up. We try to talk to them all the time in terms of you cannot block what you cannot see. So, it is important for them to be able to get a presnap look of the entire defense and what it is doing.

Now, the determination of whether it is a run or if it is a pass comes into play. When it is a run, we talk to our players about slightly rocking forward and just mentally transferring all of the weight forward. So now, they can be in more of a run mode. Their stance hasn't changed all that much. I may be in a slight rock or maybe a quarter of an inch. But, I mentally transferred all of the weight. If it is a pass, we are going to slightly rock back. The difference between run and pass is not that noticeable for those people on the sidelines or for the defensive guys on the other side of the ball. We try to talk to them all the time about this. We say, "Defensive players are dumb, but they're not stupid. They will read your stance. So, try to disguise it as much as you can." Now again, do you get that all the time? No, you don't, but it comes down to this: if you are going to give it away, whether it is a run or a pass, then you are telling me you are better than that guy. There is nothing that guy can do that you are not going to beat him, and not just beat him, but really physically and emotionally beat him. We don't spend a tremendous amount of time on stance, because everybody has to get into one that is comfortable.

Our steps are very important. Our first step as a center is no bigger than three inches. Our initial first step is no bigger than three inches. That is because I've got a nose usually sitting right on my face. For guards, tackles, and tight ends, their first step should be no bigger than six inches. That is a short six-inch step to the ball of my foot. That maintains that I can always have great power angles in my ankles, my knees, and in my hips. The common problem is that kids want to overstride or they want to overstep. The natural reaction is to step to their heels. If you step to your heel, your next movement is straight up, instead of coming out at a 45-degree angle.

The other thing we talk to our players about is that the first step is important and we have to get it on the ground. But, the most important step in terms of blocking is the second step. That is when contact will be made. So, your first step is important in terms of getting it on the ground whether it is three or six inches. It is important in landing on the balls of your feet and getting ready to have good power angles in your ankles, knees, and hips, so you can explode off the ball. The second step is the one that you are actually going to drive with. So, it has to be a short three- to six-inch step to the ball of your foot, so you can maintain and keep all of your weight underneath you. Now, the power angles in your ankles, knees, and hips can work together in terms of having an explosive nature off the ball.

When we go to strike, we tell all of the offensive linemen, "God gave you these hands and arms to be great offensive linemen." The greatest thing that football could have done was allow offensive linemen to use their hands. Everybody is going to say, "All they do is hold." That is not holding to us; it is survival. It becomes survival, but it is a game of leverage and it is a game of pad control.

Now, in most conferences in college, and I don't know about in high school, but, if you can strike within the framework of his body underneath the lips of his pads, regardless of what you do with your fingertips, you are good to go. It is that guy's fault on defense who allowed you to get in there. So, we work on a lot of fast hand drills to try to get our hands in place inside. When we go to strike, we are not windup guys. We don't wind up to go strike a blow. The reason I don't like to do this, after doing a lot of research, is this: one, it exposes your chest, and, two, it raises your body up. So, what we do is work on fast hands. We want to strike them straight from our stance, out. By throwing our hands out, what that will naturally force you to do, just to maintain your balance, is to get your first and second steps on the ground. If you don't move your feet, you are going to fall flat on your face. You can't overstride by throwing your hands out. It is like a sprinter coming out of the blocks. He comes out and throws his hands, and there is no way he can overstride. He has to get his feet on the ground so he can continue to run, then his arm action gets involved.

When we strike a blow, run or pass, it is always the same. It is with our thumbs up and our elbows in. The natural power line in your body, biomechanically, goes through your thumb, elbows, shoulders, lats, hips, knees, ankles, and to your feet. It is the natural power line of your body. It is a game of leverage. We try to control leverage.

The drive part is the next phase. We talk about driving all of the time. What we really want is for our kids to run their feet. In the old days, the coach had you out there duck walking and doing other crazy things. They had you run get-offs in your stance and starts. All of a sudden, he would have his kids come out of their stance and then chop their feet. You look at the Olympics. You don't see anybody run the 100-meter dash with their feet that wide apart. They can't run like that. So, we talk about doing this. If you can strike a blow, get great leverage and great pad control on the defender; now, it is up to you to run your feet. Use your speed to be able to maintain the block, or use your speed in terms of finishing the block. So, instead of always harping on maintaining a good, wide base after contact, we talk in terms of just running your feet. Get going in a certain direction, the faster the better.

The next part about it is the finish. We talk about finishing all of the time. Call them pancakes, or call them whatever you want to call them. They are probably one of the four great feelings in life that any of us can ever have. Flat-backing a guy is one of them. The other three are up to your imagination. When you are able to put a guy on the ground or on his back, that allows you, mentally, to establish physical domination. The thing that we try to talk about doing is this. If I am worth my salt as a defender and a blocker is into me, and if I am halfway good, at some point in time, I have to react to the ball. As that ballcarrier comes, I have to try to take the pressure off the man to make the play. Once I release the pressure, that is when my feet continue to accelerate, and I want to run through the block. That is when the decleaters or the pancakes happen. We talk about finishing all of the time. Finish the play you started.

Pass wise, we've got basically the same five components. One, it all starts with a great stance. Don't give it away. Don't give away your run and pass stance. Try to make it as close to the same as you can, so you do not have to take any false steps.

Two, how fast and how strong are our sets? Three, what is our strike like? How do we strike a blow on our defender? Again, we want to make sure that we have pad control. Every defensive guy in America, if he has a choice to run through you or around you, he is going to run around you. So, if we get our hands on you, we feel like we've got an opportunity to win.

Number four is shuffling. There is a right way and a wrong way to shuffle. We want to make sure when we shuffle that we have all of our weight up and underneath us and not out to the sides. We want to be able to change direction when they change direction.

The last part is the finish. We will finish on throws as well. We don't cut. We want to make it at one point in time when you decide it comes back to a bull-rush situation, and now we can come back and finish you. When you are trying to bat the ball down, we are going to finish you. If you try to make it just a bull rush, then we are now going to try to make a run block. We want to try to get you back to the line of scrimmage to give the quarterback more of a cushion to throw. So, we will put the physical part of the game back into protecting the passer.

Those are the five basic components. We already talked about the stance. We have three basic sets that we work on all of the time. It doesn't matter whether it is a three-step drop or a five-step drop, it is the same. We are going to set as tight to the line of scrimmage as possible. We are going to go on and do battle in this area. This is our battleground. If you happen to beat me, then that means you have to have great closing speed to get to the quarterback. This is as opposed to retreating and giving ground grudgingly. I have never seen someone give ground grudgingly. Not when you are trying to back up and he's running straight ahead. So, we are going to try to do our battle as close to the line of scrimmage as possible. If you beat us, at least the quarterback has an opportunity to move.

We have three basic sets. One is a snap set, which means we are going to set on the line of scrimmage or as tight to the line of scrimmage as we can. We have a wide outside set for any wide outside rushers. And, we have a change of pace for what we call up-kick, which means we are going to change our set point. It could be on the line of scrimmage or wide and outside. We are going to be more aggressive and go get you, just to change our set points. We also up-kick on a lot of screens, which means we are going to get into you, and then we get rid of you, then we go.

What I want to talk about is the snap set first. When we snap set, the first and most important thing in terms of protecting the passer is getting out of our stance. We must be able to put speed back into the game. Again, the defensive line is using the ball as the trigger. We know the snap count, so everything is equal. But, now, we are trying to make it a foot race. He is running forward, and I am running backward. Who is going to win? Unless I can physically get in front of the guy, he is going to win.

So when we snap set, we try to do this. First, it all starts with a good, comfortable stance. My weight is evenly distributed. A pass has been called, so I am going to rock back. I mentally transfer the weight. From that point, I want to be able to get my head back as fast and as violently as possible. As I get into my stance, the first thing I want to concentrate on is snapping my head back as hard and as fast as I can. What that naturally does, even without using any hands, is it sinks my butt down so I have great power angles in my ankles, knees, and hips. I have the weight up and underneath me. It keeps my head back from trying to get overaggressive on the defender.

The first thing in terms of snap set is head back. The second thing is hands up. I'm going to throw my hands up as tight to my body as I can. The thumbs are up, and the elbows in. I want them as tight to my body as I can. Reason being is this: jerseys are getting tighter, and some are tighter than others. There are very few kids on defense who are now getting used to grabbing cloth and using it. What are they aiming for now? They're aiming for hands. They are trying to do all of the things the NFL guys do in terms of hand fighting and then being able to throw a move. We want our hands as tight to our body because, basically, we want to invite you to us. We want you to come and try to grab cloth and expose your chest. We want you to come and try to swat our hands. That means you have to close that distance that much more. So, we want you to come to us. If they do not come to us, we just mirror them. If they want to play the game, they will come to us.

We want the head back, hands up, and our hips will naturally fall back underneath us. We want to always maintain that our feet are buzzing. It is not chopping them up and down; it is keeping them active. It is easier to move when they are moving than when they are stationary.

When we strike a blow, our guards and tackles will always try to strike inside hand first. The reason is because eventually he will have to close to me. He is a B gap rusher. He is either going to try to reach out and grab cloth or come straight through to me and bull rush me, or he is going to try to swat my hands. In any case, he is going to expose himself. As I set, my feet are buzzing. I want to keep my outside hand as tight to my body as I can. I invite him to come that way. Then, I am going to put my inside hand on him, thumbs up, elbows in, right under the lips of his pads, immediately followed by my outside hand. So, it may look like we are trying to put them both on them at the same time, when in actuality we are trying to get our inside hand on him first. We want contact on the defender. So instead of one, now there is a second one. Bang! It is going to be done very, very quickly. Now, all of the pressure goes with my outside hand. I can keep a great relationship with my outside eye with his inside eye and force him to make the next move. So, we want to make sure that we strike with our inside hand first. For our tackles, it is really important. Now, our jerseys are going to be real, real tight. We are going to keep that outside hand in and invite them to close that cushion on us and get as tight to us as they can. Now, we have them. The thing we talk to our players about is this: you can fight your man in a lecture hall, and, if you catch him, there is a great chance you are going to beat the dog out of him. But, you are expending a lot of energy just trying to catch him. Or, you can fight him in a phone booth. If he comes to your body, you can get him into that phone booth. That is where you want to do battle. Again, most defenders will try to run around you rather than run through you.

With our centers, the thing we always try to get them to do is this: we talk in terms of having a stab hand. Our stab hand is nothing but the hand without the ball. What we try to teach our centers is not only to settle back and off the ball, but to snap set. So, every time they set, they are going to settle back off the ball so they can get on the same plane as the guards. When that ball moves, that off hand is up. So simultaneously, that ball is the same direction. Ball back, hand up, and protect yourself. You are at a disadvantage anyway. One, you have a guy sitting right in your face mask. Two, you have to get a little bit of separation so you can get on the same plane as the guards. Three, you better get your off hand and stab hand on him to try to neutralize the guy in order to get your other hand up. Now, you are like the rest of the guys. When that ball just starts to come back, that hand must be out. They are the only ones who can literally lock their arms out on a defender.

On the shuffle part of it, we have two different shuffles. We always talk about shuffling the trail leg first. The first step I want to take is with my backside foot or my trail leg first. Reason being is, if I step with my lead leg first, my weight is out to the side. It is no longer up underneath me. When that guy moves, I end up ripping out my groin trying to adjust to him. I want to make sure that by shuffling the trail leg first that I have my weight up and underneath me. I can transfer the weight; I can shuffle back and forth and basically mirror the guy.

When working in terms of shuffle, we break it down from strike to shuffle. We tell them the hands lock you on the block, but your feet do all of the work. The feet do all the work. This game is played from the waist down, and it is important that your players understand that. I have seen a lot of players who could bench 500 pounds who couldn't play dead. That is because they don't know how to use their legs.

When we vertically shuffle, it is the same set as when we are outside. If I have a defender wide, a lot of people teach a kick step. That is the same thing that has just taken place when you shuffle lead leg first. What ends up happening when you kick step is your second step ends up coming to flat. Or, it ends up coming too deep. So on your third step, you will end up dropping it to your own goal line, which creates a natural pass-rush lane, or shortens the corner for that defensive end. We are going to set with our inside foot. We are trying to get depth on our first step and width with our second step. For an offensive tackle, the best thing you can ever have is to have a guy on the outside shade such as a 5 technique, 6 technique, whatever you call it. Now, you are in that box. I can get my hands on you, and I can physically beat you.

My only chance is to get to that junction point where contact can be made. Then, I can get my hands on you, and we can go ahead and work it. It all starts with the set. Again, I'm going to stay heavy on my inside leg. I get depth and width. Now, I am basically on my second step, which is the original position I was in my stance. If he is a little wider, inside out, I still have my weight underneath me. All of my weight is on my inside leg, so if he does want to come back inside, I still have a great strong post foot.

When contact is made, they have to keep the pass rushers on the line of scrimmage so the quarterback has someplace to go. The tackles have to be the athletes. They are responsible for the width of the pocket. They are naturally going to create throwing lanes, if you can widen the guy. When contact is made, he is talking about being a C gap or outside rusher. He is the contained rusher. He is always going to stay outside. So, if I can widen him by working the vertical, I am forcing him that much farther away from the quarterback. As opposed to this, I drop my foot to my own goal line and I turn and open. Now, I have done nothing to that throwing lane. I have created nowhere for that quarterback to go but up. We term that working the vertical. The shoulders are square, outside hand in, and I am going to strike with my inside hand, trail leg first, trying to get depth and width on my footwork. I can always maintain that original position that I was in my stance.

Let me move to pass-rush moves that defenders have. Again, the guys who you are going to play aren't going to use them all. They may not even use some of them. But, if you understand how many there are and you have an answer for it before it ever arises, you look like you know what you are doing. That is the thing as coaches that we are trying to get people to do.

The thing that we talk about is this: a defense has only about four pass-rush moves. They have a bull or power rush and a swim move. He has the move of the 90s, which is the speed rip. Then, they have a spin move. We tell our guys even though there are only four moves how many are they going to be good at? You can't be good at all four moves. You are going to be a mediocre player, because it is a game of reaction. So, they are probably only going to be good off two of them. Each of those moves all work off each other. If you are a bull rusher, you can swim or spin or rip. You can rip and spin, but it is real difficult to rip and swim or to rip and bull. You can't swim and spin, or you just end up spinning yourself into the ground. So, they all kind of balance out and work together. We try to talk about each of those moves and which ones they can be good at.

We only give our guys five days to think. They can think about the scheme, but they have to get to the point where they can react to the move. It is a game of reaction. Just like a golfer, it is the same being a pass protector. A lot goes into that swing. There are a lot of things that can go wrong, but the great ones are the ones who make it a natural reaction. It is the same thing in terms of pass protection. If you are thinking about it, then you are not going to be able to get it done. You have to be able to react to each of the moves that he throws a second ago in order to get your body into position to go out and get it done.

They are not very difficult to stop, but it is a reaction that you have to get your kids to do. I'm a firm believer in reps. We are very, very repetitive. We are creatures of habit. We do everything in our lives the same. When I talk about being creatures of habit, I tell the line this: what is the first thing you do when you wake up in the morning? I go to the bathroom; that is the first thing. It doesn't matter if you're 15 or 55, that is the first thing you do. You have trained your body to do that. You have trained your mind and body to react to the same thing at the same time. It is the same with being a good pass protector and good run blocker. You have to train your mind and body to react to the same thing at the same time.

Move-wise, it is four basic moves we use to stop them. The thing you have to remember is this. It is not all that difficult to stop them, but the thing you must get your kids to do is to react. The first thing we work on is a gunfighter drill. Which means, we will get two kids to stand chest to chest, basically, hands down. All that we will do is, as fast as we can, once he sees movement, he is going to try to put his hands on his chest. So, it is really fast. We really work on shooting our hands inside. Once we get our hands inside, we are going to work on clinching. We want to be able to grab that plastic. We try to work on getting our hands inside as fast as we can. This will cause your kid's fingers to be sore, but they have to get used to it, because they will be hitting someone every single time.

Now, the bull rusher. Remember I talked about snap set, head back, butt down, and my hands up and inside. I want to keep them as tight to my body as I can. What he has to make sure that he does is he is going to try to get his hands inside on me. If he sees my hands inside, where are his hands going to go? They will go out. If he sees my hands outside, where are they going to go? They will go inside. So, if I can keep my hands tight to the body, as he starts to come, I want to make sure that I can strike right under the lips of those pads and get a piece of that plastic. As he continues to try to bull rush me, it means he's just going to try to walk me straight back to the quarterback. What I want to make sure that I can do is to get his chest, regardless of his height, in the air. It is that little V that comes down where his shoulder pads tie together. We talk in terms of shoving that thing into the guy's throat. It never happens, but it sounds good. We are going to try to shove his chest in the air to get him up. If we can get him up, and again it is a game of leverage, if I can get his chest in the air, regardless of whether I get that V in his throat or not, I can win. When I strike up, my hips will naturally sink down and he no longer has any forward thrust. So, the best way to stop a bull rusher is to get his chest in the air. Then, get ready to counter any move he has.

The next move is the swim move. Again, they're going to reach out and grab cloth, or they will try to grab the triceps and turn your body. They try to get you to go someplace that he is not going. The one thing that is important to tell your kids is this. A short swimmer is not going to try to swim a tall guy. We talk in terms of pressure. Whether he is trying to grab or swat, you fight that pressure. Remember, your hands are inside tight. They are still slightly bent at the elbows. When you feel it, you lock it out. You may not get it locked out, but you have started to straighten his body back out. So, when you feel pressure, you fight pressure. Now, as he either tries to come over the top or punch through, there is a major body part that is exposed, and that is his lats. We want to get that open palm and jam it into his ribs as physically hard as we possibly can. Another term, we want to try to sauce a rib.

Once your hands are locked up, your feet have to do all of the work. Again, it is not real difficult, but it is training your mind and body to react to the same thing at the same time.

The third move is the move of the 90s, the rip move. Speed guys love the rip. Tall guys, short guys, everybody can rip. Basically, what they are going to try to do is to try to get under you and create a mismatch in terms of speed. You are running backward; I am running forward. I am going to try to create a mismatch. My only hope is not to run through your body. You hear defensive line guys talk all of the time about working one half of the man. Don't work the whole man, but work one half of the man. So, as he tries to come through on that rip, he is going to rip that thing through and try to get his momentum to get vertically up the field. Then, he is going to teach the rusher about leaning into him and running the hoops and trying to get back to the quarterback.

We have two thoughts where that happens. When they first started throwing the rip move, the original way of trying to stop it was this. As soon as he ripped it, coaches talked about keeping the arm locked out straight. Get your inside hand and put it to his hip. The thing that you ended up having was a lot of kids who couldn't physically change the pass rush by going to the hip hard. Or, as he continued to run up the field and he went to the hip, all he did was basically help him by. I got tired of being called for holding because my arms are on his neck. If you are not going to allow us to do this, then why don't you outlaw the move? They are not going to do that. So, what we will do when we have the rip guys is this. It is called clamping a guy. If the opponent is coming on me and contact is made, he is going to rip me half a man. What he is trying to do is to force my elbow up high so he can continue to run through me.

His coach has told him to make this fat guy work his feet. But, what does the offensive line coach tell him? "You are not fat, you are an athlete." There are skilled guys, and there are athletes. Have you ever seen a skilled guy block an athlete? It can't be done. Have you ever seen an athlete try to catch a ball? It can't be done. There are skilled guys, and there are athletic guys. That is us; we are the athletic guys. We don't want to work our feet. We want to get this guy in a phone booth. So, as he rips through, instead of going to the hip, I am going to get his elbow and I am going to clamp it as hard to my ribs and my hip as I can. That forces him to play back into my body. Is it holding? No! Why? He got himself in that position; I didn't. We will clamp it so he has to work his little body into my big body. If I do not clamp hard, he will continue to rip it up. So, we work on this drill all of the time. We are both standing up and we have him sprint up the field. He has to clamp him and then shuffle vertically. We talk about the clamp all of the time. Now, where does our off hand go? Same place as it would if he was trying to swim me. I don't want to go low, because if I go low, my elbow will go up. I don't want it to go high, because now my elbow will go down, and he has my shoulder. It has to be right in the middle of his back, and what I want to do is to squeeze him and force him back to my body.

The last move is the spin. They can come off a bull rush or they can be off a rip, but they are all basically the same. A good spin guy is going to reach out, grab, and take the extra step, plant, accelerate, and try to get that fist with momentum to get himself vertically up the field. Whatever he hits along the way, that is great. The guys who don't try to build momentum, like a discus thrower or shot-putter who tries to block out, they are the ones who never go anywhere. They just stay in the same place going around in circles. If he gets a good clamp on me, it is real hard for me to try to pull that clamp out of there. Eventually, I do have to let go, and I will, but initially for him to try to gain speed and momentum, it is tough. If he is loose with it, and he does pull off, remember, he has to release all of the pressure off you in order to spin. So when he releases the pressure off, you want to push and settle back inside.

We tell our line the defense will never spin away from the quarterback. If they do, let them go. Just turn them loose, because they are stupid. They will always spin to the quarterback. So, if I am a right tackle, he is only going to spin inside. If he goes away from the quarterback, let him go. The quarterback still has someplace to move. Center, you are in a bind because you are right in the middle. They only spin away. You always want to push and settle back inside. The key thing is this: you don't want to settle out early. You want to be able to push and settle.

Those are the moves we use. We talk to our kids in terms of this. Each one of those moves will always revert back to the same move, which is the bull rush. They revert back to it.

19

Zone Blocking Concepts

Dan Young
University of Nebraska
1994

Thank you. I appreciate the opportunity to come to this fine clinic. It was not that many years ago that I was a high school coach at Omaha West Side High School. I was invited to the Minneapolis Coach of the Year Clinic. I especially like the clinic manual, because it was something you could keep from year to year and continue to look back at. You can grow from the information from other clinics that you do not have the opportunity to attend.

We really had an outstanding year at Nebraska. We had a group of players that believed in what they were doing. They found a way to win all of the games except the last one. We took Florida State down to the wire without coming up with a victory. We have another outstanding group of players coming back next year. I am looking forward to next year's season. We start spring practice March 28. We have a clinic on April 8 and 9. Don Nehlen of West Virginia will be one of the speakers. It is a very good clinic, and I am sure you will get your money's worth. We used to have great door prizes at our clinic. We gave away boats, La-Z-Boy chairs, and diamond rings. The NCAA made us stop giving out those things, but we still have a great clinic. We used to have people come from all over to attend our clinic, just for the door prizes. We had one coach that got some great door prizes, and the coaches really enjoyed that part of the program.

I am not going to talk much about stats, but more about techniques. I will cover what we do at Nebraska and give you the zone package we use. At Nebraska, we have two offensive line coaches: Coach Milt Tenopir and myself. I work with the kickers, centers, and special teams. During that time, Milt is down working with the tackles and guards. On other days, Milt has the tight ends and tackles. When I bring my group down to join his group, I will take the tackles and he will take the guards and centers on combination blocks. Then, we do individual blocking with the centers, guards, and tackles. Generally, I work on the pass blocking and Milt handles the run blocking.

When we have just the linemen, we work against different fronts. I will take the pass phase, and Milt takes the run part. We usually have a one and a two group, and then we switch around. That is how we get prepared. When we come up to the field, we have a kicking period. Then, we have about three team stations. We have an option, run, and a pass station. This is all team work. That is how we split things up at Nebraska.

We grade each play after the games. In spring practice, we grade every scrimmage. We scrimmage on Wednesday and Saturday. The way we grade our plays is this: If they go to the right spot and do the right thing and make the right block, they get a two. If they go to the right place, but do not do the right thing, they get a one. If they go the wrong way or screw up their block, they get a zero. That is our grading system. We hope our players can get efficient enough to grade out to about 1.9. That is about 95 percent efficiency. You must have players that know what they are doing and they have to be dedicated and unselfish. They are not going to get a lot of glory. One of the reasons we like to run the football is because it highlights our offensive linemen. We can look at the stats and see where we stand as compared with other teams in the NCAA. They take a lot of pride in our standings in running the ball.

Since I work in the passing game, we take a lot of pride in the low number of sacks we give up. The pro coaches tell me that if they can only give up five percent sacks they feel they are efficient. In the last year, our line gave up six sacks in 220 passes. That comes out to about 2.65 percent. That means we did a good job protecting the passer. It is a little easier to protect our quarterback because a lot of our passes are play-action verses the drop back pass.

The first thing our players get after the game is their grade. Next, they get the average grade for the entire team. We tell them if they can get close to a 1.9 average they have done well as a unit. The first thing we look at is perfect plays. To use that is where all five linemen grade a two on the play. We like to have our players in the 65 to 70 percent category there. We look at knockdowns, or pancakes, and the number of times we put people flat on their back. Our goal as a team is to get 100 knockdowns. We want our offensive line to get between 50 and 60 knockdowns. It shows we are aggressive if we have a lot of knockdowns. When you go against good teams, it is hard to get knockdowns. Against UCLA, we had 24, and against Florida State, we had 34. The better the teams, the more difficult it is to get knockdowns. We still set a high goal and strive to get our average.

Next, we look at penalties. These are penalties that are caused by offensive linemen. We try to get that down to zero. Only in one game did we have zero penalties on the offensive line. Against Florida State, we had two offensive penalties. These are the things we look at as offensive line coaches.

I do not want to spend a lot of time on penalties. I heard a story about a man that drowned in a river where the average depth was only 2.5 feet deep. Stats do not always tell the whole story. This is how we break down our offense at Nebraska. Run plays are like the toss sweep, draws, fullback traps, and those kind of plays. You can see that was about 50 percent of our offense. Options were about 20 percent of our offense. Passes/runs are plays where the quarterback ran the bootleg or had to scramble on the play. Our quarterback is a good runner, and he made a lot of yards on plays where pass plays were called. You can see our passing game was effective with over 51 percent completion.

Plays	Attempts	Yards	Average
Runs	441	2244	5.21
Options	141	410	6.45
Pass/Run	37	164	4.40
Total	619	3373	5.45
Average	51	281	40 Touchdowns

Passing Attempts = 226 - 116 - 8
Yards   51%   1711   7.57
Average   18   142   17 Touchdowns
Offensive Line - Sacks = 6 = 7.65

In the Orange Bowl, we had a high percentage of third down conversions. One reason for that is because of the type of offense we run. We keep the defense off balance. On third-and-long, we are going to run the ball as much as we are going to throw the ball. You can see we run the ball about half of the time. The actual passes and the called passes are about 30 percent of the time. This will give you an idea where we are coming from when we talk about our offense.

When I first got hired at Nebraska, coach Osborne called me in and told me to go see a farmer out in western Nebraska. He was a big supporter of the team, and coach Osborne wanted me to spend some time with him. I did my homework and got ready to go see the farmer. I went to see him and gave him a run down on what my duties would be as a new coach at Nebraska. Next, I gave him a run down on the seniors and what players would be expected to have big years. Next, I took each game and went over the opponents and told him how I thought we would be able to accomplish against them. I went on and on for over one hour. I could see the farmer was starting to lose interest. Finally, I asked the farmer what he thought. He said, "Coach, I know you know your football. I am a farmer, but I do know one thing." I said, "What is that, sir?" He said, "Well, coach, when I feed my cattle each night, I do not give them the whole damn truck load at one time." Sometimes, coaches get tempted to do that when they get up to lecture. I may get tempted to do that here, but this is what I want to cover with you today.

This is our zone offensive package. We went to this three years ago. We like the zone concept. We wanted to develop a blocking concept we could use for a number of different plays. We did not want a different blocking scheme for every play. We wanted to cut down on the amount of time Milt and I were spending trying to scheme plays rather than teaching players their techniques. We talked to the Bengals and Chiefs and watched a lot of film. We came up with something on our own as well. We went to this three years ago. We have won the Big Eight the last three years. It has been a good package for us.

Most teams today will put their best players on defense. I know when we sign a defensive tackle and he gets to us in fall practice and we find out that he runs a 5.4 for 40 yards, coach Osborne meets him about halfway coming back to tell him he is now a member of the offensive line. Those are the kind of players that end up on offense. They do not have the size and speed to play defense. This year we played with two tight ends. One was a converted wingback, and the other one was a walk-on. They ended up being good players for us. The point is this: our best outside linebackers are rush ends, but they could also be tight ends. However, we put our best players on defense to make things happen for us. It is not as easy to block those types as it use to be. That is another reason we went to the zone concept.

We run four different plays from the inside zone concept. We run our dive, give to the fullback off our pitch action. Then, we run the give to the fullback off our dive option action. Then, we run our one back dive from the one back set, which is a zone read. It is from an I back set where he cuts it back or stays onside. The other play is a two back draw, where we can run it to the tight end side or the split end side. When we run to the tight end side, we have two different ways to run the draw.

We run four different plays from the outside zone concept. We run the toss sweep, a one back outside dive, a pure outside option off our dive option action, and our speed option out of our one back set. Those four plays are all packaged off our outside zone concept.

Then, we have misdirection plays. We run our dive pass where the quarterback comes out naked and a draw pass where it looks like zone action, and we pull the uncovered lineman out to the backside. We also have a little shovel pass where we bring the wingback around back underneath, off our dive one way, and bring the wingback underneath. Then, we run our tackle trap where we look like we are running dive one way, but it is a designated cutback. We trap with the tackle either on the linebacker or the 2 technique, depending on the kind of look we face. This is what I would like to go over with you today.

This is what our zone offensive package looks like. Hopefully, you will be able to see what we are trying to accomplish with our zone blocking scheme.

Inside Zone Series

- Covered—stretch base
- Uncovered—stretch double
- 33-37 dive, fullback give from pitch action
- 11-19 dive, fullback give from dive-option action
- 43-47 dive, 1 back dive
- 43-47 draw, 2 back fullback lead
    - Openside
    - Tight end side

Outside Zone Series

- Covered rip-reach
- Uncovered pull and overtake
- 41-49 pitch, toss sweep
    - Openside
    - Tightside
- 41-49 outside, one back outside dive
    - Openside
    - Tight end side
- 11-19 base option, dive option action

- ○ Openside
- ○ Tight end side
- 31-39 sprint option, one back sprint option
  - ○ Openside
  - ○ Tight end side

Misdirection

- 43-47 dive pass, dive action naked boot
- 43-47 draw pass, the 2 back draw action—uncovered lineman lead
- 43-47 dive wingback shovel pass
- 43-47 tackle trap, designated I back cutback

The reason we like the zone concept is because it is simple. We just tell our linemen they have to know two things, basically. They need to know if they are *covered* or *uncovered*. If you are covered and we run an inside zone, you do what we call a stretch base. If you are uncovered, you come and help another blocker. We call that a stretch double. We are thinking double-team where one of the two will come off late for the linebacker. If you are covered and the backside man is also covered, we know we have a stretch base, but we are not going to get any help. That is the play. That is all they have to know. When we get into the draw, we have to know who the fullback is blocking, so we have a small adjustment there. Basically, that is the concept we use: covered or uncovered.

If I am covered, the first thing I want to do is to take a stretched step. That is a quick lateral. We do not want to come upfield. It all depends where the defender is as to how big the step will be. If the defender is on the blocker, it will be a simple change of weight on the feet. We use to step, and the defense would step to the side, and we ended up with no leverage. We want to get our belly upfield. We want to keep our heels pointed toward the goal line as long as we can. So, the first step is all determined by where the defender is aligned. If he is wider, I will take a longer stretch. It will be a quick lateral step. The second step is right in the middle of his cylinder. We step without crossing over. The young players tend to crossover and then lose their base. The second step is in the middle. We bring up the hands in the middle of the defenders cylinder and start driving him. If we have help, we are eye balling the linebacker all of the time this is happening. If you do not have help, you stay with the defender all the way. It is a stretch step, second step to the middle, do not crossover, rip up. We try to invite movement. We do not care if they are running. That is fine. If they want to run, we will get back underneath them. We do not have to knock them on their back and cut them off, and all of that. We invite movement and just run them. That is the covered principle.

If I am uncovered, this is what we do. We tell him to take a 45-degree step and aim for a point on the back of the hip of the defender. If he gets to the man and the hip is still there, he stays with it. If the hip disappears, he goes up to the linebacker. If he gets to the hip of the lineman, he does not come off until he gets to linebacker's depth. So often, what happens is they want to come off the block too early. The most important thing is to get movement at the line. Sometimes, we drive the lineman into the linebacker. You have to eyeball the linebacker to see what happens. We do not have to worry about who is going to block each man if they slant. We drill it over and over again, and it becomes automatic for our linemen. You will see in our films teams that try to slant and play games against us just take themselves out of the play. We have good running backs at Nebraska, and they can read the blocks up front. They can cut off the blocks. We just get the defense moving and take them the way they want to go.

The center has a tough block if the backside guard is covered. He knows he is not getting help from the backside guard, even though the nose is lined up six inches away. Sometimes, we will have the center scramble block rather than take the man one-on-one with this stretch base scheme. Since the center has to make quick contact, we will overstretch the center at times to make sure we get penetration stopped. The thing that hurts the inside zone play more than anything else is penetration. If you can keep the defense at the line of scrimmage and get them running, the backs can find a place to run the ball.

If the guard is uncovered, the backside tackle will check out. If the play is going away from him, he will check down the line. If a man is there, he runs him down the line. If the man is stretched, we run with him. If we can cut him off, we will.

All of this looks easy, but it takes a lot of time to perfect. That is why we have gone to this scheme, because we feel we can spend more time working on technique. It takes a lot of repetitions. Our splits on the outside zone is tighter than on our inside zone. We split one foot on the outside zone and a foot and one-half on the inside zone. If the split is big, you have a bigger chance for penetration. The technique we use on our outside zone has to be tight.

We have two fullback give plays, either off our dive option action or off our pitch action. We used to run the pitch like Florida State and Auburn runs it. We have hit so many three linebacker setups we had to change the way we run the pitch. When I get to the outside zone, I will go over that. Our fullback aims a little wider than he did before on our pitch toss sweep play. On our dive option action, the fullback aims at the butt of the guard. The fullback comes off his butt, and we read the onside crease. If the play is not open, he is not going to cut until he gets up into the hole. We tell the back to get to a heel's depth of the lineman before he cuts. We do not want them to start cutting back too soon. If people start playing the cutback too soon, it will not work. The deeper you can get the backup in the hole, the better you will be. We tell them smooth to the hole and then speed through the hole.

The defense we see more than any other is the offset 4-3 look. You can see the rules as they apply on our dive option versus an even front. Then, look at the play against the odd front. Now, the center has the nose by himself.

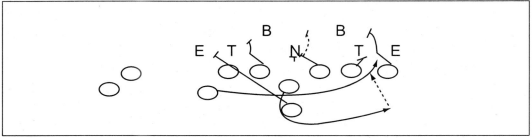

Diagram 1. Dive option versus even

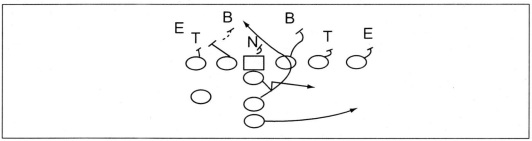

Diagram 2. Dive option versus odd

It is a simple concept of who is blocking who. The players cannot say they do not know who they are blocking. You get a body on a body. You do not have people unblocked. This has helped us a great deal.

The next play is the lead draw. This gives us an effective running play to the splitside. On a 4-3 setup, we want the fullback to block the outside linebacker to the onside. You do not have to use a different rule to the other side. You can have the same rule to the tight end side, and all you have to do is to have the tight end release to force. To the openside, we bring the fullback on the outside linebacker. The onside guard and center work on the nose and middle linebacker.

If we get a split six look, we still get the fullback as an extra blocker on the linebacker. The tight end makes an out call. We end up coming over one man. Our fullback is five yards deep, and the tailback is eight yards deep on their alignment. The quarterback gives the back the ball as deep in the backfield as he can.

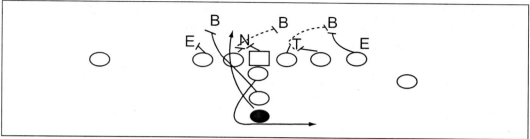

Diagram 3. Lead draw openside versus even

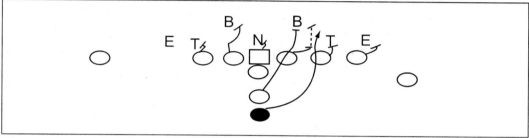

Diagram 4. Lead draw to tight end versus odd

Next, I want to go over what we do on the outside zone. Again, it is the same concept. It is covered or uncovered principle. If you are covered, we say you are going to rip reach, and, if you have backside help, you are going to escape. If you are uncovered, you are going to pull and overtake. That is all the linemen have to know, who is covered and who is uncovered. If I am covered and the play is going to my side, then I am going to rip reach and escape to the linebacker. We are going to try to get the play outside with this scheme. We are running the toss sweep, the outside dive option, the speed option, or the pitch outside. We are running our outside zone play. It is very similar blocking. The covered man takes a stretch, and then he crosses over and tries to get belly up field. We want to rip with the hand when we get to the defender to help the other blocker pick him up. The split is only about one foot. We want the uncovered man to pick him up. The man that is pulling just keeps pulling, but he must eye the linebacker. If the linebacker plays under, he comes off and picks him up. If he doesn't come off, the puller will end up going around the man that is rip reaching.

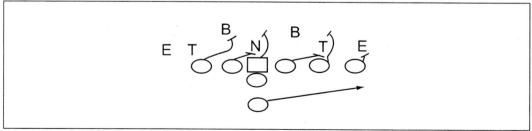

Diagram 5. One man set sweep versus odd

Let me give you the two back toss sweep against the odd front. Now, we have the fullback lead the play. We do run the play to both sides: tight end or open side.

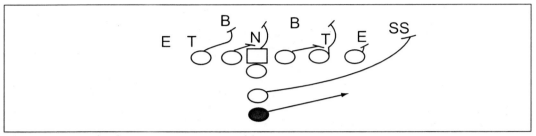

Diagram 6. Two back toss sweep versus odd

We used to run the toss sweep like Florida State runs it. When we played teams like Miami and Florida State, the Sam linebacker would have a hay day. We could not run the play. We went to the outside zone concept, and it has helped us a great deal.

The next thing we look at is our sprint and dive option action. Our rule is this: If we go to the split end side, we are going to pitch off the end man. If we go to the tight end side, we are going to pitch off the force man.

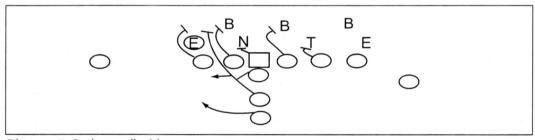

Diagram 7. Option—split side

If we are running the option to the tight end side, we pitch off the force man. This is a good play against third down situations when teams are playing the pass. The one back sprint option was more effective than the two back option.

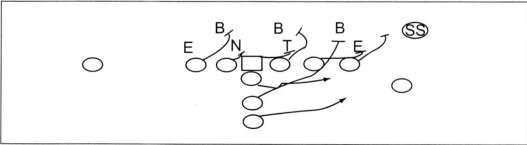

Diagram 8. Option—tight end side

If we are going to run dive option action, it is the same deal. We have the luxury of having the fullback to help on anyone that filters through our line. Let's see the film on the outside zone.

Let me cover our misdirection off our zone action. The plays include the dive passes, the draw passes, and the tackle trap, and the wingback shovel pass. A lot of times, we run our dive passes out of our ace formation, where we keep our tight end in to block and the quarterback is not completely naked. We give the line this rule on naked. Everyone pulls one man to the call. If there is no one there, block the man on you. That is where the rule ends. One man to the called side. If the tackle is uncovered and the defense has two men outside, the tackle can give the guard a call and we will pull two men to the called side. They are the only two that would pull to the call. Normally, we pull one man to the call. If you are covered, block the man on you. We try to make the play look like we are running the inside zone action. The quarterback goes naked away from the action. The end runs an 18-yard comeback route. The pro back runs a horn on the other side. Those are the two receivers the quarterback looks for.

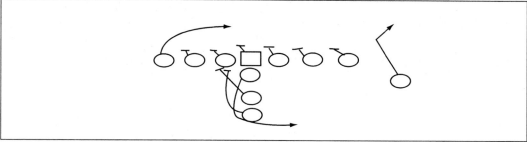

Diagram 9. Naked bootleg

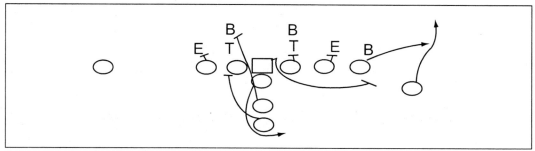

Diagram 10. Naked bootleg versus even

If we face an even look, the center pulls. We can have a delay route with the tight end. The split end is coming across. We like to get a man out leading the quarterback.

Next is the shovel pass. We run it off the dive. The fullback blocks to the side the wingback is lined up. The wingback and quarterback must read the defensive end. If the end drops off, the wingback may end up blocking him and the quarterback keeps the ball on a run. It is a simple play that has worked very well for us. We can run this play from the shotgun formation.

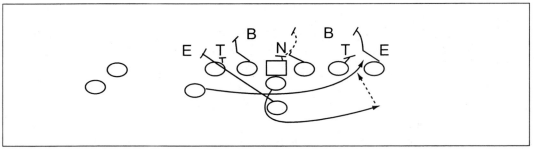

Diagram 11. Shovel pass

The last misdirection we run is a designated cutback that we run where we trap with the tackle. We bring either the guard or center off on the linebacker. The I back gets the ball about three yards from the line. He cuts it back underneath, keying the block of the tackle. If we are going to the right, we call the play 43, so it looks like we are running 43 draw. It is a designated cutback for the I back. When you get to running the zone play very effectively, everyone starts running to the ball. If you have tackles that can pull like we have, they will love this play. We can trap the down lineman and let the end block the linebacker.

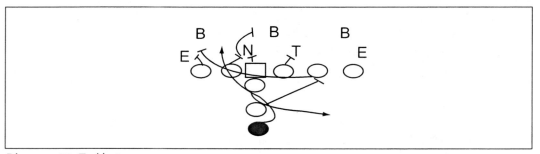

Diagram 12. Tackle trap

Those are our misdirection plays off the zone action. Let's see the film on them. Thank you.

About the Editor

Earl Browning, the editor of the "By the Experts Series," is a native of Logan, West Virginia. He currently serves as president of Telecoach, Inc.—an organization that conducts football clinics and produces the Coach of the Year Clinics Football Manuals. A 1958 graduate of Marshall University, he earned his M.Ed. and Rank I education certification from the University of Louisville. From 1958 to 1975, he coached football at various Louisville-area high schools. Among the honors he has been accorded are his appointments to the National Football Foundation and to the College Hall of Fame Advisory Committee on moving the museum to South Bend, Indiana. He was named to the Greater Louisville Football Coaches Association Hall of Legends in 1998.